Bikers

Bikers

Culture, Politics and Power

Suzanne McDonald-Walker

Oxford • New York

First published in 2000 by
Berg
Editorial offices:
150 Cowley Road, Oxford, OX4 1JJ, UK
838 Broadway, Third Floor, New York, NY 10003-4812, USA

Berg is an imprint of Oxford International Publishers Ltd.

Library of Congress Cataloging-in-Publication Data
A catalogue record for this book is available from the Library of Congress.

British Library Cataloguing-in-Publication Data
A catalogue record for this book is available from the British Library.

ISBN 1 85973 351 4 (Cloth)
1 85973 356 5 (Paper)

Typeset by JS Typesetting, Wellingborough, Northants
Printed in the United Kingdom by Biddles Ltd, Guildford and King's Lynn

Contents

Contents

Abbreviations

ACU	Auto Cycle Union
BMF	British Motorcyclists' Federation
DSA	Driving Standards Agency
DVLA	Driver and Vehicle Licensing Agency
EMA	European Motorcyclists' Association
EU	European Union
FEM	Federation of European Motorcyclists
FEMA	Federation of European Motorcyclists' Associations
FENOMSEE	Federation of National and One-Make Motorcycle Clubs
FIM	Féderation Internationale Motocyclisme
MAG	Motorcycle Action Group
MCIA	Motor Cycle Industry Association
MCN	*Motor Cycle News*
RRO	riders'-rights organisation

Acknowledgements

There are many people to whom I owe a debt of gratitude for their contributions to this work – a debt both of quantity and quality, for never before have I experienced such unqualified co-operation and willingness to help as I encountered during the course of this research.

Firstly, I wish to thank University College Northampton for both research funding and sabbaticals; clearly, without that material support this book could not have been written. Particular thanks must go to Professor Helen Rainbird for her support; especially in the early phase when everyone else merely smirked when I told them about my latest research project. I also would like to thank my office mate, Stuart Smith, for allowing me to bounce ideas about, and Clive Norris from the University of Hull for his useful and positive comments on the draft. My publishers, Berg, have also been tremendously supportive throughout the preparation period, particularly Editorial Director, Kathryn Earle, whose E-mails were a lifeline.

Secondly, my appreciation goes to those Members of the European Parliament who found time to see me and who provided an invaluable insight into the workings of the European Union. Thanks must also go to the various organisations, and individuals within them, that have helped in data collection. In this regard, thanks to Paul Fowler of the former Motorcycle Media Bureau, Richard Schofield of EMAP National Publications Ltd., Angela at the Driver and Vehicle Licensing Agency and Stewart Bembridge at the Driving Standards Agency. Warren Dickson of Carole Nash provided some much-needed accident statistics and a jolly good chat. A particular expression of gratitude goes to Frank Finch, formerly of the Motor Cycle Industry Association, for allowing me to interrupt his day on numerous occasions over recent years and, more recently, to Maria Garcia. Many thanks also to Sean Warwick, former editor of *Motor Cycle News* for a great day out at the 500 Grand Prix at Donington, and for allowing me to gatecrash Brother Justin of the Haringey CX500 Brotherhood.

Thirdly, the biggest debt of gratitude goes to the many riders who allowed me to inveigle my way into their homes for interviews. Rarely have I spent a more agreeable summer: never has fieldwork been so much fun. Particular thanks for contributions beyond the call of duty go to the BMF's Jeff Stone for ongoing support and ideas and MAG's Ian Mutch, especially for the lunches and gardening tips. Most importantly, without the help of the FEMA's Simon Milward, Christina

Acknowledgements

Gésios and Bob Tomlins this book could not have been completed. Extra-special thanks go to Jeff, Ian, Simon, Mandy and Phil Barton for allowing me to take my pick of their photograph collections.

Clearly, thanks go to all of my friends whose mere presence has contributed to the whole thing over a significant number of years. A particular 'thank-you' goes, of course, to my husband, Ruaraidh, for inadvertently giving me the idea in the first place (and whilst bleeding profusely), for putting up with me during the project and for finally restoring my Guzzi. Thanks also to Baines Racing of Silverstone for subsequently repairing said bike after he crashed it. Lastly, thanks to Karen at Zak Leathers for keeping my arse in one piece long enough to write this.

Any complaints, blame her.

Prologue

It is that time of year again, when a Sunday morning finds us heading east along the A14 and north up the A605 to the BMF Show. It is a trip full of anticipation for, as the miles click round we encounter a steadily rising number of bikes on the road. Not all of them are headed in the same direction. Some groups, heavily laden with camping gear, are making their way to the M1 and, thence, home. Most, however, like us, are making for Peterborough. By the time the A605 is reached, the trickle of bikes is becoming a torrent. Like bees, whose numbers multiply as one approaches the hive, by the time we near the Show the bikes have become a swarm.

It is a profoundly moving sight, seeing, and hearing, so many bikes at once. It is infinitely more exhilarating than the Bike Show where, stationary, they are reduced to just so many pounds of metal, plastic and rubber, denied their full expression. Here, on the road, that fundamental essence is clear. Something unidentifiably Japanese whirrs past; well, they all look the same. A noise like a high-speed flatulent cow announces the presence of a Ducati. A Moto Guzzi, coming towards us, makes that unmistakably agricultural *clonk* as it changes gear. It is nice to know that I do not possess the only eccentric Guzzi gearbox.

This year, the journey is quicker than in the past. A new route in, clearly marked lanes and more police and marshals serve to ease the traffic into the ground. It may be more efficient, but I miss the motorcycle traffic jams of previous years, where one had time to examine the myriad collection of bikes. Once on foot, we enter the mêlée. Between 60,000 and 70,000 people are usually expected to attend, and the density of the crowd makes this believable, people coming to a halt in particularly congested areas.

The weather is just right for a change. Last year, in sweltering heat, riders strolled around in almost visibly melting leathers, lolling on the grass, too enervated to move. Two years previously, a cold wind and drizzle seemed to penetrate that protective layer and send people scuttling for cover. Today, warm but overcast, the crowd seem more energetic, exploring all of the stands and tents and lounging outside the beer tents, enjoying a drink.

People attend the Show for many reasons. For, perhaps, the majority, it is an excuse for a ride – not that bikers generally need one. For others, it is an opportunity to pick up clothes or parts at good prices. We were particularly pleased to find a TRT (or a 'turny-roundy-thing', to give the technical term) for the garage. Yet some people are here just to be part of the thing.

Personally, this last is the most important for, whilst it is nice to stroll around the stands, to watch the races and stunts, all the while breathing in air which smells a curious mix of hot-dog and hot oil, the social side is crucial – particularly catching-up with people who live at a distance. My formal arrival is attended by the traditional hug from Andy, which he follows by shaking Ruaraidh's hand in a suitably manly fashion; no soppy hugging for the guys. We all hang around chatting and our conversation demonstrates the dual nature of the Show for, whilst there is obviously much talk about bikes, this is also a social occasion and the topics roam over a wide terrain. Trevor talks of cats and his latest Green Paper. Well, it is a paper, and it has a green cover, interestingly picked-out with blue lettering so that it matches his leathers. One is hovering around the edges of the strange inner world of the compulsive Trekkie here. Best to beat a hasty retreat. I make it so. Simon discusses flying and the best way to obtain a pilot's licence. Jeff's upgraded his 888 to a 995 Fogarty Replica because, as he says, you cannot take it with you so you may as well enjoy it now. Wincing slightly at the price, we applaud this sentiment whilst Ruaraidh, desperate for an 888, sulks because Jeff did not offer it to him first before he sold it. Jeff pretends to be contrite. I pretend to believe in his contrition. Ruaraidh does that 'last puppy in the pet shop' look which men, in the face of all evidence to the contrary, think works.

One of the best parts of the day is seeing Simon and, when he finally shows up, Bob, for whilst E-mail is all well and good, in the last instance it is hard to socialise with someone who lives in Brussels. Simon is deeply into his plans for his round-the-world bike ride for charity. I listen in a kind of horrified admiration and then, because he is a good chap and because I have a mean streak, spend ten minutes listing all of the terrors that can befall a lone rider in some of the more isolated parts of our globe. He does not listen. Well, so long as he has a 6mm Allen key, to my mind the most vital tool to possess, he should be able to fight off the heavily armed mountain bandits he will, no doubt, encounter. I came, I tried, he is a stubborn little sod.

We saunter some more and I, being a traditionalist, take time to deplore the virulent leathers being sported by the older generation these days. We watch some more races, chat some more and then head off home without, as it seems about to rain, stopping at that nice little pub on the A605 which offers a great vantage point for some serious bike-watching.

Back home, beer in hand, I ponder on the day with mixed feelings. I am struck by a trend about which I have had many discussions recently with friends and activists: namely, the declining numbers of bikers who salute each other on the road. In the past, every biker one passed would wave, nod or flash their lights. Increasingly they do not. One wonders whether this signals a decline in camaraderie between bikers, a sense of community which traditionally helped affirm us as 'Us'.

Perhaps it is a good trend, indicating that we no longer feel such a beleaguered, outcast community. Yet I miss the sense of affinity that used to unite us whatever we rode. Similarly, I had spent much of the day talking with bikers and was surprised at how many who were enjoying the hospitality of the BMF knew little about its activities other than this annual event. The Show is the interface, where bikers interact with those active in the riders'-rights lobby, yet it would seem that many riders hardly know these activists exist, or what they do for biking as a whole.

What is extraordinary about this is that everywhere one looked at the Show one saw marshals, people running stalls, organising the programme of events – people who largely were giving up their time voluntarily to throw a party for tens of thousands of riders. For me, as a biker, academic and former activist, the crucial question is thus how and why do some people come to give of themselves to act on behalf of all?

Introduction

This research springs from two interrelated questions. Firstly, it is concerned with the ways in which individuals identify their interests and come to political action and, secondly, how a social movement is born and develops from these concerns within changing social circumstances. These two are seen as fundamentally intertwined in that movements and organisations are seen as shaped by the actions taken by participants, actions undertaken in the light of the conditions which surround them. It is in this sense that we can understand how, for the purposes of this study, concerned individuals are perceived as knowledgeable and capable actors who are both created by, and create and change, their environment. Thus, whilst individuals may find themselves confronted by situations not of their making, they seek to change these circumstances in ways that will be more favourable for them: people act in the present to change their future.

Yet these questions must be located within another issue of current concern: namely, the arguments that contemporary political involvement is, and has been, undergoing transformation. Such ideas are rooted in the belief that we are entering a 'post-political age' wherein, due to the disrepute and contempt in which politicians are held, the 'central focus of new thinking and collective activity is moving away from the political party' (Perryman 1994:1) and towards other forms of political expression. Consequently, it is held that there has been a decline in membership of conventional political parties due to people's disenchantment with traditional politics and a move towards what are called 'new social movements'; that is, single-issue politics and/or alternative forms of lifestyle.

The research upon which this work is based, therefore, is an attempt to unravel these issues through an examination of a specific social group which has only recently entered the political arena: motorcyclists. Those familiar with the limited, and dated, British data may find this a strange choice in that the best-known works on riders, carried out in the 1960s, hardly present a picture of knowledgeable actors capable of political action. Thus, for example, S. Cohen, in the later edition of his work on mods and rockers, argues that 'there are just the same (rather poor) sources of information from the same (often inarticulate) informants' (1980:ii). Similarly, Willis, whilst portraying bikers as having outrageous style and attitudes, sees them as offering no political challenge or critique to change society but, instead, as manifesting 'an inability to break from cultural forms into any kind of political activity or power struggle' (1978:6).

Clearly, we cannot subject these comments to rigorous critique in that we cannot establish their accuracy some twenty or thirty years on. Further, two points make any such challenge impossible. The first, historical, point is that they were both writing in the years when riders'-rights organisations (RROs) – that is, organisations dedicated politically to the rights of *motorcyclists* rather than concerned purely with *motorcycling* – were in their infancy and thus riders may not have been generally aware of 'biker politics'. The second, theoretical, point is that political challenges at that time were generally seen as valid only to the extent that they could be seen as concerned with the inequalities of the class structure, that is as portraying features of the 'old social movements' of the labour struggle. Indeed, at that time, non-class politics tended to be seen as no politics at all. Now, however, due to the rise of new social movements such as the civil rights, feminist and gay movements, a much broader definition of what constitutes political action is in general usage – a more inclusive definition which, it is believed, befits the subject matter under discussion.

As such, we need to establish the extent to which the motorcycling community and the RROs may be judged as 'qualifying' as a new social movement. However, we do not seek here to provide a detailed theoretical exploration of the entire body of relevant literature, and that for three reasons. The first, simply, is that these are to be found, and in a much more competent form, elsewhere. Secondly, such reviews tend to be 'framed as confrontations between competing paradigms' (Klandermans 1997:199) through which, by attacking the works of others, authors have 'added more heat than light in this area of study' (Tarrow 1994:2). Consequently, rather than introducing ideas merely to disagree with them, only those works that have provided positive and constructive help shall be used. Thirdly, it is believed that academia should not be a 'closed shop' in which researchers merely talk with one another, but that it should open up debates to a fuller audience of interested 'lay-people' with whom we have interests in common. With that in mind, overly abstract, and lengthy, discussion may only act as a disincentive. Thus, whilst this work must be placed in some kind of theoretical context, this shall be kept to a minimum (and may be passed over if desired), for as Seidman so aptly argues, 'much sociological theory is unconnected to current research programs, divorced from current social movements and political struggles. . . . Sociological theory has become the domain of theory specialists, with its own technical problems and vocabularies. . . . Needless to say, few people except for theorists read sociological theory texts' (1992:47). Thus, it is believed, too often theory mystifies its substance, in this instance people's political involvement, concealing more than it reveals, and provoking more questions than answers. Rather, theory should not shroud people's lives, obscuring them to outsiders, but make them transparent in a way which enlightens non-members.

That said, we do need to explain how the data are understood. The first question to be answered is the extent to which we can understand bikers, their community and their political organisations as fitting definitions of either a social movement or a pressure group. Scott, for example, argues that a social movement is:

> ... a collective actor constituted by individuals who understand themselves to have common interests and, for at least some significant part of their social existence, a common identity. Social movements are distinguished from other collective actors, such as political parties and pressure groups, in that they have mass mobilisation, or the threat of mobilisation, as their prime source of social sanction, and hence of power. They are further distinguished from other collectivities, such as voluntary associations or clubs, in being chiefly concerned to defend or change society, or the relative position of the group in society (1990:6).

As we shall discover, the first part of this definition may be seen as corresponding to a community generally, which has interests and identity in common. Yet the second part refers more narrowly to political activities seeking change. This more confrontational aspect is caught by Tarrow, for example, who defines social movements as '*collective challenges by people with common purposes and solidarity in sustained interaction with elites, opponents and authorities*' (1994:3–4. Author's emphasis). Such a definition casts social movements primarily in oppositional terms, as a unified group with 'enemies'. However, the idea of political engagement with elites, and the potentiality for mass mobilisation identified by Scott would perhaps be more properly characteristic of the RROs, which fulfil definitions of social movement *organisations*, the goals of which fit in with that of a broader movement. Consequently, within the wider movement, concentrated at its core, may be the political arm, which may be better understood as a pressure group.

Smith informs us that pressure groups 'are organisations that seek to represent the interests of particular sections of society in order to influence public policy. Pressure groups are distinguished from political parties in that they do not usually seek election to office' (1995:7). Furthermore, in accordance with the notion that traditional politics are in decline, pressure groups are seen as becoming increasingly important as individuals choose to align due to identity or beliefs, for example with gay rights or ecologism, rather than through class position with conservatives, socialists or whatever. What this means, therefore, is that 'we are entering an era of anti-politics in which pressure groups are the dominant mode of political representation and expression' (Mulgan 1994:1). Yet within these broad definitions we may draw a further distinction between sectional groups, which protect the interests of a particular section of society, and promotional groups, which promote causes arising from a given set of attitudes or beliefs (Willetts 1982); that is, between groups whose cause is a type of person and groups whose cause is a cause. This distinction helps us identify riders as belonging to a specific type of sectional group, more bounded in its membership than a promotional one – such as the environmental movement.

Such distinctions between social movements and pressure groups are not definitive, however, for social movements form a continuum from informal networks through to formal associations (Scott 1990). It is in this light that we can understand Melucci's (1989) argument that social movements are rarely seen, as most action is submerged in the social networks of everyday life. As such, we must distinguish between visible behaviour, when a group engages in public action, and latent behaviour which occurs 'invisibly', out of the public eye. Consequently, rather than seeing the biking community and the RROs as a movement and as pressure group respectively, we can see them both as part of a continuum, as a dynamic process of involvement. Thus, for example, the differences between a summer evening's ride with friends and riding on a demonstration should be seen as a difference of degree, not of kind. Social movements shall be seen, therefore, as growing from the rootedness of everyday life and experience.

This, of course, begs the question of why people become involved. This contains two aspects: namely, to determine the nature of participants' demands and the processes through which they become engaged in a movement. In relation to the first of these, the new social-movement literature argues that there has been a decline in the importance of class and, relatedly, of class politics due to the growing complexity of society and of people's lives. This means that people increasingly find themselves with 'a plurality of memberships arising from the multiplication of social positions, associative networks, and reference groups' (Melucci 1989:108) and align politically on the basis of other forms of identification than merely class, such as patterns of consumption (Bocock 1992). In the contemporary period, therefore, political activity is not necessarily determined by who people are, but by their preferences – what has been called the 'politics of choice'. To this end, contemporary political aims are seen as qualitatively different from those of the old labour tradition; seeking not material goals, such as the redistribution of wealth, but more amorphous rewards based on 'post-material', intangible values (Inglehart 1977).

The common theme to the goals sought by new political groups is that they are characterised as cultural, in that many of 'these struggles take place within the realm of civil society, that is, those areas of society that are neither part of the processes of material production in the economy nor part of state-funded organis-ations' (Routledge 1995:273). Thus, for example, goals may include 'the autonomy and dignity of diverse individuals and groups', who seek an enhanced 'quality of life' (Routledge 1995:272). In this sense, people seek autonomy in order to fulfil themselves, either to be able to chose personal identities (Plotke 1995) or achieve self-realisation (Melucci 1989). Relatedly, movements may seek social justice, that they may enjoy the same rights as others (Perryman 1994). There has also been a tendency to view these 'new' forms of political expression as different in structure and organisation, being anti-hierarchical, grass-roots movements with democratic decision-making structures and non-conventional forms of action. Such movements are seen as having little to do with traditional political concerns about the extension of citizenship and more to do with lifestyles and cultural codes (Koopmans 1995).

However, it may be argued that such debates over-state the differences between 'old' and 'new' forms of politics. Thus, for example, the work of Barrington Moore (1978) indicates that, among German workers in the mid-nineteenth and early twentieth centuries, one could find the expression of non-material values running through economic struggles – a demand for 'decent moral treatment' which bears close resemblance to goals found among the new social movements and, indeed, as we shall see later, among bikers. Further, Scott (1990) argues that all social movements are also political in that they are about political integration and access to decision-making processes. Thus what may appear as social demands may feed into the state in that they may require political negotiation between politicians and pressure groups, set new political agendas and involve allocation of state resources. For example, whilst a woman's right to choose abortion is clearly a personal one, it carries ramifications for NHS funding and so on. In this sense, there is no easy distinction between the social and the political. As Scott argues, 'the personal is not political merely in the sense that power relations are embedded in personal ones, but also in the sense that demands for personal autonomy, freedom, etc., are political in nature' (1990:23). Consequently, he argues, new social movements sit at the interface between state and civil society. Such conclusions are supported by Koopmans, who argues that some new movements have managed to have their concerns become part of political agendas and have influenced the programmes of established political parties. As such, they are not merely cultural but are 'thoroughly shaped by their political environment. . . . In most cases, the new social movements have not hesitated to use the political opportunities offered to them: litigation in courts, attempts to influence political parties, the media and the government . . . and demonstrations aimed at concrete objectives have been typical for the mainstream of the new social movements' (1995:232).

We can conclude, therefore, that the new social movements overlap with the old in that whilst they may seek non-material goals they do this through interaction with institutionalised politics. This leaves us with our final and, in terms of the nature of this work, most important question: namely, that of determining why people become drawn into a group and thence on to movement participation. Early attempts at theorisation tended to see the emergence of movements as due either to grievances which indicated structural strains in society or to look at how movements emerged due to an increase in resources which made action possible. Yet, as Melucci (1989) argues, such theories fail to explain the process by which individuals come to identify with a movement; that is, the process by which actors become drawn into a group and into activism.

Clearly, there are some groups that one has no choice about joining, even if individuals may seek to circumvent this – what sex or colour one is, for example. In other groups, however, decisions about whether or not to participate are optional, and depend upon an individual's preferences. In such instances, therefore, membership involves a conscious choice. When this is the case, individuals' ideas, beliefs and experiences become 'important for understanding the motivations to participate in social movements' (della Porta 1992:188). Thus we need to examine the reasons for participation among individuals, as it is through this participation that they come to take on the collective identity of a group and become integrated within it.

Klandermans gives us a detailed analysis of the processes through which this occurs. When individuals become part of a group they must first become familiar with its collective beliefs, a process which becomes reinforced as participation continues. Group membership, therefore, creates a group identity. He argues:

> The way in which collective beliefs are formed and transformed depends to a great extent on the fact that they are, by definition, shared. Obviously, collective beliefs are not created by individuals in isolation but in interpersonal interaction. In these social exchanges, events and new information are discussed, interpreted and commented on. . . . Interpersonal interaction, then, is crucial in the construction and reconstruction of collective beliefs. This kind of interaction depends on the existence of a social identity – that is, the way an individual defines himself or herself as a member of a group or category. . . . Because they identify with a particular group, individuals may willingly adopt the beliefs and norms that define the group (1997:5).

Yet this collective belief system, which he calls a 'collective action frame' is not static, but changes in time/space. Klandermans continues:

> A movement's collective action frame is continuously under construction. In public discourse, during confrontations with its opponents, and in interaction with its constituency it is moulded, elaborated, specified and expanded; and, while they are appropriating beliefs, individual movement supporters create their own versions of the collective action frame, thus making their contributions to the ongoing construction of the movement's collective action frame (1997:63).

Through membership and ongoing participation within a group, individuals thus become integrated into the collectivity yet, at the same time, input into the way in which the group's beliefs develop over time in response to changing circumstances. Movements are thus dynamic systems composed of individual parts. Further, this dynamism continues over time in that, with ongoing participation in a movement, people must respond to changes both in society and the political opportunity structure which will affect their beliefs, tactics and goals. Both individuals and movements are thus moulded by events. It is the interrelatedness of individual identity and politics which forms the basis for this research. This entails, as Brunt argues, an examination of both activists' experiences and the circumstances which help them develop as they do. To this end, she argues:

> The starting point I'd suggest for any politics of identity is the issue of 'representation': both how our identities are represented in and through culture and assigned particular categories; and also who or what politically represents us, speaks and acts on our behalf. These two senses of 'representation' alert us to the whole area of culture and ideology as we live it and as it is lived and directly experienced by us. They help us think how we both 'make sense' of the world and get a sense of our 'place' in it – a place of many, and increasing identities (1990:152).

To sum-up this discussion, the aims of this research are threefold. Firstly, we seek to undertake a micro-level analysis of why and how individuals make the decisions they do about group membership and how, through this, they come to the identities and beliefs they do. Secondly, an exploration will be made of what draws members further into organisational activism, and the problems and rewards of political involvement, and, lastly, how this is located within the larger set of structural constraints determined by the political sphere. Yet, whilst these questions are primarily political, it is believed that politics comes from, is informed by and informs, the rooted experience of everyday life. It is this sense that there is believed to be no categorical distinction between the cultural and the political, for both are seen as growing from, and into, each other. As such, it is through the stories of individual lives that we can understand these broader social processes and gain a fuller understanding of how, through people's actions, a social movement is created and reproduced.

It is due to this fundamental task – the attempt to understand what brings people to a group, why they become active and the consequences of their actions for the creation and development of movements and organisations – that an ethnographic approach has been used in carrying out this research, for it believed that only through such techniques can one fully understand the processes through which individuals develop into activists. What is of concern, therefore, it not so much the 'factual' history of the development of the riders'-rights organisations and the wider biking community, but how this is perceived by those within it and how, through knowledgeable and capable action, they come to change their world. It is through the personal histories of these individuals that we can thus see the interrelationship between objective and subjective, and structure and agency. Clearly there are weaknesses within such an approach that are typically levelled at qualitative research; the primary ones being of the reliability and comparability of data and the representativeness of the sample. The former criticisms are concerned with whether people, consciously or unconsciously, give the 'truth', for they might forget, distort or whatever, and of whether it is possible to compare such unique, individual stories. The latter of these makes the point that by using ethnographic data one cannot fully determine whether those interviewed represent the whole population – in this case whether they reflect the general biking community. Further criticisms come from Klandermans (1997), who feels that using only participants within a movement tells us nothing about those who do not participate, nor how activists' beliefs are changed by participation, and from Friedman, who argues that the problem with ethnographic research is that the researcher determines what is said and that this may consequently mean that 'we ultimately force him [*sic*] to speak through our categories' (1992:322).

In order to access the validity of this work it therefore becomes important to discuss the methodological approach used. In terms of fieldwork methods, this research was conducted through a combination of participant observation or, rather, participation over a period of many years, informal interviews with bikers and forty in-depth taped interviews with activists, ranging from occasional participants through local, regional, national and international officers. Thus, whilst one may never completely be sure that one's results are reliable, it is believed that the time-scale and wide variety of individuals involved, and the general consensus given, preclude the probability of distortion. Primarily, however, for the in-depth interviews, only activists were used. Yet this is not held to be the weakness Klandermans suggests, for two reasons. Firstly, activists *are* the target population, for it is precisely activism which is under discussion. Secondly, whilst they are also used for the general discussion on biking and the biking community, as bikers their feelings and experiences accord with that of the wider community. His second point, how activism changes people, can be addressed only by identifying people before they become active and following them over many years, or by asking them. Acting on the premise, discussed above, that people are knowledgeable subjects, the latter approach was adopted. However, his criticisms, and also that made by Friedman, can be minimalised by adopting certain strategies, della Porta (1992) informs us. Firstly, we should engage in interviews until we have reached saturation – that is, the point at which no significant new information is being discovered. Secondly, we can compare stories to try to ensure that they fit with the general picture and by seeking participants who have considerable experience. Thirdly, she suggests that if the researcher has good background knowledge in the area they may be able to determine what is relevant from the interviews, but also, we may add, help assess whether data are reliable and help avoid imposing categories in data selection.

As has been noted above, the first of these two criteria were observed in terms of the variety of people involved, the time-scale of research and the years of experience that many respondents had in the area. In relation to the last point, it may be useful to state that I have ridden motorcycles since my teens, and that I have, in the past, been active within a riders' rights organisation. Consequently, all information provided was assessed in the light of this, and, to counter Friedman, if I have imposed categories on the data, hopefully I have imposed these as a biker and not an academic. As such, these are not 'unconnected' data with no real meaning for me as a researcher, for I have experienced personally the changes and events to which my respondents refer and continue to experience the threats posed by anti-motorcycling legislation, just as do they. My life, therefore, has infused this fieldwork as, indeed, this fieldwork has infused my life. Thus the stories which others narrate are also my stories, just as this book is also theirs.

Part I
Bikers and the Biking Community

–1–

On Becoming a Biker

Primary questions in any investigation into a social group must include what drew an individual to that community or activity, what meanings being part of that group hold and what rewards are gained. In this chapter, we shall seek to explore why people become drawn to motorcycling, the enjoyments and frustrations that are associated with it, but also how these factors have changed since the pre-war years; for such issues are not necessarily constant in time, and may vary between different periods as social conditions change. Further, like other material objects, motorcycles exist not only in themselves, but as bearers of symbolic meaning and identification – that is, that they carry social 'messages' to others. What we shall examine is how these have both positive and negative consequences for riders, that what draws individuals to motorcycling is, at times, the very same thing which is used to denigrate and marginalise bikers as a community within the wider social context

Clearly, individuals assume many different roles and identities in the course of their lives, some of which are determined by external forces, such as gender or ethnicity, for example (Bocock 1992), whereas others are chosen voluntarily. Just as clearly, motorcycling is a chosen identification. This being the case, we must therefore examine what factors lead individuals to make the choices they do in that, as Klandermans argues, 'if we consider that . . . there is no inherent reason why an individual should identify with one category rather than another, we will see that we need to find more specific factors to explain social identification' (1997:159). As a form of consumer choice, motorcycling exists in a domain of relative autonomy, dependent only upon financial means and retail possibilities. Yet consumption may also be seen as not just about material purchases but as a form of self-expression – a means by which individuals 'express their sense of freedom, their personal power' (Tomlinson 1990:6), and as a mechanism through which riders seek 'to preserve the autonomy and individuality of his [sic] existence in the face of overwhelming social forces' (Bocock 1992:126). Riding a motorcycle, therefore, may not be merely an activity, but also a mode of being.

However, although a form of individual expression, motorcycling is also inherently social in nature, in that our membership of particular social groups binds us into collective identities and beliefs, that is that 'people derive their identity (their sense of self, the self-concept) in great part from the social categories to which they belong' (Hogg and Abrams 1988:18–19). As Klandermans explains, people 'employ distinct sets of beliefs in difference circumstances and in doing so draw from the beliefs that are available . . . Individual beliefs, then, are appropriated collective beliefs.' (Klandermans 1997:43–4). In this sense, motorcycling functions also as a means of 'constructing identity, constructing the self, and constructing relations with others' (Bauman 1992:223).

This latter factor is significant for, whilst part of one's identity may come from relations with other bikers, it stems from relations with non-bikers; for a community does not exist in a social vacuum but forms part of a wider society, and relations across that boundary between the in-group and out-group also carry consequences for the collectivity as a whole. This is not to argue that the circumstances confronting the motorcycling community have remained static, for social conditions and attitudes change both for riders and non-riders. It is thus necessary to view the community as a dynamic phenomenon, which evolves as its members' actions act to either perpetuate or change the community in time/space (Giddens 1979). For the purposes of this study, therefore, what is of importance is how the motorcycling community responds over time to perceptions of motorcyclists that hold general social currency.

Consequently, we need to explore the reasons why one chooses to ride a bike, ones experiences of riding, and the relations in which one engages when 'being a biker', for all of these factors provide us with significant data with which to understand motorcyclists. Further, through such an understanding, we can lay the basis for an exploration of the community itself for, if individuals are inextricably linked into the collectivity, then any analysis of a social movement must depend upon its fundamental building block, the individual group member.

Three main reasons are primarily identified as underlying a person's decision to start riding: friends, family and a feeling that motorcycles are a source of both romance and exhilaration. Motivating factors are thus both situational and symbolic. Only one rider within the sample knew of no other motorcyclists when she first started. For most, therefore, there was a pre-existing climate within which motorcycling becomes a possibility, that is that riders 'have to be made aware of them as an option'. As such, individuals must be able to 'access' the group to which they wish to belong (Melucci 1989). Yet, without doubt, this social setting is also one within which the motorcycle is appreciated as offering positive rewards. Consequently, motivations are likely to overlap. One noticeable factor is that family played a more crucial part in bringing young men to riding among older riders. The following quotation, from a man in his late fifties, indicates the importance of family for older riders:

> I first started riding bikes when I was fourteen, which was dad's little runabout – because dad had always had motorbikes. He'd had motorbikes from when he was a lad. And so even though we had a car, he'd bought himself a little BSA Bantam to go backwards

and forwards to work. And so he let me have my first ride on that when I was fourteen, on some private land . . . And then I couldn't wait until I was sixteen. But then, the first bike I had, dad had then gone off using a bike for work, but he had a little two-stroke, James Captain 200cc, and so he let me have that as my learner bike.

Figure 1 Cafe racers on Kettering market place, 1965

Among younger riders there is less of a sense of motorcycles as part of a specific male culture one enters during adolescence, and a smaller role is played by family members. Thus the first quotation, which portrays motorcycling as part of a post-war climate in which cars were not necessarily the primary mode of transport, may no longer reflect general experience, which indicates a decrease of fathers riding among those of the sample born in the 1960s and 1970s. The following two quotations, from younger men, instead stress the role of friends or siblings, thus indicating a break in generational socialisation within the family and a greater role for peer groups. The first comes from a 45-year-old who was brought up without his father, and thus was not part of the male motorcycling culture, and the second from someone born in 1965:

I think it all started when I was fifteen and I was doing a holiday job at a local electrical engineers, during the school holidays. And a lot of the young men there had motorcycles, because we're talking about 1965–66, and it was a normal thing for young men to have bikes before they went onto cars. So they were starting to change then. And there was one lad who had a 500 Velocette, which was regarded as an extremely potent machine at the time, but by modern standards it would be regarded as somewhat gutless. And he gave me a lift home on the back of that, and I think I was sold on motorcycles after that. I was never allowed to have a motorcycle, at that time I was being brought-up by my grandmother, who was extremely hostile, and every time I mentioned motorcycles she would tell me horror stories about people having accidents and all that. And it wasn't until probably about a year after she died, when I was about twenty-four, when I actually first bought a motorcycle.

It was just something that well, I don't know, when you're, sort of, quite a young teenager, I just got interested in it because it seemed like an exciting thing, I suppose. And there were a few people around where I lived who had bikes, or their older brothers had bikes, and that sort of thing, and they were very exciting.

This 'pursuit of excitement' (Downes and Rock 1982:145), and of the romance of the motorcycle, is caught by one rider, who encapsulates how motorcycling may fire the imagination by its promise of the unknown:

I started in '69 on a BSA500, single-cylinder, sidecar outfit. As a kid I didn't have a big thing about bikes. I had an uncle who owned one, and it seemed like quite an exciting thing. But I wasn't interested in them mechanically, I wasn't, sort of, 'Wow, there goes a Norton' or whatever. It wasn't until I was sixteen that it dawned on me that I could *buy* motorised transport, that I thought, 'This might be quite fun.' And then I saw some of these old war films like *The Great Escape*, where there always these characters careering around on sidecar outfits, looking pretty eccentric, and I thought, 'That looks like a lot of fun.' And I thought I could carry a lot with me, because travel was what I wanted to do, I wasn't very interested in speed, and so I bought the sidecar outfit, because I convinced my parents that it was very safe. They were dead against it, but I managed to convince them sufficiently to let me have this thing, because the accident record of sidecar outfits was very, very good, better than cars. But I think it had more to do with the fact that it was mostly old duffers, either carting around a ladder and a bucket and mop, or their families in them, [who owned them]. It was a very exciting time. I can remember being at school in the sixth form and looking out of the window of the science lab., three floors up, and in one direction you could see the docks, Dagenham docks I suppose it was, and you could see the cranes in the distance – I'd never been there, the docks were something extremely nasty that I never had anything to do with – and if you looked in the other direction where the land rises to the north of the Thames Valley – Hainault and Chigwell and that way – you could see these hills. And there was a *tremendous* fascination in just seeing hills and thinking, 'I must get to those hills and see what lies beyond.' And I set off in the summer of 1970, June, when I'd finished my A'levels, swearing I'd never do anything academic again, anything that involved opening an instruction book, and just set off with total optimism and about probably £7 or £8, and headed for Devon, that I particularly liked, the south-west peninsula always held a great attraction. I think partly the Arthurian legends and the mythology associated,

Glastonbury and all that. And a friend of mine [came along], it was just when Mungo Jerry had brought out 'In the Summertime', and I thought this was great, and I wanted to have side-burns like Lee Dawsey. That really seemed a fantastic time, and we set-off, no helmet law then, I remember I was wearing a beret, and we set-off at midnight.

Yet the romance of the motorcycle need not be focused on the 'machine' as such, that is it is not necessarily confined to those who are primarily interested in all things mechanical. Indeed, the technological side to motorcycling may be no more than a necessary evil. The same rider continues:

I've no interest in spanners *whatsoever*. The first few weeks I had that bike, I hadn't a spanner on it, and eventually I was out, there were four of us on it, two on the bike, two in the sidecar, and it was a little over-stressed. And it stopped, the bike just stopped. And we looked at it, and smoke was *pouring* off it. And I undid this sort of tap or something on the side, I wasn't sure what it was, looked inside, and there was this empty space with smoke pouring out of it. It was the oil tank, and it was empty. And, I remember, we pushed it, and we found a garage, and there was a guy with a load of oil in a tray under an engine, filthy oil out of the sump, and we gathered all of our money together and we had a shilling. Well, we got this shilling together and poured about a pint of this filth into it, and it unseized and off we went on it. So, no, I wasn't a mechanic!

This self-acknowledged lack of interest in the mechanics of the motorcycle is another aspect which appears to have changed over time. Older riders are usually keen to emphasise that the present-day rider is not so intimately involved in the workings of their motorcycle as was formerly the case. Much of this is seen to be due to the changes in technology, as is intimated below, a factor which, as we shall see elsewhere, may be one of the reasons that the profile of the motorcyclist is changing:

When I was a lad you did all your own maintenance on bikes. You *had* to understand how they worked. You took them apart, you repaired them etc. etc.. People today, they buy a motorbike and they take it to the dealer, as they would the car, to have it serviced. They haven't got a *clue* what makes it work, how it works or whatever. They just want the oil changed, the plugs changed. Japanese bikes are incredibly reliable, you don't *need* to know how they work to enable you to go on your holidays or whatever.

The type of bikes themselves have become very expensive. Their ability to work on those bikes, to maintain them service them, has reduced dramatically. I mean, to do major work on a bike when I was a kid was easy. To do it on a 250 overhead camshaft Honda, even something like a Dream, is difficult. You need real skills.

Clearly, many motorcyclists are involved with the maintenance, restoration and customising of their machines, and this plays a large part of the attraction of motorcycling for the mechanically minded yet, in the last instance, it is the experiential nature of riding itself which most explicitly demonstrates the attitude of riders to their bikes. For motorcyclists, it is the immediacy and sense of unity with the machine that provides the most pleasure. Thus, whilst for contemporary society technology may often be seen as something independent of societal intervention, outside our control (Tester 1993), a force which may be, perhaps, deplored, feared, but which cannot be gainsaid, for motorcyclists, it is the interrelationship between the rider and the motorcycle which is the source of esoteric gratification:

> You are part of the bike, whereas you're *in* a car, and you have a screen in front of you, and I always think, when I'm driving the car, I could just have been looking at a video game. You've got *no* contact with it. Whereas, with a bike, you've got full feeling of what's going on around you. You've got a lot more perception of what's *happening*.

> That feeling of being out there, and you're moving, and you can go from one place to another, completely uninhibited, and the tarmac is six inches under your feet, and you're there, you're in it . . . it's interactive with the world around you in a way that isn't achievable through any other mode of transport.

There is a crucial sense here in which a motorcycle's role as a mode of transport appears to be almost of less interest to riders than the more intrinsic aspects of enjoyment that come from it, that is that it would appear that motorcyclists do not have an instrumental attitude to their vehicles purely as objects of transportation. The following comments all allude to things which have little to do with mere mobility:

> I'm just as happy with a small bike as I am with a big one. Even when I've had big bikes, I've had performance bikes, a GT550, the Suzuki two-stroke, which was pretty nifty. After that I had a Honda 125 then for a year, and that was just as much fun. In fact, I had an old BSA side-valve after that, which was flat-out at fifty, and that was great, I loved it. I just like riding. It's as simple as that. I get just as much enjoyment pottering around country lanes at a sedate pace, and through towns, weaving in and out of traffic, which you couldn't do on a big bike, as I do from riding at a sensible speed along a nice, fast A-road. I don't like dual-carriageways and motorways at all on a bike.

> It's a personal thing, isn't it? I mean, I know why *I'm* enthusiastic about motorcycles. Me? It's all the old ones, you know. I need transport. I can't get to work without transport. I would prefer to do it by motorcycle because I'm the only one who arrives at work with a *smile* on my face. I actually *enjoy* my ride to work. I don't like it when I'm *there* much. You know, it's great that I can come home again. And when I get home I might go straight back out again. I actually enjoy *riding* it. It's *great* fun, yeah? I enjoy doing it.

This enthusiasm for motorcycles is seen to separate them from other road users. As one rider informs us:

> Most people who drive cars do it for practical reasons only: to transport themselves or goods. People who ride motorcycles tend to be enthusiasts. And so there is a clear divide there. And because enthusiasm is one of the other common denominators which unites bikers . . . the possibilities of there being some kind of gregarious instinct or recognition of a social common ground is greater than it would be between car drivers.

Yet whilst this enjoyment marks riders off from, at least, the majority of car drivers, it does unite them with other people who are passionate; whatever the object of their enthusiasm:

> Do they have something in common? Yeah. But it's no different from your local modelling club, or local camera club, they've all got something in common as well, haven't they? And that's *enthusiasm* for something. And it's *that* that they have in common. It's enthusiasm for what they do that they have in common. What they *haven't* got in common, and why they all look down on each other, is their *object* of enthusiasm is different, or slightly different from the other people's. The motorcyclist would call the local camera club 'anoraks'. One of my brothers, Richard, he's involved in all levels of the BMF, beavering away in the background, is called an anorak by his wife, because all he does is motorbikes. 'It's motorbikes. It's motorbikes all the time. You're a bloody anorak!' Because she's a non-motorcyclist, looking at what he does, and he's obsessed with motorcycles as far as she's concerned. He's an anorak. So, what has he got in common? He's got this *enthusiasm* for something.

However, if riders see themselves merely as people with a particular interest, in common with all other people with specialised interests, clearly the form of their interest is specific, that is whilst they have the *attitude* in common with others, the *focus* of that attitude draws a distinction between them. Consequently, whilst any activity for which an individual feels a passionate attachment must play a part in the enrichment of that person's life, what is of interest is, given the complexity of daily life, what role motorcycling plays for riders. The most obvious component to be identified about motorcycles would appear to be that they are extremely vulnerable to the world around them, whether from inclement weather, an unexpected pothole, an unobservant car driver or whatever. This quality is, to a large part, one of the attractions of motorcycling for those of a suitable disposition. As one motorcycle journalist argues:

> This is something you'll find with quite a lot of motorcyclists, they don't just do motorcycling. In fact, the prime example of that is off-road motorcycle racers. That isn't all they do. They're into lots of other, what people might call 'adrenaline sports' or

Figure 2 The BMF's Phil Barton perfects his James Dean impress

dangerous sports, and that could be anything from downhill mountain bicycling, which is something I do, to race cars or probably something that involves quite a lot of fitness.

This is not to say that all motorcyclists would undertake all types of dangerous activity, but merely that they would do so to accomplish a specified aim, as the following quotation indicates:

> The pleasure of doing it, once you've discovered it, the pleasure of doing it far outweighs the possibilities of being injured, if you like. Some people do bungee-jumping, which I would never dream of doing, thank you very much indeed. But people have their own views of what limits they'll go up to to enjoy [themselves].

Whatever extent it may be to which individuals are prepared to go, however, there is a sense in which danger is inseparable from motorcycling's image of romance, as encapsulated by a sense of excitement and gratification:

> I think, certainly, there is a bit of romantic in everybody that rides a motorcycle. Danger and romance are inseparable. And when people show you something awful, like the consequences of a fatal accident, and ask, 'Where is the pleasure in that, and the

excitement, and the romance?' it's in the exhilaration of a form of propulsion that's so personalised, so *you*.

It is, perhaps, this flirtation with danger as an ever-present variable which may account, at least partially, for the hedonistic image associated with biking, that is that the assumption may be that people prepared to live with, or positively encourage, dangerous circumstances are somehow different, less safe, than those who do not. One rider offers his own explanation for the effects of the risk of danger on the attitudes of motorcyclists:

> We know we're more vulnerable and we know that, in order to combat that, we have to be more aware of what we're doing when we're riding. And I would be very surprised if that doesn't rub off into other areas of our lives . . . It is about how that difference filters into other areas of life as well, not just how we are different, but the *effect* of that difference, I'd like to think that we party harder than your average. There's the risk-taking side of it . . . There's a madness to bikers that takes us over the edge in all kinds of ways . . . We're *less* safe because we have to be *more* safe. It's almost risk compensation. Because we have to be more safe on the road, we're less safe in the rest of our lives. [People who would say motorcycling is unsafe to begin with] haven't quite sussed that it's not bikes that are dangerous, it's cars that are dangerous. It's bikes that are vulnerable, and bikers that are vulnerable. So bikers tend to be more aware of their vulnerability, when they're riding. And when they're not, I think the way that plays out is, 'Oh, I'm not riding my bike now, I must be invulnerable!'

Relatedly, it is also feasible to argue that this awareness of risk, and of rationally considering that risk, means that, to some extent, motorcyclists are gamblers. This position is argued by the rider below, and also linked intrinsically to the entire experience and enjoyment of riding:

> To give you an example, right, you can get a biker who wants to go to a rally, the rally's three-hundred miles away, his bike has certain mechanical problems, let's say. He sits down on a Thursday evening, he works through, maybe, till early Friday morning to get those mechanical problems fixed. He *thinks* he's fixed them, he's not absolutely sure and he won't know until he gets fifty miles, or a hundred miles up the road, right. He thinks he's done it. He sets out for the rally on the Friday night and he's, basically, investing, then, his trust in his own abilities. And if he's got it wrong, he's got to cope with the consequences. And the consequences can be very expensive, and very uncomfortable . . . That biker who's done that, right, let's say he's going to ride a six-hundred-mile round trip. And the bike goes wrong, at the extreme end, three-hundred miles away, and he ain't got any breakdown cover because he's, perhaps, not very flush with cash, and he hasn't paid for his AA cover, or his RAC cover, he's got to get his bike back by some way or another. It might cost him £200 to do it, you know, pay out for the Rescue Service if he breaks down without cover. Now, that's like saying, 'I am

prepared to gamble £200 to have a good weekend doing what I enjoy.' You say to the average member of Joe Public, 'To have an enjoyable weekend this weekend, will you gamble £200?' whether putting it on a horse, playing with cards, playing poker or whatever, and most people will say, 'No.' So you've got to be a bit of a gambler as well, I think, to be a biker. I think it takes a certain amount of tough-mindedness to gamble for high stakes as well. You see, again, most motorcyclists are smart enough to know what the accident statistics are. So being a biker is a gamble to start with. I *know* it, I *accept* it. As far as I'm concerned it's a gamble that's worth it. I wouldn't enjoy life as much if I didn't ride a motorcycle anyway, so I don't see the point of not taking the chance. You take the chance, the gamble makes it better. And I don't want someone to take away my right to gamble. I'm not talking about a stupid gamble, I'm not talking about riding up the road with your eyes shut and hoping that you don't hit ouwt. What you do is you try and improve the odds in your favour. You're trying to improve the odds, so you leave yourself a good stopping distance. You see somebody at a junction, you weigh-up what they're doing. You watch them. You figure out your escape route if they pull out, all this kind of thing. Well, that's all part of it as well.

As such, the implication is not that riders are unaware of the risks they take, but merely that some risks are acceptable if the rewards they bring outweigh possible disadvantages. Risk awareness, therefore, is a subjective assessment dependant upon social priorities. What is of further interest, however, as Adams argues below, is how the perception of risk may differ between certain types of people and communities:

> . . . risk is culturally constructed. . . . Slipping and falling on ice, for example, is a game for young children, but a potentially fatal accident for an old person. And the probability of such an event is influenced both by a person's perception of the probability, and by whether they see it as fun or dangerous. For example, because old people see the risk of slipping on an icy road to be high, they take avoiding action, thereby reducing the probability. Young people slipping and sliding on the ice, and old people striving to avoid the same, belong to separate and distinct *cultures*. They *construct* reality out of their experience of it. They see the world differently and behave differently; they tend to associate with kindred spirits, who reinforce their distinctive perspectives on reality in general and risk in particular (1995:9).

Motorcycling, therefore, is about calculating risks, potentially life-threatening ones. Yet another part of this, and intrinsically bound up in this sense of danger, is the heightened awareness this gives the individual of 'living life' – an awareness that confines itself not merely to dangerous scenarios but to motorcycling generally. As one rider observes, 'it's just to do it. The risk factor you're introducing, *aware* that there is a risk of your own mortality, but *needing desperately* to be near the edge of it', means that there is an intensity to the experience beyond the common-ality of life – a 'being in the world' more powerful and more gratifying than that of routine existence, and which can be found only in extreme conditions:

> I think [riding a bike changes people]. Partly, because it does bring you into contact with the elements, that's one important thing. When it gets cold, you know it's getting cold because you're get colder. Whereas if you're driving a car you adjust your heater, and you still climb out of it in a short-sleeved shirt if you feel like it, in the middle of winter. And that fundamental is a big, big difference. When somebody's cut the grass at the side of the road you can *smell* it more easily. When the road is wet, you have to be much more careful. To a great extent, you step back in time, you're like the cowboy riding the range, and you're looking out for Indians all of the time. Or the explorer, who's going to the Arctic, and voluntarily exposes himself to risk, or the lone yachtsman, or any kind of yachtsman for that matter, going down to the Southern Ocean, and doing crazy things like that. . . . I think, these days, because life has become so comfortable, everything from running water to central heating, the human race, certainly in the West, finds discomfort almost as unacceptable as it finds danger. And motorcyclists deny both of those, or fly in the face of both those anxieties *voluntarily*. So *that* provides a unifying force between them.

Part of the calculation for motorcyclists, therefore, is that other benefits from riding outweigh potential dangers. From this we can see that, in many ways, bikers see biking in the same light as others in society. The difference is that what for non-riders are seen as negative qualities appear positively for riders. Thus, for example, the perception of danger which ensures many people would not ride a motorcycle, can be part of the attraction for riders. As such, bikers are those who view the risks as, at the least, worthwhile, or at most, exhilarating. Bikers may thus be seen as 'different', in the sense of pursuing minority interests and of belonging to a specific culture, wherein pleasure and excitement provide strong motivating forces. Yet, further, in what many riders perceive as a conformist world, biking allows for feelings of individualism. For the following rider, this is partly a consumer issue, in that the wide variety of motorcycles on offer at affordable prices means that there is a wider choice of goods through which riders may express themselves than in other areas of the market:

> Every person is an individual. And motorcycling brings out that individuality. If you go to a motorcycle showroom, you can see so many different sorts of bikes. . . . Whereas, you go to a car showroom, you see nice, shiny, clean bodywork. Don't matter whether it's a Ford or a Vauxhall. There is hardly any difference in the shape. [There's a huge difference between a Ferrari and a Peugeot 205 but] nobody can afford a Ferrari. Everybody can afford a motorcycle.

Therefore, 'as a motorcyclist, you can bring out your individuality with your bike and your clothing and your style of life'. This idea of difference as something positive, enhancing individuality, is expressed by the feeling that riders 'want to be seen to be different, or that they value their individuality . . . or they don't want to fit into the crowd'. It is in this sense that we can understand Rutherford's comment that difference, otherness, is sought for 'its exoticism and the pleasures, thrills and adventures it can offer' (1990:11).

This individualism may also be seen as connecting with another quality that riders view positively in that, as the one man states, they 'want to be different, and that can be interpreted as rebellious'. Another rider maintains, 'there's got to be, among motorcyclists, or at least some of them, the underlying hooligan, rebel trend as well. . . . Motorcycling's a really easy way of not conforming.' This does not necessarily mean that motorcyclists are social deviants or rebels, there is no need to actually *be* rebellious; the bike itself is sufficient for the appearance and feeling of being *risqué*:

> Maybe that's why a lot of people do ride bikes, because they see a little bit of the rebel in themselves coming out. Even if they don't speed. Even if they don't do hair-raising things. People who drive down the road on a Harley at thirty miles an hour can imagine that they're Marlon Brando. And the devil is coming out of them even though they're doing absolutely *nothing* wrong. And they'll have the biggest grin on their face that you can imagine.

It can be seen here that, as with other minority communities, there is a sense of play, of self-deprecating humour in this which means that the 'hooligan' aspect is not usually taken seriously (K. Thompson 1992). Further, however, the image of a biker, which we shall explore more fully below, is something that can be used self-consciously when desired or necessary:

> People do like to live-up to the image as well, it's part of the fun, in a way, to do it. To rev. the bike loudly at traffic lights, or to overtake somebody on one wheel. You know, that sort of thing.

> Occasionally it is nice to play on it. Occasionally, if you are in a threatening situation, it is nice that I am who I am and that I have a motorcycle helmet with me, because, suddenly, I gain *much* more respect, let's say *physical* respect, than I certainly deserve. I'm *certainly* not a big person. I'm *severely* lacking any sort of masculine physique. But, when I have a leather jacket on, I've suddenly gained three stone and a torso. Which can be very handy. Yes, symbolically, I do gain, and it is nice, occasionally, to *use* the myth for my own ends. . . . I don't want to upset people and everything, and I really do have a problem with annoying people, *but* I do also enjoy being looked at. I can't deny that. So I play it both ways. I always play it both ways. Everybody always does, I think. Everybody can turn around when they need to. On the whole I try not to, but I've got to admit that there are times when I want to turn it all on its head and I do want to be noticed.

Overall, therefore, various qualities are identified as being associated with biking, and as making it a pleasurable activity, qualities which, whilst being related to the physical and subjective pleasures of riding a motorcycle, are also social in nature – that part of the attraction of riding is the feelings of freedom, difference, individuality and rebelliousness that prevent riders from living a dull conformity seen as characterising mainstream society. In a sense, we can understand this as a hedonism which rejects, if for only a while, social responsibilities. Yet social responsibilities are a consequence of maturity. That is, as adults, individuals are expected to fulfil social duties and obligations. Consequently, by trying to underplay these responsibilities riders are, to a certain extent, also rejecting adulthood. Therefore, as will be discussed more fully later, it may be argued that motorcyclists exhibit a 'denial of age' which indicates that their chronological age may be 'discredited as an indicator of inevitable age norms and lifestyles' (Featherstone and Hepworth 1991:374). Bikers are not normal 'grown-ups'.

What is also clearly indicated above is that, unlike other social activities or collective affiliations, bikers are bikers because they *chose* so to be, that 'it is a positive choice, riding a bike'. As such, they fit in with current speculations about the 'politics of choice' perhaps more than other socio-political groupings, in that membership can be readily withdrawn unlike, perhaps, members of other minority communities. Three quotations provide examples of this. What is of interest is how this choice is seen as symbolically encapsulated in common themes – personal freedom, social non-conformity or individual difference – which we shall meet again later when discussing reasons for political engagement:

It *is* a buzz. I mean, the thing that people fail to recognise about it, I mean, I've been riding bikes virtually all my life and when I rode in here this morning, and I *chose* the road I came in because it's got four or five really nice bends on it, and I didn't go mad, I didn't ride dangerously, I wasn't scraping footrests or anything, but I actually got a *buzz* coming in here this morning. I *really* did. I went through a series of bends, quite fast, on a nice line, and I felt *good*. And, I mean, motorcycling is, primarily, about *freedom*.

The very perception that they are anti-social, motorbikes, *that* in itself brings you together. But it's a positive *choice*. You're making a *statement*. In many ways, you're seeking not to conform, with a motorbike, even when reasons for using the motorbike are entirely practical, like getting to work cheaply, or avoiding jams or whatever the case may be.

I tend to think that motorcyclists *are* individualists, as far as they can be. In my experience, there's something about them that sets them apart. In other words, I think that everyone I know as a motorcyclist can also drive a car. So it's a real *choice*. It's not through necessity that they've got a motorbike. They actually *prefer* this motorbike for whatever reason it is. Whether it's the performance of the thing, whether it's being out in the fresh air, whether it's mobility, whether it's posing; whatever the hell it happens to be. Their *preferred* mode of transport is a motorcycle. Now, I think it *does* say something about the person as an individual that they're *not* part of the herd. They either *want* to be seen to be different, or they're *prepared* to be seen to be different.

Overall, however, these reasons given by riders for the attractiveness of biking are also the same factors that they believe are responsible for the negative responses they believe they receive from the wider society. It is not necessarily the case, therefore, that bikers reject what they believe others hold against them, but merely that they interpret things differently. It must also be borne in mind that societal images of bikers are not static, but caught in the complex dynamism of time/space, that is that rather than there being a universal attitude to riders, this is seen as varying in different times and places (Perryman 1994). Contemporary negative attitudes are consequently viewed as not having always been prevalent nor, indeed, as prevalent now as they once were. Imagery surrounding motorcycling is viewed as responding to changes within the material circumstances of riding. In order to examine this more fully, therefore, we need to explore changes within motorcycling since its rise earlier in the century.

Figure 3

Whilst data do not allow us to confirm this statistically, it is commonly believed amongst riders that, prior to the Second World War, motorcycling had a very different profile in Great Britain: namely, that it had a higher social-class profile and was thus associated with privilege to a greater extent than was the case after 1945. As one rider remarks:

It was much more of a sort of gentleman's pursuit, or something. It was just, you know, like going fishing or something for the weekend . . . it wasn't, initially, in the very early days of motorcycling [a lower class thing], it really was a gentleman's thing. It was what people like Lawrence of Arabia did. I mean, they were quite expensive, I guess, the really performance motorcycles. I mean, it was a completely different thing.

There is an opinion that, due to the high sporting profile and activities of dispatch riders during the war, motorcycling was prestigious and, consequently, enjoyed a positive image:

Prior to the coverage of . . . mods and rockers etc., motorcycling was probably viewed much more positively. Motorcycle sport in various forms was very well supported by spectators, motorcycles were a sign of personal affluence in an era before most people seemed to have a car, motorcycle manufacture was a significant exporting industry.

What you've got to remember is that the army used dispatch riders in both wars and, you know, dispatch riders were very much courageous people. Lawrence of Arabia was into motorbikes and, in fact, he was killed on a Brough Superior.

The following 70-year-old rider links the use of motorcycles by elite members of society to previous social acceptability, and how the change came as motorcycles became more prevalent:

In the '20s, I think, King George VI, who was then the Prince of Wales, was a Douglas rider when he was at Cambridge University. Well, you know, nowadays, I can't see the Prince of Wales riding a motorbike. There's been a *change* in emphasis. Once upon a time, motorcycling, because it would cost money, was the prerogative of the professional classes. . . . I can never remember being, in my younger days, until the '60s possibly, motorcyclists being banned. Because, of course, you've got to change the culture. When, in the '20s, a motorcyclist was bound to be a gentleman or a solicitor or somebody like that, they were welcome anywhere.

One possible argument for change is that the expansion of car ownership meant that motorcycles were no longer viewed as the prerogative of the privileged, and thus their elite image was undermined. The following quotation is from someone who started riding in the 1950s:

[If you reflect] back about seventy years ago . . . if you were very poor in resources, as far as transport goes, you walked everywhere or used the bus, if you were lucky, or your pony and trap or whatever happened to be around. As things improved, people got bicycles. You were doing really well if you could afford a *motorbike*, that really was something. All sorts of people in society had motorbikes in the early days, in the '20s. If you were doing *extremely* well, you'd have a car. . . . At one time it was the *norm* to have a motorcycle, and this probably went up to pre-war. I mean, motorbikes and sidecars were still popular *after* the war, and no-one looked *down* on them. They were just a way for people of getting around. And then, in this class-ridden society of ours, I suppose, they started to be looked down on when the post-war cars became more accessible. Ford brought out things like the Ford Popular. It was the cheapest car you could get. I can't remember the figures, but I remember it being very cheap, and I remember dad talking about it, 'How do they make a car this cheap?' It was the first stepping stone, get people off the motorbike and sidecar, get them into a car. So I think 'keeping up with the Joneses' then started. And so, I think, a *snob* element then came in. Perhaps the '50s-ish, it starts to come in. Certainly the '60s.

It is among older riders that we see how, in the 1950s, the motorcycle was to become the only potentially affordable way of becoming geographically mobile for those on lower incomes. This sense that motorcycling and working-class culture were entwined in the post-war period is explicitly recognised by riders:

In the '50s . . . motorcycling, to a large extent, was regarded as a working-class activity. Which means that the movers and shakers tend to look down their nose at it, in that, when cars weren't readily affordable, and motorcycles were cheap transport, you would tend to have a bike. If you got married and you had a family, you'd attach a sidecar on it, and maybe then, later on, you might be able to afford a car, or you might go on forever with the sidecar outfit.

The bike *used* to be the working-man's form of transport. I mean, with a sidecar on it, it was the working-man's answer to a car he couldn't afford.

In the following quotation, we are given a keen insight not only into how this was experienced by young men of the period, but also into the way in which motorcycles formed an intrinsic part of working-class youth culture in the years after the Second World War:

It was the only *affordable* form of transport when I was a young man. I mean, young men of my background, my class, couldn't afford cars. Apprentices' wages were very, very poor. They were poorly paid for six years and the only way you could get to work without pedalling your bicycle was by buying a little motorcycle. And that's how it started. I mean, there was a genuine *culture* around motorcycles then. You know, young men *bought* motorcycles, *rode* motorcycles. Without wishing in any way to sound arty-farty or pseudo-psychological, it was part of the *rite of passage*. It was part of *growing-up*. And it gave you independence, and you became responsible for your own actions for keeping the thing running. It gave you the opportunity to practise a *range* of manual skills; doing your tappets every weekend and that sort of thing. . . . I mean, for me, getting a motorbike at sixteen years of age, seventeen years of age, was the done thing. And it was a *practical* consideration and a *cultural* consideration. I mean, it really did provide the *rite of passage*.

It was only in the 1960s that the image of motorcycling was to take a definite downward trend. Three factors are seen as underlying this development: the mods and rockers of the early 1960s, media images and Hollywood. These are often explicitly linked. Already, by this time, motorcycling's image was taking a downward turn due to the activities of some bikers:

> Well, they were getting a bad image because of the 'ton-up boy' days, because they used to have ton-up races in between the cafes and things like that, and the famous chicken runs.

This was to worsen, however, after the alleged infamous bank-holiday clashes between mods and rockers. Two riders, one in his sixties and the other in his late forties who had been at both Brighton and Great Yarmouth, describe how they saw events and the suspected role of media:

> If you go back to the early '60s, there was this mods and rockers thing at Brighton . . . and there was a big, big fuss about this warfare at the weekend down at Brighton. And [a friend] went down, there'd been so many motorcyclists arrested, God knows why, and there was open warfare virtually, and he went down. . . . It turned out that one had turned-up on a bike because he'd nicked one in London, one had got a scooter because his dad had bought him one for his birthday, and the rest of them had either turned-up in cars or on the train from London! But, according to the press, there was this open warfare between motorcyclists and scooterists. [So the whole thing was a lie].

> It was very well conceived by the press to look like *everybody* there in a parka or a leather jacket was thumping hell out of each other. I didn't thump anyone. I just hung around, driving bikes up and down the prom. Bikes would go one way. Scooters would go the other way . . . we did hear rumours that it was conjured up by certain press people to get people running along the beach and causing mayhem. But we could never really prove that that happened.

As such, there is a belief amongst motorcyclists that the moral panic over the mods and rockers, the main cause in this country of negative imagery towards bikers, was merely hyped-up by the media. The second rider quoted above, a self-confessed rocker, tells us about the aftermath of events and, interestingly for our later discussion, how it affected him:

> We were regularly turned away from public houses locally because of that and, if we wanted a run out to Skegness, the police wouldn't let us park on the promenade. We had to park some way away in a carpark, and things like that. And that's when I thought, 'Well, get more involved with the BMF and try and do something to fight people's attitudes.'

Yet, he continues, the stereotype being created at that time did not meet the reality of the motorcycling community as a whole:

> In the '60s, by and large, the average biker, as perceived by the press, was a teenager. In reality, probably the vast majority of people that rode bikes were probably mid-twenties to mid-thirties. He used to just ride a bike backwards and forwards to work. [So the image wasn't right], not even then. But the spotty teenager who used to go thundering up and down the road from one cafe to another got the publicity. He was probably 5 per cent of the motorcyclists. They got all the publicity because it was good press, because we did things that were exciting. We went down the road at 100 miles an hour and we went along Brighton beach. But the poor chappie who went to work on his bike and came home at night, and got up the next morning and went to work on his bike and came home on his bike, never got a *look* in the press because that was totally *boring*. But 75 per cent of motorcycling was that in the '60s. Getting up, going to work on your bike, coming home on you bike. And the rest was us exciting people.

It was the minority image, however, that was to prevail. Yet the media are not merely held to be responsible in the sense of hyping the reporting of events, but also for the fact that, due to the spread of a new kind of mass media, more of the general population were able to access such images:

> Early '60s, television was just becoming big. Everybody had a television then. I mean, in the '50s, when the ton-up boys were about, there weren't too many televisions about. Just the middle class and the better-off had a television. But, in the '60s, working-class people started to get televisions, so more people saw these mods and rockers running along the beach. And everybody just automatically gave the rockers the bad image. Because *they* were the leather-jacketed thugs, and these other old boys [had] these nice, clean, polished scooters.

Consequently, it was this understanding of bikers which was to gain social currency. Another biker argues:

> . . . the old mods and rockers from the '60s and the Hell's Angels from the '70s is still in a lot of people's minds. Whereas anybody who's got half a brain could see that they were still only a very small percentage of the people who rode motorcycles.

This is supported by a retired member of the police:

> . . . they had a very negative image. A lot of it ill-founded, certainly, but in the '60s and the '70s, following on from the late '50s and '60s, of course, for any teenager to prove that he was 'hip', he had to wear a leather jacket. A leather jacket was associated with motorcycles, so when there was aggravation, as there always will be with a percentage with young people, when they were wearing leather jackets, they were seen as

motorcyclists, very often. And it always annoyed me, certainly as a law enforcement officer, that most of the pillocks that you meet wearing a leather had never been near a motorcycle, wouldn't know what to do with one. But the image was always there, of course, always re-inforced by the average television depiction of how to depict a hooligan, give him a black leather jacket and preferably make motorcycle noises in the background.

This period, therefore, was one wherein the stereotype of the biker was largely created: 'the classic stereotype of someone who's perhaps greasy, long-haired, grubby, dangerous, aggressive'. This is not to argue, however, that there were not people who found the new rebellious Hollywood image, where 'everybody was a long-haired lout and biting the heads off ferrets and things like that', attractive. A rider in his fifties informs us:

> [During the 1960s], over the pond in America, you got then the Marlon Brando 'Wild One' image, the first beginnings of the Hell's Angels [*sic*] and God knows what else, and these were rebels. As I called them the other day, 'Rebels with a cause, not without a cause'. Their cause was motorcycling. This was the way that they would show that they were *different*. So 'I'll have a motorbike. I'm going to make noise. I'm going to show I'm tough. I'm not going to have one of these tin boxes.' Different to mum and dad. So I think a rebel element started then which just wasn't around pre-war. No-one ever thought of rebels on motorbikes. It was people on motorbikes. So, it became a minority thing and you had to be tough to have a motorbike.

Nor is it to argue that the stereotype did not exist in real life. One national official from the British Motorcyclists' Federation (BMF) recalls the 1970s and early 1980s:

> I wore the dirtiest, filthiest, rancid-ist jeans you could ever think of. My leather would walk around on its own almost. My hair was as long as it now, and I had a massive, great, long beard, and I wasn't very clean and this sort of thing. All of my mates were like that. Really, really, *rebellious*. They didn't want to be rockers – *they* were smart, with their shiny studs and badges, with their nice quiff and their shiny Triton – they didn't want to be like that. They wanted to be *different*, really *different*. Different like the punks were different. But even the punks were clean. They might have spat at each other but at least they were clean. . . . What's happened now is that really dirty, filthy, disgusting image has gradually changed. Now, people, instead of wearing dirty, filthy, rancid jeans, will wear decent leather jeans. They might be scuffed, they might be oily, but they're *clean*-ish. [It's because we've got older but also] because you realised that the complaints that you were getting lodged against you by the landlords of pubs when you walked in, saying, 'I don't want you sitting on my chairs in my pub because you stink. I ain't having you coming in here because people think you will cause trouble,' regardless of whether you did or you didn't, it's immaterial, they *thought* you would, the whole blooming lot, you realise, 'Yeah, he's actually right, you know. I can hardly blame him. I want to sit on the chair in his pub and I stink, and I'm dripping oil.'

What is being suggested is that such stereotypes were over-played, both qualitatively and quantitatively, that is that it is believed the actuality did not meet the stereotype either in its essential characteristics nor in the numbers of motor-cyclists whom it represented. Clearly, by their very nature, stereotypes do not provide detailed understandings but simple, easily understood caricatures. Nor are they necessarily factual in representation for, as Lash argues, we make sense of the world by classifying phenomena, yet the process by which we do this may also involve making value judgements about those things classified, and consequently 'invidious distinctions' may be drawn which do injustice to the thing or group being classified (1990:19). This may be particularly the case when dealing with a group about which we know comparatively little for, as Goffman informs us, such 'stereotyping is classically reserved for . . . persons who fall into very broad categories and who may be passing strangers to us' (1963:68). Such conclusions are supported by Hogg and Abrams (1988), who inform us that people are willing to define social groups in terms of only a few crude characteristics. As such, the complex and multi-layered nature of reality is both simplified and reduced by such portrayals (Aronowitz 1992). Further, if groups are socially marginalised or there is tension between different social groups, then stereotypes can manifest a pronounced hostility in content and tone.

Such negative stereotyping can best be described as meaning that an individual or group is subject to stigmatisation, that is that people so defined are 'disqualified from full social acceptance' (Goffman 1963:9). We can see, perhaps, how such a

Figure 4 One of the thousands of Harley photos in Mr Mutch's collection

process may have occurred in the 1960s, during a period wherein there was social concern surrounding people on powered two-wheelers – a process which resulted in motorcyclists being stigmatised for their activities. This stigmatisation is seen as then being continued from this period to disadvantage bikers socially. Unfortunately, Hogg and Abrams also argue that stereotypes are generally only slow to change and do so only in response to social, political or economic change. Consequently, not only will a stereotype be a distorted characterisation of a group, but there may also be a 'time-lag' involved in that, if the social group changes, the stereotype does not change automatically with it. In the short-term, therefore, the falsity of the representation may increase.

For motorcyclists, the most commonly cited culprits in the perpetuation of negative stereotypes are the media in that, perhaps, the general appearance of the motorcyclist makes it an ideal persona to construct in media representations. However, 'the media are not neutral in the symbols that they will receive and transmit' (Tarrow 1994:126). As one rider informs us:

> . . . what we are, and the way we have to clothe ourselves and whatnot to actually do what we want to do, makes us really nice, cosy, little candidates for being the bad guys. It's the black leather, it's the thumping machinery, the speed, the general sort of excitement and thrilling side of things that you can tie into motorcycling quite easily without too much effort. So if you've got a bad guy image you want to portray, we can fit it without too much difficulty because of the way we *appear*. How we are as people, the way we think and how we live our lives doesn't necessarily have to be involved in that. The way we look can be used to portray quite a nice sort of wicked image. I think quite a lot of public perception is from the media. . . . That reinforces us as maybe being Untouchables a little bit, from the normal public point of view, in that we do something that's a bit dangerous, a bit different, and it involves looking grubby most of the time, because, let's face it, a bike doesn't go through a carwash very easily!

If such symbolic misrepresentation is easy to sustain against riders this is, quite simply, due to the seeming paradox of their social visibility and invisibility. Goffman informs us that 'visibility, of course, is a crucial factor. That which can be told about an individual's social identity at all times during his [*sic*] daily round and by all persons he [*sic*] encounters therein will be of great importance' (1963:65). Clearly, this has great applicability for motorcyclists who are, most obviously, very easy to see on the road (leaving aside for the moment the belief that car drivers never seem to see motorcyclists when it suits their purposes), in that they may be noisier than a car (though this is increasingly less the case), have lights on, be dressed in bright colours or whatever. Yet, at the same time, they are invisible in that, beneath leathers and helmet, it is impossible for a bystander to see what a particular person is like. It is this factor which means that the general public do not know a great deal about motorcyclists. Consequently, if the media portray them as greasy, broken-nosed, long-haired, tattooed, spotty adolescents, unless a member of the public actually *knows* a rider they have no way to dispute the imagery portrayed. As such, any characteristics can be superimposed on one's visor with impunity.

Clearly, this may contain positive aspects in that, whilst on a bike, a rider may use this sense of anonymity to fantasise, becoming for a while, as will be discussed later, a rebel and hero rather than a 39-year-old wage earner with a mortgage, three children and considerably less hair and more weight than they carried twenty years ago. However, this also makes it very hard for motorcyclists to fight any label accorded them:

> There's still very much [the image of] the incredibly uneducated, greasy, dirty, skuzzy biker with no respect of society or anything else. That one hasn't existed *ever*, really. That existed in the minds of the media and was, perhaps, knocked-off in the '60s. Post-'Nam, with the Angels starting up and the original Oaklands chapter and everything [*sic*], yes, maybe, there was a group of individuals who were very much on the edge of society. Society put them there, certainly the way it treated them, if you're looking at 'Nam vets. and everything, and they reacted accordingly, you might say. But the media jumped on it, and that was that. 'I'm sorry. That's bikers. That's the way you are. You're all *exactly* the same. Tarred with the same brush. We don't really want you in our establishment. You *are* going to start fights. Nobody could possibly have a conversation with you because you're all ill-read, and probably just completely illiterate. Yeah, you might be able to strip a bike down at the side of the road, but why do you never wash afterwards?' There's still a tremendous *fear*. I mean, the media struck *fear* into the hearts of individuals. I can walk down the street and get the usual intimidation that I would do from a lot of people, for whatever reason. But if I walk down the street in my leathers, people cross the road.

This invisibility, therefore, acts negatively against riders, and may only be counteracted by personal experience that contradicts it. Again, such an idea is supported by Goffman who argues that 'the whole problem of managing stigma is influenced by the issue of whether or not the stigmatised person is known to us personally' (1963:73). He continues, 'although impersonal contacts between strangers are particularly subject to stereotypical responses, as persons come to be on closer terms with each other this categoric approach recedes and gradually sympathy, understanding, and a realistic assessment of personal qualities takes its place' (1963:68). Consequently, if people know riders their attitudes will be more favourable but, if people do not know riders, then they will rely to a greater extent on imagery from other sources for social knowledge. In such circumstances, they may accept labels that stereotype people. In the complex social circumstances of contemporary society, wherein people rely increasing on information from external sources for knowledge, rather than relying on the rooted, face-to-face experience of daily life (Giddens 1990), it thus becomes easier to demonise people. We have to trust that media sources are telling the truth in circumstances in which we cannot contradict them. However, this makes bikers vulnerable to misinterpretation for, if people are distant from the motorcycling community, it becomes easier to rely on a 'master status' (Becker 1963), a stereotype which provides one-dimensional characterisations of actual people. As those using the stereotype do not actually know any bikers they feel no responsibility for the veracity of their views. As Bauman (1989) argues, people only feel a sense of moral responsibility for those in social proximity to them; if distant from a group, that sense of responsibility is suppressed. One rider sums this up:

> I mean, for example, there's are these peace convoys. They're hippies. I mean, hippies used to be like, 'Love and Peace, man.' Laid back. Through the Thatcher years they got turned into thugs and hooligans. And people *believe* it. And their only experience was through the media. Because the chances are, they've never met any of these people, so they don't know really what they're like. . . . I think they get keyed onto 'the bloke in a leather jacket – bad person'. [So the leathers symbolise negative characteristics.] But it's easy, it's very, very easy to make someone look like a biker. Leather jacket. Pair of jeans. Pair of work boots. Wig. And that's all it is. And it's very easy to do. Cheap and easy. And it's not like the old days where you used to get 'Shock! Horror! Exposé!' of motorcycle clubs in the *News of the World*. I don't think you see anything like that anymore. Motorcycling is much more respectable than it used to be. I suppose everybody knows at least one person, or is related to at least one person, who rides a motorcycle. . . . If you lived in a little village, and you were a biker in a little village, people might not approve of crazy bikers in [general], but because they know you, because you're that old boy who drinks down the pub that's George's son, they think 'Oh, it's all right'. That he must be all right. I think people do make little exceptions for people they know. Because they know them already. . . . Once you name somebody, you put them into a category. Then they're filed with all the other people in the category. . . . Because putting a label on somebody, putting them into a category, it's like you've got some kind of control over them. In fact, going right off at a tangent, there used to be, did you hear about, like, magic, knowing somebody's true name gives a great deal of power over them. And, I suppose, if you put somebody into a category, you don't think of them as an individual, you don't have to treat them like an individual.

The consequences of this negative imagery is that riders tend to feel that the general public holds anti-biker attitudes. This does not mean all people are hostile, yet the evidence tends to support the quotation below; that is, when a member of the general public is pleasant to a rider, it is usually because they have a previous familiarity with them:

> I think people who had motorcycles, and loved motorcycles, would always stop to pass the time of day. They would always, 'Oh, I used to have one of those. Oh, that's a nice

bike you've got.' I can remember having these conversations with people coming up to me when I had British bikes. But, to people who've missed out the bikes and gone straight from school to a car, motorbikes were just dangerous, noisy horrible things, and they had no interest *whatsoever* in them.

Overall, therefore, the evidence suggests that negative attitudes are seen to be more prevalent than positive ones, that 'motorcyclists had got such a bad press people were afraid to go up to them, or they were kind of beneath everybody.' There is a feeling, again, that this has changed over time, and that 'it was at its worst in the '60s, '70s and '80s.' It is also believed that it is those members of the general public who remember those years who are still more likely to be hostile. As one rider observes:

I think the more mature members of society think back to the seaside battles at Brighton and Margate and whatever between the mods and the rockers, the skinheads and the mods or whatever. And they perceive them as a dangerous group of people. Now that might have been right for a small proportion of motorcyclists in 1968 or thereabouts, but it's *certainly* not the case now. We've most certainly [changed].

It is in this sense that we can understand the comment that 'if a robber has used a motorcycle to robber a bank, [the media] say, you know "Motorcyclist Robbed a Bank" or whatever. They never say a motorist robbed a bank and, invariably, most robbers are motorists.' Yet whilst such attitudes may be in decline, as we shall discuss below, there are still examples of riders being stigmatised due to their motorcycles. One example explains this:

. . . getting refused a bed-and-breakfast is very annoying. Getting refused served, or being *ignored* in a restaurant for, like upwards of an *hour* before anyone will come to serve you, it's very annoying. Very annoying. Not being served, and actually being asked to leave the pub is very annoying. 'We can't have your type, son.' It *does* happen, as blatantly as that. It happens a lot more very subtly, but when it's blatant and in-your-face it's almost easier to deal with, because you think, 'Sad Person'. It does [still go on] in some places. On the whole, I don't think being asked to leave is, but certainly getting a hard time is. Queuing at the bar, for *hours*, and they'll serve everybody around you again and again and again and again, making loads of eye-contact with you every time they come to you, but not serving you.

How riders manage this stigma, how they respond to negative treatment, varies. For some, riding itself compensates for any bad treatment they might meet. As one rider maintains, 'I've been riding for nearly twenty years and, in that time, I've had more enjoyment, adventure, positive receptions and good times than any of the prejudice or ignorance I've encountered could overshadow.' For others there's a feeling that they are an ambassador, and should try to provide people with evidence that counters the image. As one rider argues, 'I do try and compensate, I must admit, when I've got the full kit on. I try and be nice to people because they don't expect you to be polite.' There can also be a feeling of mild exasperation when meeting fear or prejudice. One female rider tells a tale:

> [I think that] 'If you've got a prejudice, you've got the problem, not me.' Yeah, that's very definite. I mean, I get more out of motorcycling than I get 'anti' feelings that actually register with me. There was a lovely occasion where I followed some woman into work and she'd actually got her brake light out. And we came to a nice stop in the traffic so I pulled alongside and tapped on the window, and she looked *terrified*! You know, and I'd got my visor up and everything, she still looked terrified of me! So she did wind down the window a little bit, and I said, 'I hope you don't mind me telling you, but your left-hand brake light's out. It might be worth having a look at it before a policeman stops you.' And she just went, 'Oh, really? Oh, thank you! I'll check it when I get home.' And she was so completely stunned, I mean, she was so worried to begin with, and then she had a really nice, polite, friendly involvement, and I think she was partially relieved. And you think, 'Well, you don't have to look terrified at me, dear. I'm just riding a motorcycle. I'm not that bad a problem.'

Yet, more strongly, for some riders there is a considerable indignation at the discrimination bikers face, and a feeling of injustice at stigmatisation. Like members of other social and political movements, a feeling of exclusion from 'normal' treatment and a desire to be treated 'normally' can generate aspirations for change, that a group may 'struggle to . . . gain social legitimation for their feelings, desires, and lifestyles' (Seidman 1992:52). One Motorcycle Action Group (MAG) member states:

> . . . you can still go to pubs where they can't discriminate against people going into a pub because of the colour of their skin, but you still get signs outside them saying 'no bikers'. Mind you, you also see them with 'no coach parties' but that doesn't matter! We're often viewed in a similar way as so-called football hooligans. You know, you get 'no football coaches'. It's illegal to discriminate because of race, colour and creed but there's nothing to stop them discriminating because of the form of transport you decide to use *at the time*. I know of friends, who've been to a pub on their bike and been turned away, so they've gone home, got the car and gone *back* again, and been let in. I mean, that's inherently *wrong*. I get very annoyed. It annoys me that people can have that attitude. . . . They may dislike me because of my appearance, but people should look past that. People should look past what you're wearing, and what you're riding and what you look like. . . . We're trying to change the continuing perceived attitude that because people choose to do something slightly different, that they're not outcasts, they shouldn't be classed as outcasts, they shouldn't be discriminated against. They should be treated *exactly* the same as your pin-striped bank manager who drives a Jag.

There should be *no* difference in attitude between them. They should all be viewed in the same way.

This expression of a desire for inclusion in all aspects of life (Scott 1990), and to be treated in the same way as any other citizen, is summed-up well by another activist:

> Our biggest problem at the minute is *awareness* of motorcycles everywhere. Awareness on the *road*, so we all remain alive longer, and awareness within the *media*, to accept us, because Britain is *light years* behind the rest of the world where motorcyclists are concerned, and awareness at all political levels, that we *exist*; not looking for *special* treatment, just looking for *fair* treatment. And awareness at European political levels, Commission and otherwise. Awareness, that is an all-encompassing thing, that will reduce *prejudice*. If everyone is *aware* of us, and *accepts* us as, 'Wow, once you take off your helmet and you arrive at work, you're actually that office clerk that I'd have spoken to and assumed you'd come in a car. God, you're the same person!' That's our biggest problem, awareness all over.

Yet if, as we have seen, riders are aware that public perception of them changes over time, it is also the case, as indicated above, that they believe that attitudes differ in space, that the particular experiences of British history – for example, the mods and rockers, easier access to American culture – mean that the image of a biker is different in the UK to other countries. As one officer from the Federation of European Motorcyclists' Associations (FEMA) observes, 'Europeans seem to be less prejudiced. . . . I haven't seen it in other countries like it is in the UK.' Another riders'-rights activist who spends much time abroad observes:

> . . . it's worse in this country, I think you'll find, than in other places. If I turn up at a four-star hotel, dressed as a biker, in this country, they might let me in, but I think I'd get a rather frosty response and so on. But I think they realise, on the continent, they're more attuned to the fact that tourism takes many forms and you have to put up with all kinds of peculiar people if you want their money.

One rider who, with his wife, has gone abroad camping with a motorcycle since the 1960s observes:

> The first time we went abroad we couldn't believe it. We hadn't, as I say, I'd never been turned away from anywhere in this country, but the *difference* when we went over there in the way we were treated made us realise that there *was* a brick wall up against motorcyclists in this country. . . . Everywhere we went over there, you know, you were another human being.

This sense of being accorded equal treatment in a way not experienced in Britain is explained more fully in the following quotation from a newspaper article:

> If you're reading this while stuck in a traffic jam or sitting on a train, just think; it's quicker by bike. But is biking for you? Among motorcyclists the line goes: 'There are people who are bikers and there's the rest of the world.' And as a biker in Britain, you are often made to feel like a second-class citizen. Arrive by bike at a hotel – booked in advance by credit card – and you feel the warmth of welcome reserved for the Nineties British equivalent of a leper. It does not matter that the clothes you are wearing would cost the average British worker a month's salary, or that your 150mph superbike costs the best part of £10,000. In contrast, go to the continent and you will find a warm welcome, and jealous admirers, in every town. Two outdated misconceptions concerning motorbikes are still prevalent in this country: bikes are a cheap form of transport; and they are driven [*sic*] by spotty teenagers who scream around city centres for a cheap thrill. Some memories extend back to the Sixties bank-holiday clashes between Vespa and Lambretta-borne mods and Norton or Triumph-toting rockers (*Independent*, 20/10/ 1993:16).

However, riders do feel that the last few years have witnessed the beginnings of a change in the biker image and, subsequently, in the treatment they receive from the non-biking public. Much of this change, as is discussed later, is perceived as a response to the new 'trendiness' of motorcycles, most clearly demonstrated by the new devotees currently being found among the famous. One rider remarks:

> [The image is changing] but very, very recently. And I would say as recent as two, three years, we're seeing it. Harley Davidson nearly went bankrupt but they started to revitalise themselves. They started to get people, in the States, onto Harleys. The Peter Fondas and all the rest of it.

Additionally, it is believed that the media have also picked up on this trend and have been quick to capitalise on the new image. Yet, as the next quotations also argue, these changes are not specifically aimed at bikers but are seen as part of a general change in social climate which now allows more space for those previously marginalised. The consequences for riders, however, are simple: bikers are becoming fashionable members of consumer society:

> I've obviously been biking for donkey's years now and it's *certainly* not as bad as it used to be. The difference is, everyone's picked-up on it, you see it on the TV, the media's picked-up on it, they've got some new after-shave, they put some guy on a bike, on a Harley. The image of motorcycling is *changing*. It's suddenly becoming, you know, professional, trendy, a fun thing to do, and, you know, you're really cool because you've got a bike. Even though you only use it on weekends when it's not raining. But

the image has changed or, rather, it's changing. It has changed quite a lot and that is having a positive effect. You know, twenty years ago, you couldn't have gone to Peterborough Borough Council and said to them, 'We want a bikers' festival in Peterborough.' They'd have just *laughed* at us. 'We're not having you lot coming to our town and smashing it up . . .' You know, you say to the average guy these days that you're gay, and they say, 'Oh right. Whose round is it?' They're not *interested*. Ten years ago if you'd said that, 'Ooh,' you know. People *do* change, and things are *changing*. And biking is no different from anything else. You know, the fact that you're a biker, these days, so what? 'Why are you telling me that?' You know, it doesn't even come up in conversation. Another biker will walk out and look at your bike. 'Oh, that's nice.' Whereas, before, they wouldn't. It has changed.

As motorcycling becomes more socially acceptable, so too does the image change and public perception with it. As the following quotation indicates, this may partially be due to changing technology which, as is examined elsewhere, broadens the potential scope of motorcycling by expanding markets beyond the mechanically minded who did not object to being permanently covered in oil:

You've got to give some credit to the Japanese for cleaning-up motorcycles, in that they don't leak oil, they're not smelly, they're not even noisy anymore. Now, they've become socially acceptable. They look nice and *lots* of people have said to me that Honda Goldwings really impressed them. They're not sure what they are, but people say, 'I saw a motorbike the other day. It was an amazing thing. It'd got a stereo on it and all the rest of it. It was a Honda something.' 'What, a Goldwing?' 'Don't think it was that. Something beginning with an "a".' 'Apsencade?' 'Ah, that's it. It had these bells, and whistles, and bits of chrome.' I'd say, 'Yeah.' You see, *that* has broken down barriers, because people generally got interested in them. I went to the Waterside in Stratford, where they park bikes by the Memorial Theatre because there've been complaints about motorcycles parking all over the pavement, and I met a local councillor there. Now, observing tourists and locals as they're walking along with the kids, motorcycles were not a problem to them whatsoever. They were stopping and looking at them. Not frowning at them. It didn't matter what the bike was, they were just genuinely interested in what they saw. But you've got to admit, they're very attractive looking bikes. They're in bright colours. They look the business. They look as if they could go on the race track, a lot of them. They think, 'S'truth. Look at that.' It *looks* interesting.

Further, if, as is discussed more fully elsewhere, this attracts a different type of rider to biking, then negative stereotypes will finally break down. As one rider comments:

. . . the market *is* changing towards a leisure pursuit, populated by better-off, older people . . . [and] as people meet motorcyclists who are 40-year-old company directors, rather than hooligans, they'll think 'Ooh, motorcycling's actually quite respectable.' And, you know, that is inevitable, isn't it? You can't have a stereotype persisting if all of the evidence points to the contrary.

As such, it would appear that the media, advertising and industry are exploiting perceived changes within the community. From these changes a new picture is emerging:

> If you've noticed in that last four or five years, yeah, biking is being stolen by the ad. people, and that's not the wrong thing. It's not getting the wrong sort of people into biking, either, it's getting the right sort of people into biking, because suddenly biking is stylish. The style is stylish, the machines are stylish, and I think that's coupled with the fact that people are getting fed-up with traffic congestion, and they want to explore a bit of freedom for themselves. I think that's what's getting them into biking. [The manufacturers] stole Harley's clothes, this marketing concept of the cruiser motorcyclist, which is always something associated with a slight rebelliousness. But what the manufacturers have done is give that rebelliousness a kind of acceptable edge. That coupled with PR and promotion of various products has meant that people can be an urban rebel but still be a respectable person.

What we may be witnessing, therefore, is a growing respectability and accompanied social acceptance of motorcyclists as biking becomes associated with more affluent and fashionable characteristics. Yet, as Ewen cautions us, being stylish has its disadvantages in that 'style has become an essential, inescapable instrument of cultural and political discourse. The ability for renegade styles to be reabsorbed into the consumer market may also make it an instrument of cultural and political containment' (1990:47). Absorption into the consumer market may a double-edged sword. On the one hand, the demise of the stigma against biking would greatly benefit bikers. Alternatively, the sense of 'difference' from dull social uniformity would also be lost as biking spreads to the middle-of-the-road, middle-class and middle-aged. Thus, what motorcyclists may be experiencing is a 'gentrification of rebellion', danger and excitement for a mere £10,000. If this is the case, this may adversely affect the bike's romantic, non-conformist associations in the future as it enters the mainstream of cultural expression.

For the moment the full consequences of such a trend still lie in the future. What is of importance at the present is not the extent to which riders may or may not become integrated into wider society, but the extent to which they form a community of their own, expressing feelings of commonality and unity with others who ride motorcycles.

−2−

Bikers and the Biking Community

The term 'community' is one surrounded with much confusion; being drawn upon often in an unreflexive, nebulous way that lacks detailed definition. There are two possible understandings of the term, one more easily accessible than the other. Firstly, a community may be merely the physical manifestation of a specific group – for example, a mining village is clearly a geographically situated location within which miners live. However, even here, the concept of community is politically laden for, since the growth of industrial, urban society, it has become common for academics, politicians, the media and others to comment on the 'breakdown of community' – a phrase which refers not merely to the physical decay of communal environments but which carries connotations of a collapse of sustaining ties which link members of collectivities to a mutual frame of understandings. Consequently, once beyond simplistic conceptualisations, one encounters difficulties, for 'community' is also used symbolically to describe the bonds between members of a collectivity – the sense of identity, beliefs, values or whatever which unify them. As such, for our purposes, whilst the first definition is easily established, and refers merely to those riding motorcycles, and partners or friends who associate with riders also, the second is more complex.

These long-standing concerns about community have acquired a new focus in recent debates about postmodern society. To simplify and summarise this argument briefly, changes in the nature of industrial societies are alleged to have weakened traditional communities. Firstly, the decline of manufacturing industry has weakened the work and class base of many such communities whilst, at the same time, factors such as geographical mobility, information technologies, greater educational opportunities, the media and mass consumption have loosened individuals from traditional structures of authority with the consequence that contemporary individuals rather than, for example, following the traditional tenets of family, church, trade union and so on, make their own decisions. Consequently, individuals are now regarded as having increased knowledge and, because of that, more information from which to make choices about how they lead their lives – lives which, due to the above factors, are increasingly lived not in a local, but a global context of satellite news and the Internet. Bradley explains the consequences of these developments:

> As a result of social change, people are said to be losing their sense of social belonging, of being rooted in traditional collectivities, such as class, community or the kinship network. . . . Now people draw their sense of identity from a much broader range of sources, including gender, age, marital status, sexual preference, consumer patterns (1996:23).

For the purposes of our particular discussion, these arguments largely focus on how individuals may choose membership of new types of community as traditional ties are undermined. S. Hall argues that, in the face of such changes, everyone 'needs some sense of identification and belonging' (1989:133). This is supported by Bauman (1991), who believes that individuals join new communities due to a desire for belonging in a world of ambivalence. In this sense, he sees communities as ideological brotherhoods offering succour and shelter to members and based on affective commitment (Bauman 1992), what Hebdige has called 'communities of affect' (1990). As this implies, these new communities are not necessarily based on tangible identifications as were traditional collectivities, such as class or religious affiliation, and thus are consequently less stable, as members may join or leave as they wish (Bauman 1992). Indeed, communities of affect may not have a class base or, as Pakulski (1995) argues, this may not be significant; for example, he states that although the Nazis were middle class, so were their opponents and, therefore, class did not single out one particular side of the political divide. Alternatively, new forms of identification may generate communities and movements which have a diffuse, cross-class base (Garner 1996).

It is in this sense that we can understand how it is that individuals can choose which communities they join. As Kellner argues, 'the boundaries of possible identities, of new identities, are continually expanding. . . . One can choose and make – and then remake – one's identity as fashion and life-possibilities change and expand' (1992:141–2). One's sense of community is thus a matter of self-construction by individuals who choose to identify with each other. As Bauman argues, these communities may be seen as 'neo-tribes', whose base is 'the multitude of individual acts of *self-identification*' (1992:136).

We can see clearly that the motorcycling community falls into such definitions in that membership is a deliberate choice (Bocock 1992); one chooses to become a motorcyclist, one is not born a motorcyclist. Consequently, whilst we have already examined why individuals become motorcyclists, we must also assess whether motorcyclists can be seen to form a community and whether collective membership provides the affective ties Bauman identifies as a crucial benefit to such membership.

In the first instance, and to set this in context, it must be stated that those who informed this research were not what are colloquially called 'lifestyle' bikers – a term which conjures up images of outlaw gangs (H.S. Thompson 1966; Harris 1986). Yet this distinction, between lifestyle and 'conventional' bikers (Willis 1978) is perhaps an erroneous one for, rather than the two being polarised, there appears to be a continuum along which individuals may place themselves. Therefore, whilst riders appreciate that 'for a lot of bikers, it *is* the main thing, it *is* how they define their lives,' there is also a distinction to be made between doing and being, that is that 'initially it's an activity, which *can* become a lifestyle, if you let it.' Thus, for the sample, motorcycles may be best understood as a central focus in a complex life which also involves other duties and responsibilities and that, consequently, they participate in the community in 'differentiated ways' (Hall and Held 1990: 176). It is in this context, and relating back to the comments made in the previous chapter, we can understand the comments below which indicate how, whilst daily life constrains individuals to the mundane activities of social living, motorcycles interlace that, cutting through other activities and roles in ways that enrich an individual's life:

> They know that they've got to *conform* to survive, that's something that *I* know. I mean, I've got the beard, I've got the build, I've got the hair. I ride a loud Triumph some of the time. But I know that when I get up in the morning I've got to go do my day job. I've got to be professional.

> I'm always a biker. When I'm at work, when I'm doing things at work or what have you, I identify with things that are relevant to me as a motorcyclist. Stuff that I've learnt in motorcycling helps me in my work and what have you. It's a constant thing with me. There's probably not ten minutes goes by end to end when I haven't thought about bikes at least once, because bikes are just so much a part of my life.

Consequently, we must be aware that participation within the community is a complex issue, which may change between, and within, individuals. However, there are also factors that further problematise the issue for, when addressing the difficult question of the presence, or absence of a motorcycling community, motorcyclists attest to a great deal of social diversity between riders, an observation also noted in the 1960s (Collyer 1973). Should this be the case then it may be argued that, like the society of which riders form a part, they reflect the same complexity and difference as may be found in the wider social setting. Two quotations suffice to illustrate this point, the first referring to occupational differentiation and the second to political affiliation:

> I've met so many different people through biking that it's opened up a great deal of other interests to me. In a motorcycle club you have everybody, all walks of life. Policemen, magistrates, builders, plumbers, decorators, Royal Air Force personnel, and from them you go off at a tangent and meet other people.

There are people from all walks of life, who've got different politics. You know, you get people from the extreme left, and the extreme right that'll ride bikes. And you'll get some greenies who will ride bikes.

Further, within this, motorcyclists identify not merely different groups of people, but also different types of rider, either because of the types of bike they ride, or the kinds of enjoyment their vehicles provide, as the following quotations illustrate:

> If you look at the sort of clubs that belong to the BMF, because individual members are a very disparate group anyway, but if you look at the sort of clubs that belong to the BMF, they range from the Brit. bikes, you've got the vintage owners that have very old bikes and their hobby is restoring, you've got people that ride off-road, you've got the national one-make clubs, which can be older British machinery, Italian machinery, more modern Japanese bikes. I mean, there's even a vintage Japanese club, which specialises in looking at the older Japanese bikes, and that type of thing. Then you get the touring clubs, then you get general bike clubs, particularly local clubs where people just go down there and they have weekend events, the odd camping weekend, go to rallies maybe, a lot of runs out. Just ordinary people.

> There are those who enjoy doing forty or fifty miles an hour as long as the bike looks *astounding*, it's quite loud, everybody has to turn and look. There are those who get it purely from the buzz, going out on a nice, twisty piece of road on nice, sticky race-tyres and having a fine time. Completely different what they're getting from their bikes, but they're both enjoying their bikes.

From this we can understand Tarrow's comments that communities are not homogeneous but are likely to be 'an interlocking network of small groups, social networks and the connections between them' (1994:22). For these reasons, we can understand how riders may refer to a certain snobbish quality to be found among motorcyclists, that motorcyclists do not form a unitary community of good feeling. However, it is not merely among motorcyclists that internal diversity may be found within a social group. S.L. Smith (1998), for example, discusses the internal differences to be found among road runners, and the way in which, to runners' chagrin, outsiders fail to see what, to themselves, are clear distinctions and treat all runners as similar. It is in this light that we can understand the following two quotations, from national officers in MAG and the BMF respectively:

> There's as much resentment and controversy and bitching in biking as there is outside of it. And the idea that bikers are all part of one big, happy family, that we're all singing from the same song sheet, is an illusion. And if we like to tell ourselves that it is so, then we're deceiving ourselves. Lots of bikers hate Harley riders, lots of people that ride Harleys, or who ride chops, feel no empathy with those who ride sports bikes, and conversely so. And lots of people within MAG despise people that don't join MAG,

and people outside of MAG despise people who are inside of it, for all sorts of reasons. Yeah, it's a bit like a whole load of religions in which the frictions between the religions can be far more severe than between those who subscribe to a particular religion and those who are atheists.

... there's *definitely* snobbery. The local MC club down here will look down on all other bikers. The fact that the local MC club members actually have only got a Ford blue transit van at the moment seems to be neither here nor there. They look down on all other bikers! The local vintage motorcycle guy, who's got his Thruxton 3-speed, wobbly back axle thingy, thinks it's *pointless* riding these Jap. bike because 'You don't need all that. We didn't need them when I was a kid.' And he looks *down* on you! And the guy with the £24,000 Ducati, with gold wheels or something like that, thinks we're all *oiks*. And we all do it, don't we?

Yet, as is mentioned above, these differences are seen merely as a reflection of the varying interests and proclivities which are to be expected societally:

I don't think, to be honest, it's about a difference between bikers, it's that there are different types of *people*. There are people who, like myself, enjoy putting a bike on a bench in the garage, ripping it apart, fixing it if it's broken, and putting it back together and then riding it. I get satisfaction out of mending something when it's broken and making it run. There are other people who have no inclination whatsoever to take an engine apart, they just want to run it into a garage, throw some money at the bloke running the garage and pick it up in three hours fixed. And I don't have a problem with that because the guy who's running the garage needs to earn a living. And there'll be something wrong with *my* bike at some point where I'll have to throw it into a garage to have it fixed, so it's a good thing that he's there. I don't resent anyone earning a living. I don't think that makes that biker a different type of *biker* to me, he's just a different type of *person* to me. I like fixing stuff, he doesn't. I don't have a problem with that.

It is in this context that we can understand the comment that

[We have] nothing in common besides our bikes. ... Everybody's too different. Much too different. The enjoyment of riding a bike is what it is. That's purely it, because everybody gets different enjoyment. ... And it's only their bikes that bring them all together.

Thus, to a certain extent, biking may be seen merely as a single unifying factor amongst otherwise diverse people, that

there is a common denominator there. But, what I'm saying is that they're not all the same. They have a common interest, but that interest needs to be defined. And what motivates one biker might be quite different to what motivates another.

As such, although motorcycling may be seen as manifesting 'unique qualities' (Hogg and Abrams 1988:106) binding individual motorcyclists into a coherent objective group, it may provide merely a propensity towards a subjective sense of community and fellow-feeling, all other things being equal. In this sense, motorcycling is a base line for a potential relationship and bond, but these may remain superficial if other factors do not come into play. Thus, whilst motorcyclists may always have something in common, a subject for discussion, there may be no bond beyond this. As such, we can agree with Melucci's argument that unity in a movement is 'the result and not the starting point, a fact to be explained, rather than assumed' (1989:26). At best, therefore, it provides a good starting point from which riders may discover potential friends and greater involvement within the community. One rider explains this:

You have [something in common] with some, obviously, because there are other things that link you in common, but, as a general rule, probably not. I think you get all sorts. All sorts of people, all sorts of bikes. The fact that they have bikes of *some sort* is a link in itself, and you'll find that people that you wouldn't speak to, maybe wouldn't think to speak to [you'll speak to because they have a bike]. Some you'll find you have more in common with, and you develop that. And others you find you've got nothing else in common with so you stay at that level. But . . . there's always that level, and that always means you've got something of a link, and something of an amicable link. If you say, 'nothing in common besides bikes', there's what's *drawn* you to bikes in the first place. There's lots of different bikes, and some like their ape-hangers and their four-inch pedals and all the rest of it, fair enough. And others like their drop handlebars and rear-sets and whatever you like. But something's drawn you to those bikes in the first place. What's done it is very difficult to define. I mean, some like the excitement, for some it might be a social thing, I don't think that's a strong enough reason, actually, I think that's a secondary reason. I think it's the bikes in themselves. And, I mean, some get into them because they love the mechanics, I wouldn't know where to start. . . . But some love the mechanics, some just love to ride bikes, because they're shiny, they're macho. Some like the speed. I mean, there's all sorts of different things. But there's something that's drawn you to it in the first place. And, I think, after the initial 'I've got a bike, you've got a bike' contact, probably the next level down, even if they don't realise that that's what they're talking about, is 'Why did you get it in the first place? What's your secondary interest in the bike, other than the bike? Is it the mechanics? Is it the "I did 150 down the Dolphington straight,"' you know. 'Well, I nearly came off at such-and-such.' I mean, the bike stories, I mean, you must know yourself. After the initial 'I've got a bike, you've got a bike' then it's onto the story time, isn't it? And through that they establish whether they've got anything else in common or not. And it works from there. . . . You make a certain number of probably correct assessments on the type of bike somebody's got. If they've got a Harley, there's certain very *strong* images attached to Harleys that must have drawn them to them in the first place. And it's the same with, like, a Goldwing, or a chop. You know, all these things. I think some are more nebulous, some types of bike, but there's definitely very strong lines drawn between the different types. And you can *assume* a lot about somebody from the type of bike they have. And that's what people do. Sometimes they're mistaken, but often they're not.

As such, there is considerable complexity and layers of varying affect between riders. Yet despite differences and disagreements, all riders attest that bikers do display a tolerance and empathy with others. In Britain, such ideas, which support the ideas of Pakulski (1995) and Garner (1996) discussed earlier, are often expressed as a sense of classlessness among motorcyclists – that biking is a 'great leveller.' Thus, in addition to or, perhaps, because of losing its post-war working-class associations, biking acts to undermine social divisions, that, as one man in his fifties observes, 'that *cultural*, almost *class* experience of biking that *I* had is gone.' The following quotations, from a man in his fifties and a man in his forties respectively, illustrate this point:

[Class is] non-important to a great extent. The subject matter is all important. It's the talk about the bikes and sharing the pleasures of motorcycling. So it's a very interesting bridge there. It's odd, because you're so accessible on a motorbike, it breaks down barriers anyway. The barriers that we used to have in England and still linger on, and some social thing that motorcycles are a poor man's transport and 'Can't you afford a car?' and all the rest of it, I think, at long last, that is dying away.

I would say motorcycling takes in the whole spectrum of class and so on, and it tends to be relatively classless when you get in. Now, I think the differences tend to come in in the sorts of bike people that ride. There isn't quite so much attitude of turning one's nose up at one another as there used to be, that's dropped off considerably in my opinion . . . it tends to be a leveller of class.

What is more important is the bond of motorcycling, irrespective of the particular form this may take. Two quotations express this:

I find there's a little bit of sort of, like, 'We're Brit. bike riders, and you ride Japanese stuff,' but, at the end of the day, we're all motorcyclists. And it's not a *hostile* thing.

When I used to do BMF road shows, going to all sorts of little provincial motorbike shows. Just these little weekend jobs. It was very interesting because you move around the country. You'd meet what, today, would be called the bikers' lifestyle, but I'd just call them, ten years ago or more, just enthusiastic young motorcyclists. They'd live for their bike. That is what they spent *all* of their money on. They'd camp in a field, without any proper gear, it was muddy and all the rest of it. Love it, and they loved their bike. But that's not to say that the guy whose got half a dozen cars and a Ducati, [doesn't love his]. He still loves his Ducati, gets a hell of a buzz out of riding it. Doesn't ride every day. Hasn't got the time to ride it every day. Doesn't particularly enjoy going out in the rain. But so what? He fits the dictionary definition of a motorcyclist when he's sitting on a motorcycle and riding the thing. And you *are* a motorcyclist once you're riding a powered two-wheeler of over 100cc, aren't you? I think that's then a motorcyclist.

Yet, although, at a fundamental level, the biking community is merely the total number of differing types of people on powered two-wheelers, a different point repeatedly made by riders argues that, at another level, respondents also view the community as much more than the sum of its parts. That, alongside the physical community, *is* a symbolic one based on affinity and comradeship:

> The catalyst is that you're sitting there on two wheels, you're out in the open, you go past another biker and nine times out of ten they wave. And so there's that. And when you pull up, I mean, motorcyclists are interested in what they and other motorcyclists ride. Even if they would never ride it, they will still go across and look, and ask questions about it and that sort of thing. And, I mean, *that* binds. . . . We do not have much in common other than the machines we ride, but *that* is a significant bond. . . . What you *get* from riding a motorbike, what you have with you when you *come* to riding a motorbike, is, I think, a real *bond*.

Thus it would appear that difference is rendered irrelevant by similarity. Additionally, this is compounded also by a sense in which, as A.P. Cohen (1985) argues, community is felt greater across the boundary, and thus difference between each other is of less importance than a perceived difference between themselves and non-riders. On one level this is purely practical, that the very differing experiences they have to other road-users gives them different skills, yet, as can be seen below, this is also held to be accompanied by other qualities:

> 'We probably are [different to non-bikers] in a lot of ways. I think your average biker is a better car driver when *he* gets in a car than a car driver who's never ridden a bike. Because your average biker, for example, is far more aware of the road surface; because you can fall off a bike, you can't fall off a car. Certainly you can roll a car, but you've got to really drive it to extremes to roll it. You've got to be very stupid as well. But you crank a bike over on a corner that's covered in gravel and you're going to be on the deck. If you do it in a car, the car might skid and all the rest of it. You'd be *very* unlucky to come out of it in a bad way. So I think bikers are more aware of the road surface for a start-off. Bikers are more aware of weather conditions. I can't ever remember a multi-bike pile-up on a motorway, whereas you get car drivers who blithely steam down the motorway into banks of fog that they can't see through. So, I think purely on a level of *motoring* bikers are different. I think bikers are also, they're not necessarily different from everybody, but I think that there are certain *mental* characteristics that are more common amongst motorcyclists, it's certainly not true of every biker, but I think bikers

tends to be more, what I would call, tough-minded than a non-biker. I think bikers, well, most of the people I know, are capable of making hard decisions and sticking by them, and putting-up with the consequences of them.

As such, there is some disagreement expressed, often within the arguments of the same person, about whether or not there is a commonality among bikers. Despite all of the above, however, it can also be said that whilst disparate and diverse on one level, at another, fundamental, level a sense of similarity between motorcyclists was also expressed. Additionally, however, for many there are social benefits that accrue to riding a motorcycle that are an intrinsic part of being a biker. Most importantly, within such advantages, is the sense of community riders experience.

The tolerance and empathy to be found among other riders, alluded to above, are commonly referred to by riders as a feeling that among other bikers one can 'be more oneself'. Two riders make this point:

I'm probably more me when I'm hanging around with bikers I can relax with.

I mean, I'm not particularly outgoing and I do feel that I can talk with somebody who rides a bike more easily than I can [with someone who doesn't].

As such, there is a sense in which one can 'fit in' and 'get on' more easily surrounded by people who have similar interests – a point which supports that mentioned earlier that, within the community, one is assured of at least a superficial relationship with others. At a basic level, therefore, the motorcycling community provides an individual with an immediate surrogate family. Another rider makes a similar point:

And you've gone through that initial contact barrier so much more easily, you know, because you've already got something you can talk about. It's obvious. ... There's never a barrier in there by the different sort of criteria of bike you're riding. The fact that you ride one, and you're out there enjoying yourself on it, is enough to make you all right to sit down and talk to.

This confirms that, despite the many differences between bikers, there can still be a strong sense of comradeship. The 'immediate family' and comradeship concepts are drawn together by one rider:

Enjoying life and having a good time, I think, is probably the most common thread. I haven't met a biker yet that doesn't know how to get down and party, and doesn't like sitting down and doing the 'fishermen's tale' bit over the bikes and stuff. Oh, yeah! 'How fast did you manage to get this?' Forget that the clock only goes round to such and such, and is delimited to a certain point. 'How much did you manage to get out of it?' There's always a little bit of that. . . . I think there's quite a lot of camaraderie. Sort of pack mentality. It's nice to be around other bikers. It's a nice, comfy feeling, and you know you've all got something you can have a good yarn about to each other without any real effort at all. You can walk into a pub full of bikers, and you can sit down with any of them and strike up a conversation. So we've got a sort of ability to announce ourselves to other people as who we are, to make that first step of breaking down any sort of social barriers. So you know it's another biker, so you know you can talk to them. It's not a problem. You can sit down and get on with them at whatever level. Whereas if you're just in ordinary clothes in a pub, you're surrounded by other people in ordinary clothes, and you've got no means of measuring where to make the mark to begin with to strike up something. So it's a little bit more difficult to get a conversation going, because you've got nothing you can obviously key it in with. It's quite a nice hang to get a conversation going. And you strike up a friendship normally quite quickly. You know, you can get a really nice, easy attitude going. A nice conversation. All right, you get bad attitudes in biking as you do anywhere else, that's just something you live with. You get some grumpy sod who doesn't want to talk to you because you've spotted him as a biker and you want to sit down and talk to him, that happens. But, as I say, I think it's just a really nice sort of lifestyle thing. You know, it's friendly, it's fun.

In the last instance, therefore, whilst there can be difference and distinction between bikers, at a fundamental level there is seen to be a commonality of interest which belies more obvious cleavages.

I suppose because we're all in a common situation, I suppose, so we try to get on. . . . Sometimes you meet people, you've never seen them before, and you say something really *rude* about them, and they just *laugh*, and give a good answer back. Whereas if you did that with people that weren't bikers, you know, they'd be rearing-up at you. You know, they'd be really angry.

In my experience, if you ride something with a wheel at the front and a wheel at the back or, in my case, a wheel at the front and two at the back, then you're all there for the same thing. You're all enjoying biking, in *any* form. I mean, I've had scooters and all sorts of things. They're all the same to me. Yes. I've had a Zündapp Bella in fact!

Bikers are individuals but they're part of the tribe. The big thing you notice is, a car is sat at the side of the road, it's broken down. It's a bloke in his mid-twenties, mid-thirties, he's broken down at the side of the road. What's the chances of another car stopping to help him? Pretty slim. Same bloke, motorbike broken down. What's the chances of another motorbike stopping? Very good. That's the difference. Because they can relate to each other. I don't think it's because they're a minority, I think it's because they *know* that the guy's going to be on the same *level* as them. The guy is going to talk a *similar*, if not the same, language. The fact that the guy might need a hand. The fact that they have a little bit of paranoia, in a manner of speaking, everybody else is out to get us so we've got to help each other.

There is a sense here that 'community' is not the same as 'commonality', that a group does not need to be a monolithic mass to experience a feeling of solidarity and collective identity. It would therefore, appear that 'community' can be experienced despite many internal differences between its membership. If such is the case, diversity is not a barrier to community and the concept of 'common interests', so often used theoretically to imply the social homogeneity of a group, may over-simplify a much more complex actuality. One very clear social division may provide evidence of how difference may be accepted, or not, within the motorcycling community: female riders.

–3–

Women Riders and the Motorcycling Community

As we shall see elsewhere, statistical data on the composition of the motorcycling community in Great Britain are not ideal, yet such as there are indicate that women still compromise a small minority of riders, some 13 per cent (AA Report 1995). The MINTEL Report (1993) indicates that, within this, women who do ride powered two-wheelers are heavily concentrated in the under 125cc categories (57 per cent). Only 14 per cent of women riders have machines over 500cc. There are signs, however, that the overall figure is rising. Research carried out by the Driving Standards Agency indicates that between 1993/4 and 1998/9 the percentage of women taking their motorcycle test increased from 12.1 per cent to 19 per cent of the total number of tests taken. This is supported by research carried out by the Federation of European Motorcyclists (FEM) into motorcycle training schemes in the European Union which shows that women now comprise 20 per cent of those taking their motorcycle licence.

Women riders themselves point to the increasing amount of female riders, and how this is leading to a greater tolerance of those that do. The following quotations show how this change is held to have led to a new attitude:

I think bikes are still seen as physical, male-dominated methods of transport. It's always been perceived that you need biceps, or bollocks if you like. But I think that, again, has changed. When I first used to ride a bike it was almost sort of, 'Good God, it's a woman!' Or some had the attitude of 'What a waste of a good bike.' Which really goes down a barrel of laughs. But I think there are so many women now riding bikes, and the bikes are being made more with women in mind, that we're not the minority that we once were.

Nowadays, no-one gives me a second look, as a female rider. When I first started, and it wasn't all that long ago, only in the early '80s, people were quite surprised. So there's been a great change in a very short time, really. I think it's because there are more of us. I know, when I first started, I didn't know any women who rode bikes at all. And then I got to meet one, and then I got to meet two. Now, I know a dozen that I could just ring up and we could have a party here with a dozen girls who ride bikes just like that [snap of fingers].

Unfortunately, whilst this may imply that women will increasingly become part of the community, for the moment, until such trends become more clear, we may merely confine ourselves to an attempt to understand why some women choose to overcome the statistical odds to become motorcyclists.

Clearly, at the outset women generally find they have a certain problem to overcome before considering buying a motorcycle: namely, that in terms of strength and size a motorcycle is initially a daunting prospect. This could be the major reason that women are concentrated among the smaller capacity sizes for, as one rider remarks, 'I mean, I must admit, I wouldn't want a big bike that I could drop without picking it up. So I don't know if that probably puts some women off.' Another tells us how this is just something to be accepted when one is first riding. 'When you're first new to bikes, especially women, we haven't got much upper body strength have we, and quite a few times it's just [dropped]. And it's easier to let it go down and then pick it up than try and struggle with it.'

As such, one may argue that a woman's motorcycling 'career' is not as likely as that of a man to progress up through the capacities, for women have to consider factors that most male riders do not when making decisions about the purchase of a vehicle. A female rider discusses one aspect of this:

Believe it or not, when I got the 400/4 I was terrified of it. I mean, *now*, with the Z and everything else, and I ride Graham's bike from time to time, I look at my little Honda, and it's such a tiny little thing. But when I first got it, I remember, I left here one morning, the first time I went for a real ride on it, I left here half past five, six o'clock in the morning on a Sunday and went for a ride from here out to Romford in a circle and back, because I was just so frightened to ride it in traffic in case I dropped it. All the time it was, 'What if I drop it?' That's what was in my mind. *Any* bike I'm fine riding but, with my Z, I'm up on tip-toes. I can ride it anywhere you like, but when I have to *stop*, and I'm looking not only at the junction and what have you, but I'm looking at the road *camber* as well, and 'Is there any gravel there?' And, you know, my road positioning is not just, 'How am I going to pull away from the traffic lights?' or 'Is that car turning left?' I've also got to look, 'Is there a hole that my foot might need to go into?' Because I can't hold the damn bike up if it goes over a certain angle. And I *have* to let it go down and pick it up again. Which I've done. If it goes, I've had it.

Beyond this fundamental problem, reasons for taking up biking fall into two main areas, one practical and prosaic and the other more liberative, although the two overlap. One primary reason for women riding is that they now have the financial independence to be able so to do; more women ride 'because they've got more money. They've got the money to buy the bikes.' Yet this may be linked to a need for women to travel safely. One rider informs us:

You see loads, especially in London, for commuting. Commuting is the thing where it seems to be hitting home for women who, I think, are finding the same thing as *I* do.

That the independence and freedom from fear, I mean, you've still got to worry about the daft car drivers and what have you, but you haven't got to worry about doing half an hour's overtime. 'When's the next train? How am I going to get home? It's getting dark,' or anything like. You can just, it sounds like a shampoo thing, but you can just 'get on and go' sort of thing. You haven't got to rely on anyone *and,* once you've got your lid on and your jacket on and everything else, even with someone with a slight physique . . . no-one would know, if you didn't want them to, that you were female. So, you know, it's *so* much safer.

This rider explains how she decided to get a motorcycle:

One day I was coming home from work and I was attacked, and I thumped hell out of him as well, so he was a bit sorry. But after that I thought, 'I'm not going to use trains and buses anymore. This is totally ridiculous.' Because I'd felt nervous a few other times travelling home late at night on public transport on my own. And that just put the tin lid on it. . . . So I had to look for a more secure way to travel, which is why I went to a motorbike shop and bought a Yamaha Passola, gold, with a little shopping basket on the front.

Yet this is not to argue that women merely ride from fear, for motorcycles give them a greater degree of control over their lives. Independence is a key factor in this equation. For women who discover it, it becomes hard to then relinquish control again:

I had a real thing, when I first went out with Phil, who had this big custom thing, and I thought, 'I'm not going pillion. I'm not being a floozy on the back. I've got my own bike. I'm taking the little 125.' And he'd say, 'Fine.' So he used to turn-up on his, I can't remember what it was, he'll hate me for that, anyway, he used to turn-up with this big fairing on this big custom thing, and there was me on my little yellow 125. But I thought, 'That's *my* bike. I've got to be on *my* bike.' And I just had a real thing about that.

As such, we can see that it appears that there are a variety of factors, linking the practical to the liberative, lying behind the decision to buy a motorcycle. As one rider comments, 'It's personal mobility. A little bit more freedom. A bit more independence. I think there's a lot more confidence generally.'

The issue of confidence comes in two forms. Firstly, that owning a bike may enhance a woman's confidence in that the skill of doing something that is physically demanding is a positive force in a woman's life. As one rider observes:

I think I've got more comfortable with my life since I've been around something that I get a real buzz out of. I mean, motorcycling, to me, it's not about the going fast, and getting oily and greasy and putting the machinery together. It's about the ability that I *can* do it, and I can *ride* that bike and I can *enjoy* that bike. And I think, really at the time when I started getting involved . . . I don't think I'd got the confidence in myself.

Yet this confidence does not merely come from the vehicle, for the decision to cut against the norm by buying one in the first instance indicates that women who ride motorcycles are not representative of women as a whole. As we shall see in the next chapter, it is felt by riders, female and male, that a woman rider is not as other women.

Figure 5

The first question that should be dealt with is raised by the above quotation, namely whether female motorcyclists buy their vehicles primarily due to an interest in mechanics or engineering. Whilst most certainly this may apply to some, for those women involved in the research this would appear not to be the case. Indeed, it may be argued that one of the reasons we may be seeing an increase in women on motorcycles is precisely because of the change in attitude and technology which means that motorcycles are now not necessarily maintained by their owners. In this, women would thus be classified with the born-again or *nouveau* rider whose interest in motorcycling is perceived to be experiential and social rather than mechanical, as the following comments illustrate:

It's been seen as a man's domain, I think. Again, this leftover of, like, girls and women not going into industry really. It doesn't matter what you say about these things, there is that thing, girls are not engineers, as I say, as a generality, are they? It's just not their thing. It just probably doesn't seem to suit their outlook. So in the old days, the people needing to be an engineer to maintain a bike and understand the thing, I suppose *that's* built into it. [But now, as a consumer, who takes the bike to the garage, women] can do that.

Bikes don't break down as often as they used to, so I don't think that somebody necessarily has to feel that they've got to have a level of mechanical knowledge. It's not being patronising to women motorcyclists, but the majority of women I know with bikes still get their husbands and boyfriends to fix them. But if a bike doesn't need fixing that often anymore, if it's more 'user-friendly', let's say, then it doesn't matter if she's got a husband or a boyfriend who *can* fix it, or even *wants* to fix it, because it just isn't going to break down these days, if you get a modern Jap. bike.

A further quotation indicates two factors. Firstly, women may merely not be interested in mechanics because they find it tedious. Relatedly, and in line with the idea above that women, like returnees (that is, those returning to motorcycling after a period of absence), view their bikes at least partially as a consumer item, whilst, in the past, women may have felt they needed to be able to mend their bikes at a time when that was more generally prevalent among the community, now they can avoid this if they wish:

Most, in the [early 1980s], used to be up to their elbows in engine oil, and it was, 'I can do anything they can do.' And I think, 'Yeah, I probably could too. But I don't feel I need to prove that.' But I was very pleased to find a couple of blokes that rode bikes that also didn't want to get up to their elbows in engine oil, so we formed our own little group, the 'we don't do our engines at weekends' group. But there are blokes like me we knew, anyway, that just don't like doing bike maintenance. Well, I *hate* it. It's *boring*. I mean, I sometimes sit – especially if Graham's doing my bike so I feel almost obliged to keep him company – so I sit in the garage and watch him do it, and I think, "I've done some boring jobs in my time. But to sit there and undo all those nuts, open all that stuff up. Fiddle about with all those bits. How utterly *boring*. Not difficult, boring."

As a consequence a trade-off is made, whereby each partner may concentrate on what they do best. As can be seen below, this does not necessarily imply that it is the male partner who undertakes the maintenance and repair of the bike:

I tend to the housekeeping, not the cooking and cleaning, I can't be bothered with all that, but things like the bills, correspondence . . . because that's something *I'm* good at. So I do the household admin., if you like, and he works in the garage. There are people who do it the other way round. Sarah . . . there've been times when she used to live in London and we'd call round at her house, and she'd be there fiddling about with her bike, and Dave would be inside cooking the food. You don't think twice about it. That's what they've decided to do. She enjoys it. Very strange woman!

Yet if women are not drawn to bikes because they are mechanically minded, we need to explore what does attract them to motorcycles. Obviously, motorcycles themselves are seen as attractive or otherwise women would not ride in the first place. However, a further major factor identified by female riders is a sense of being genderless on a bike which is not normally experienced in society, this despite, as can be seen below, that biking is still a male preserve which can present women, initially, with some difficulties. The most overt reason why women can feel genderless is that, due to leathers, it is not necessarily easily discernible, that 'you can also disguise your gender'.

To a certain extent, this sense of genderlessness is due to the perception that one must try and fit in with the majority of the community:

. . . because if you're in a male-orientated environment, the best way to get on is the *try* and be one of the lads, to a certain extent. I'm not saying you've got to be male, or have male characteristics but, on the other hand, they don't like *fussy* women. That, 'Oh, no. I've got grease and, you know, I've broken my finger nail,' and all that. I mean, I do it as a joke, when I break a nail, I go, 'Oh, I've just broken another nail.' But I can do that as a joke now, with people that know me.

It is for this reason that female riders see themselves as not fitting into any clearly delineated sense of gender. One rider explains how she and her sister evolved a theory:

. . . we're actually the third sex. But there's, like, the girlies, and then there's the blokes, and we're sort of in the middle. Neither one thing or the other. And, I mean, I was a tomboy, and my sister was a tomboy, and we used to drink pints, and wear jeans, and we'd just think, 'Sod this.'

Yet this does not mean that gender is totally denied. Whilst, clearly, one cannot describe the usual attire of thermals, leathers and waterproofs as 'feminine' in any way, female riders are aware that men find the idea of women on a bike attractive and that, additionally, this may give women an ego boost. The two following quotations address such points:

> I ride bikes because I like it, and because of the buzz it gives me, and because it *does* make you an individualist. You *are* one up above the cars, and it is a bit of an ego boost. And the fact that you're female in that is also something extra.

> I think girls on bikes have always been seen as a bit daring. And I think we still are. I think because it's seen as a macho thing, to have a bike. Guys see it as a macho thing to have a bike, and it's quite a cool, daring kind of image. Add to that a girl on a bike is still something they see as unusual, even though there's a lot of women out there now. I think it's difficult because men's perception of men, I can't judge, but men's perception of women, it's definitely, 'Wow!'

However, whilst bearing this in mind, the following quotations all indicate that the biking community, although overwhelmingly male, is seen as less sexist than wider society, and that gender matters less than the more important ties coming from motorcycling. As one male national officer remarks:

> What I think is healthy among MAG activists is the general acceptance that women have just as much right to take part in MAG and motorcycling as men, and an essential distaste for discrimination in general.

On a practical level, in terms of being allowed to be an official member of motorcycling's various institutions this is supported by a female national officer:

> We don't have a major problem with discrimination against women within motorcycling generally though. I've never had a woman phone me up and say, 'I've been barred from a bike club because I'm a female,' or 'They'll only allow females to be associate members.' There's been a few that whinged that females are not allowed to be full members of clubs because they're pillions, because they don't have a full licence. But I think that's fair enough. And it's not just the women that aren't allowed. Any man who doesn't have a full licence isn't allowed in certain clubs.

Yet this formal egalitarianism may not necessarily be matched by informal acceptance. Clearly, it is hard to demonstrate whether the theory is matched in practice. However, support for the idea of an atmosphere of tolerance and mutual co-operation comes from the women themselves:

> I think, to large extent also, if you're a girl with a bike, and you're in a group of bikers, if you're at a rally, or something like that, you are *treated* as more of a peer by the guys than you are in normal life. I think they just see you as more of one of them. Because you ride a bike, and that's a link, that's an immediate link.

> I just do it because I like it. A few years ago they talked about having a women's section to the BMF. I said, 'God, no! No!' I said, 'Why? I ride a bike. The fact that I'm female is completely irrelevant, I just ride a bike.' I have enough trouble sometimes with people noticing I'm female and it'll just make it worse. Okay, it would be quite nice if I could get jeans that fit, boots that fit but, apart from that, you know. . . . I want to be treated, if I ride a bike, for the quality of my riding, how good I am.

Most confirm that their male colleagues largely do not seem to overtly discriminate. That dubious honour, as many attest, goes largely to motorcycle shops who, in their persistent attempts to patronise women, top the list of dislikes:

> The only places I've encountered problems is in *bike shops*. I won't even *go* in them. It's not *quite* so bad if I go in on my own, although they can be a bit patronising, but if I go in with a bloke they'll just look straight past me and ask whoever I'm with, 'Can I help you, mate?' 'But it's *me* that's come to buy something!' You go and buy a bulb and they think you're going to find a crash helmet to match your leathers or something.

It is perhaps a consequence of the perception that male motorcyclists are seen to treat women in a less discriminatory fashion that female riders feel more secure amongst riders. As such, there are social ramifications in that women frequently allude to feeling safer in the biking community than they do in wider society:

> I've only ever been afforded the utmost courtesy when I've been at rallies. I'm terrified to walk around here during the day, in my own sort of area, but at a rally, I wander round there at midnight, even if I've had a few drinks, and I would not worry for my safety. And I think that's great. And most women who do get involved in bikes tend to find that and comment to me *how* safe, how much safer they feel at a rally than they do if they go to, I don't know, some pop concert or something. You don't get the petty theft. You don't get the harassment. You don't get any of that.

If women feel that the motorcycling community is qualitatively different from the wider society, underlying this is also a view held, universally, across all respondents, that women riders also are qualitatively different, in terms of personality and orientation, from women more generally. In part this idea that female riders are different is seen as rooted within their response to the negative aspects to being a woman on a motorcycle; the main factor being that motorcycling has, historically, been a male preserve, which makes it hard for a woman to establish herself. Consequently, the type of woman who is prepared to engage with that needs to have a certain mental outlook. There is still an attitude, which is said to be declining, that women should not be on motorcycles. One rider remarks,

I mean, people say to me, 'Oh, you're a girl, how can *you* ride a bike?' I mean I still get that. You wouldn't think you'd get that now. I mean, it's not unusual to see woman on a bike. But you still get people say, 'Oh, how did you get into that then?'

One consequence of such an attitude is that a woman has to be able to push herself into what is still a predominantly male community:

I had one girlfriend who, before I met her, she got a bike, she passed her test, she got a bigger bike, she wanted to get involved with motorcycling groups and she went along to various clubs and that, and they didn't really know what to do with her. The men didn't really particularly want to talk to her, the men who rode the rides. And the women, who were predominantly pillions in some of these clubs, couldn't really talk to her either. So she ended up in limbo. And, perhaps, things are beginning to change but it's a difficult situation for the sort of woman who wants to ride her own bike. Very often the women who tend to sustain it, seem to be either ones who seem to be *extremely* bloody-minded and they will do it come what may.

One rider compares this to women who ride pillion when they state, 'Looking at the women who are in our group, or come to all our rallies. There are one or two mice, but they tend to be attached to people and don't have their own bikes.' This does not, of course, mean that all women pillions are regarded in a derogatory way, but that women who initially become associated with the community through a relationship with a male rider either get interested, and thus may buy their own bike, or get bored and leave. One rider sums up both scenarios:

They started off, they met the boy who had the bike, they rode pillion, now this is what usually happens. I mean, like with Sarah, she came to a BMF meeting with Dave, proudly sitting on the back of his bike, and then there were a couple of women there who rode their own bikes. And she suddenly thought, 'Why am I sitting on the back?' It hadn't occurred to her before. 'Why the hell I am sitting on the back of this bike?' And then she went out and rode a bike. But you've still got to have the mind that says, 'I'm going to get my own. Sod this!' . . . There seem to be a lot of bikers out there who haven't got partners, and I suspect a lot of that has to do with the bike. A lot of my friends have been going out with a girl for a little while and then she finishes with him. I think it's the whole thing. Everything seems to be centred around bikes, doesn't it? So he gets together with just a couple of us in the pub, although we might not be talking about engines, because I forbid anything like that because it's terribly boring, we're still talking about what's the last rally we went to, what was the last great road you rode down, you know, who did we bump into at High Beach the other day, we might even get onto how far we've gone with the Multi-Directive yet, you never know, but it's all centred around the friendship involved in biking, the riding of the bikes. So if you're not really into it, it must be so boring.

As such, the women who survive the 'trial by tedium' are those who are committed to riding and, further, who are fighters, prepared to struggle for their rights to ride. As one male national officer maintains, 'most of the people who have bikes are ballsy females. . . . They'll stand up for what they want and don't take any shit.' A female rider supports this:

> I think women who ride bikes tend to be strong characters, definitely. You don't get many little mice on bikes. It's because it's going against the flow. I think it's always been accepted that boys in their rebellious youth and all the rest of it they all like bikes and this sort of thing. It's still not accepted that *girls* in their rebellious youth are going to like bikes. [Girls in their rebellious youth like boys who have bikes], but don't like riding bikes themselves. I don't mind riding pillion, but I far more enjoy riding my own bike. It's less boring. And also, I like to be in charge!

The following quotation also alludes to the idea, expressed above, that women riders do not reflect the norm:

> *Any* female I know who rides a motorbike seems to be confident, independent, assertive, knows what she wants. . . . And I get on *so* well with female bike riders. There's seems to be something about us that makes us a little bit different, a little bit independent. Maybe you've got to have a certain spirit even to get on the bike.

Yet another aspect that comes from this is the idea, as seen above, that women riders like to be in control of their lives and independent. Linked to this is the view expressed by some respondents that women riders may be more likely to choose not to have children. Clearly, this is undemonstrable, although one respondent, who is a national official, said that of all her biking friends only one of them had children, and this friend had started off as a pillion rider rather than, as with the rest, having always ridden her own bike. Part of this is seen as due to the perceived difficulties in fulfilling domestic tasks with small children in tow if one has a bike:

> I think mostly [women don't ride] because they're in the car with the kids. I mean, I know when I had Philip, I mean, even when I first bought the bike, I used to think twice about using it for local errands because it would be easier to take the car with Philip. I mean, even when Steve was at work, I could have easily, you know, thought about getting next door to watch Philip for an hour while I took the bike round to Tesco's, which would probably have been a lot easier than taking Philip in the car, and finding a parking place, you know, just to get a few bits. It's just something you wouldn't consider.

Figure 6 Bike Show models take note: how a girl drapes herself over a bike when she *really* wants to get it into bed

Others relate this to the attitudes held by female riders. One quotation picks up on this theme:

Often it's the women, anyway, who ride the bikes are the ones who are not going to have a family. I can remember going to a meeting once and there was a lady stood up, it was her birthday, I think it was her fortieth birthday or something like that, and she said, 'Thank you for the birthday card. Thank you very much.' I can't remember exactly the quote but basically she said, 'I've decided to have motorbikes instead of children.' And I thought, 'Yeah.' Whether it goes along with that sort of attitude, I don't know. . . . I think it's a case of the attitude you have before-hand. It's just not going along with the norm. You don't leave school at eighteen, do this, do that, find a nice little husband. It's just a case of you just don't do exactly [what's expected]. I didn't deliberately set-out to do things that weren't expected of me, I just did it because I liked it. I think that goes along with it. You don't feel pressurised into doing something that, perhaps, you think you *ought* to do. Like, the number of times people have said, 'What you really need is a nice car.' Well, actually, no, what I'd really *like* is a bigger bike. And that, I think, goes along with that you're not pressurised into doing something you really don't want to do because you feel you *ought* to. You'd think, 'Well, maybe I shouldn't ride a motorbike because it's not very ladylike. And you can't wear nice clothes when you get there . . .' And I think that's partly what it is, that they don't feel pushed into doing something that society expects them to do.

Most of the factors discussed above are summed up by MAG's National Chairman, Neil Liversidge, who then relates the type of woman who becomes a rider to the reasons for political activism:

> The sort of girl that rides a motorcycle, right, has probably got a bit more bottle than the average, for a start off, right. I mean, most of the girls I work with wouldn't ever *dream* of riding a bike. They're terrified of, like, the nasty, oily, dirty things and all the rest of it. They've all got nice, clean office jobs. They go out to nice, posh discotheques of a night, all this sort of thing. They like driving their Renault Clios and pretending to be Nicole, right. But, and then you've got this 'but', then you've got the kind of girls who *don't* mind getting their hands dirty, they *don't* mind camping, they're not bothered if they get out of a tent of a morning looking a bit rough. They don't need to spend two hours in a beauty parlour before they'll show their face, and all the rest of it. They're people with a bit more bottle, and because they've got a bit bottle, they don't like being told what to do, *therefore*, they tend to be active in motorcyclists' political organisations. You know, one thing follows from the other. People with bottle don't like taking crap, and people who don't like taking crap generally tend to get involved.

The issue of activism generally will be discussed later, yet it is pertinent to raise some points which refer specifically of the role of women as activists. As we shall see, given the ever-changing nature of office holders within the RROs, it is impossible to ascertain an accurate figure about female activism, yet sources indicate that not only are women taking a full role within organisations, but that, proportionately to their numbers within the motorcycling community generally, women are *more* likely to be active than men. As one Regional Rep argues,

> It's not something MAG's been instrumental in, but it's something that's reflected in MAG, in that you've got a lot of MAG Reps now are women. Quite a large percentage of the National Committee. Quite a lot of women are Regional Reps.

Estimates from officials about the representation of women within activist positions vary from 33 to 40 per cent of the total. Further, within this, one Group Secretary argues that not just quantitatively, but qualitatively also, women are taking a higher role:

> . . . women are more prepared to get on and organise things. And I think, to be honest, in a lot of cases, they're maybe better at juggling several things at once. ... I tend to find, in work and life in general, men like to do one task and then another one. Most of them are happiest to do that. They like to complete something and then go on to the next thing. Whereas, again, sweeping generalisation, and it doesn't apply to all, but most women can do two or three [tasks], and sort of have them all working at the same time. If you give guys a few things to do then they'll forget some of them because they can't do them at once. They have to do them one after another. It's just a different way

of thinking, I think. And some guys are great at doing several things at once but, in general, they do seem to prefer to do it one at a time. If you look at, for instance, our committee I think there's about four women out of about ten posts, or something like that; 40 per cent. *But* if you look at the work that's done, the women are all doing their job. Now, some of the others aren't. They say they're Social Secretary or something and they've done absolutely bugger all. And if somebody's *not* doing their job, for whatever reason, they might have an entirely good reason then, basically the group takes it. So, I would say, in general, that if the women in our group take on a job, they will do it.

The question thus becomes, why are women more likely to become active in a riders'-rights organisation? Various factors are indicated. Firstly, in relation to the points made above it would appear that, as in society generally, women are moving more into official roles and also that women still have to try harder. The two following quotations both reflect these points respectively. The first coming from a female office holder, and the second from a male:

> I think things have definitely changed. I mean, it's not the accepted norm now, it hasn't been for a long time, for people to stay at home with their kids. It's an accepted thing that you have a career. It's getting more accepted that women will be managers and get high positions in companies and this kind of thing. I think it has changed enormously, I mean, even since I've been working. And it carries on. We're just a reflection of what's happening in a wider social setting.

> I think it's the same kind of situation for women in motorcycling as it is for society as a whole. In order to get accepted as competent, they've probably got to be a lot better than the equivalent men. Better. Otherwise men would be looking at them and criticising everything they do.

Other women interviewed see their activism not merely as reflecting wider social relations, but also in terms of their own attitudes. As one officer comments, 'I think the majority are [managing females], and that's why we have a higher profile in organising groups and things as well.' A local officer explains this further:

> I think the women who *do* get involved are natural organisers. The men that are there – you tend to think of fellas, even in this day and age, as sort of the managers, and the leaders, and the more senior end of the scale. I mean, even in business its still rare to see a woman in a fairly hefty role within the management structure. So I think you'd probably find that people would probably look to a fella taking over that sort of role without thinking too much about it, and accept it quite happily. I think, as a girl, you probably have to prove yourself a little bit more. Mine is the fact that I'm a bossy cow and, you know, I'm a pretty damned good administrator, so I'm fairly good at organising these people.

As such, as we shall see elsewhere, women draw on the skills learnt in other areas of their lives, in this context attitudinal and professional, to help perform their duties. But they would also seem to suggest that they can draw on a more specific skill additionally – that of being a woman. Some of this refers to a feeling that the very fact of having to fight harder to get where they are means women are taken more seriously. As one woman observes, 'it's a bit like women getting on in any form of life, because you're *not* at the kitchen sink, you tend to be taken more seriously because they think you've had to fight more to get what you want.' This is supported by a male officer, who states, 'in my years that I've been active, I've known a number of women who've been very active, and they're always good to have. If you can get them involved then they do a damn sight better job than a lot of the blokes. They're more into it, if you like.'

Further, women believe that their presence can have a positive effect on events; whether dealing with their organisations or, more particularly, when confronting the non-motorcycling community:

It's nice if you're meeting someone, for the first time, in a position of authority, whether they're councillors, MPs or whatever, that're likely to have a fairly heavy preconceived idea of what they're going to be meeting. And from the general perspective of motorcycling, it's quite nice to shift the balance before you go in there. We've been known to go along in threes. One fella in bike gear, one girl in bike gear and one girl in full office dress. And that throws the balance completely to begin with, so any preconceived ideas they've got, they can't work with, because they can't hang on to them because what they're seeing in front of them is completely different to what they expect to see. So you can actually make that balance really work for you, and you can get them really concentrated, totally thrown from anything that they might have thought before they got into that meeting with you, and you can make them just sit down and listen to you as people. So that's quite a nice little way of doing it. But it would be nice not to have to do it in the first place. Just be able to wander in like Joe Bloggs and just sit down and talk to them. Not to have to redress the balance before you go in there, just to make sure that any preconceived ideas they've got are neutralised by what they see in front of them.

Yet although data indicate that women riders are strong individually, socially and organisationally, none of those interviewed would describe themselves as a feminist. Indeed, as is indicated by the following quotation, it would seem that, for female riders, feminism is seen as focusing on unnecessary trivia. This is not to say that the women are blind to gender, but that it is not something which is of relevance to all aspects of their lives:

We even had this debate over the title 'Chairman'. You know, people saying, 'Do you want to be known as Chairman, Chairwoman, Chairperson, Chair?' I said, 'The title was good enough for the people that had it before. So why should I be fussy?' . . . it's a title, isn't it? It's word that just happens to have the letters 'M-A-N' at the end, really. You know, I am *not* terrified of people referring to me as Chairman. In fact, I prefer it because that's the title for the job. I hate people who are really pedantic about things like this, you know. I mean, that's really stupid. *That's* the title, *that's* the job and *that's* the job I'm doing. What gender I am is irrelevant from that point of view. But it *is* relevant when it comes to physical strength. Manhandling bikes, and all the rest of it.

It can tentatively be argued, therefore, bearing in mind the difficulties associated with a lack of statistical evidence and numerical strength, that women seem to be coming into motorcycling in greater numbers and that they are doing so for both practical and more esoteric reasons. Further, that the type of woman who is drawn into riding is not 'typical' of the wider society but that this is of positive benefit to riders' rights as a whole in that their skills and attitudes make them good candidates for office-holding. The picture is not wholly a rosy one. There would seem to be indications that women still have to try harder than men to be accepted into the biking community, but the women themselves are optimistic and ask only to be given an equal chance to prove themselves, on and off the road. For women riders, feminism and gender is not an issue, and they merely ask that their male counter-parts see things the same way. Most confirm, as we have seen from some of the respondents above, that their male colleagues largely do not seem to overtly discriminate, yet there is an awareness that women generally see the community as male-dominated and that this may prevent women from motorcycling and, through that involvement, being able to appreciate the positive aspects of the community. Female riders are also aware, however, that as the community is still largely male any attempts to try and make the community more attractive to women must be countered by the need that, in so doing, they do not alienate their male colleagues. The dilemma is thus to encourage female involvement without discouraging male involvement:

> I'm very pleased that there are more women coming into motorcycling. I'd like there to be more, so therefore I think there should be a climate where women would feel they are *welcome*. So I'm glad that we don't have tits in the magazine anymore . . . you want to create a climate where women are going to feel more welcome. But, on the other hand, if we start turning it into a magazine more aimed towards women we're going to alienate the majority of our members. So, again, it's question of balance.

Overall, the picture that emerges is one of a community that is characterised by both similarity and difference but, within which, individuals may take differ-entiated positions dependent upon commitment to riding generally. Critical to this is the factor of personal choice. Clearly, this choice is an individual decision, whether to join what is still a minority group, to be exposed to the vulnerability of

Figure 7 Corrugated Dave showing that, contrary to public opinion, bikers prefer raw steak to live chicken

riding or whatever. Further, it is a choice which must be both taken with a firm understandings of the potential drawbacks, that is of injury, death or of social stigmatisation. Just as clearly, these choices are perceived to be worth making. For the purposes of this study, what is of interest is that the issue of choice may be one reason why the motorcycle lobby is so opposed to legislation, that is that restrictions on motorcycles clearly undermine an individual's right to make fundamental choices about their motorcycles. In the following chapters we shall examine the nature of the political claims of the RROs and of the meaning of political engagement for activists.

Part II
Riders and the National
Riders'-Rights Organisations

—4—

The National Riders'-Rights Organisations

If the motorcycling community may be taken to refer both to the objective number of bikers within the country and, at the same time, the symbolic sense of collective unity felt between such individuals then, within this, the riders'-rights organisations hold a specific position in that, as Klandermans argues, 'movement organisations play a significant role in the construction and reconstruction of collective beliefs and in the transformation of discontent into collective action and the maintenance of movement commitment' (1997:9). In this sense, we may see the RROs as forming a central focus that both concentrates and directs the political manifestation of the biking community. Whether as actual members or merely as readers of motorcycling literature carrying press releases from the RROs, British motorcyclists are both directly and indirectly affected by messages coming from these organisations. However, following Blasius (1994), not all riders within the motorcycling community have made the transition from merely 'being a biker' to 'being a biker politically' through membership of an RRO, this latter being 'a form of collective action which involves *solidarity*, that is, actors' mutual recognition that they are part of a single social unit' (Melucci 1989:29). As such, we need to examine what these organisations are, how they have developed, how they interact and continue to respond to motorcycling issues, in order to understand what lies at the heart of the community.

In terms of the relevant 'multi-organisational field', that is, all of the potential organisations within a specific area of interest, we are dealing with a limited arena in that whilst there are various transport-related agencies, Britain contains only two organisations explicitly aimed at riders' rights, that is organisations dedicated to pursuing riders' political rights as opposed to, for example, a one-make club which is concerned with all aspects of a particular brand of motorcycle. Thus, whilst as a rider of, for example, a Moto Guzzi, one might join the Moto Guzzi Club GB in order to be with like-minded people who enjoy the riding experience of the Guzzi, exchange stories of the joy and despair of owning one, pick-up hints about what to do about specific problems and the right place to go for parts or services, an RRO aims to further the rights of all motorcyclists on the road, whether fighting legislation aimed at motorcyclists, trying to get a better deal on insurance, gaining access to bus lanes or whatever.

Figure 8 Anti-helmet demo, Glasgow

The two organisations in Britain are the British Motorcyclists' Federation and the Motorcycle Action Group, both of which are voluntary organisations run by motorcyclist activists on behalf of all riders. Yet they were founded in different periods and for slightly different reasons, ones which have coloured the ways in which each organisation has grown, is perceived and their interrelationship. Consequently, we need to examine these foundations to see what accounts for the development of the riders'-rights movement in that, as Scott (1990) argues, whilst certain preconditions are necessary, such as activities of authorities, emotive issues, potential leaders and the reactions of those who may or may not become active, these are not necessarily sufficient for a social movement to become active. It is in this sense that, as Tarrow informs us, 'the "when" of social movement mobilisation . . . goes a long way to explaining its "why"' (1994:17).

The BMF was the first to be formed, in 1960, in response both to negative publicity facing motorcyclists and a need for an organisation which dealt with *riders* rather than with motorcycles and riding. As Geoff Wilson informs us in the *BMF Handbook* (1982):

> . . . in the Spring of 1960 the Vincent Owners' Club had urged that one-make clubs should band together as a national motorcycling organisation. The VOC was not happy with the way that the Auto-Cycle Union [ACU] dwelled predominantly on the sporting side of motorcycling, and motorcycling was getting a particularly bad name from the

Ace Cafe, ton-up, Rocker sensationalism that the press capitalised on, and which we still feel the shock waves from today.

One BMF regional officer, who was present, puts a more 'homely' spin on the official line:

> The BMF started about 1960 at Mallory Park. It started because the projectionist didn't turn up, would you believe? It was an industry's weekend. And one of the things that we were going to do on the Saturday night was we were going to have a film show, using the projector on the side of the timing box. And he didn't turn up. And we were all kind of sat around in the middle of the track, drinking coffee. And some guy said, 'You know what we want?' We said, 'What?' 'We want an organisation that'll fight for bikers' rights . . .' We said, 'Oh, that sounds interesting, yeah.' We were talking about it and then somebody said, 'Well, what would you call it?' And the guy that had first come up with the suggestion, we didn't realise at the time that it was his friend, says, 'Oh, you'd call it . . .' and he come out with a load of letters. 'What on earth's that?' 'Well, the Federation of National and One-Make Motorcycle Clubs.' 'Oh, that sounds interesting.'

Wilson informs us that FENOMSEE was to confront early attempts at restrictive legislation on motorcyclists in its first few years, with the Cronin Bill, aimed at compulsory passenger insurance for all policies in 1961, the Road Traffic Bill debate in 1962, and the campaign by the Minister of Transport, Ernest Marples, to encourage the use of crash helmets. In 1965, FENOMSEE changed its name to the British Motorcyclists' Federation and, through the formation of the Fellowship of Riders as an associate member section, opened its door for the first time to individual members. Wilson informs us that 'the prime reason for the change was to give those riders a more direct association with the BMF in name' (BMF Handbook 1982), yet another reason has been suggested which indicates that already, in its early years, the BMF was facing the financial difficulties common to voluntary organisations:

> They started off, they did it wrong really. Having said that, I don't know how else they would have done it. But they formed the Federation of National and One-Make Motorcycle Clubs. Clubs were notorious for being hard-up for money . . . [and] because they were always short of money, they were always squealing about how they couldn't afford to pay the affiliation any more money. So the result was there was a big upheaval and it was decided it would have to become the British Motorcyclists' Federation, so they could have individual members.

The BMF continued as the only riders'-rights organisation until the issue of crash helmets came to a climax in the 1973. The BMF view was that it was pointless to continue fighting on an issue with which motorcyclists were already mainly pre-complying:

> When the helmet law came along it *was* opposed, and it was opposed by the BMF. And it was lost. It was lost simply because how can you argue against a law which 90-odd per cent of people were complying with anyway? Most people were wearing helmets. You know, there was very few people didn't wear helmets.

Yet for others, the issue of compulsory wear was too important to be accepted without stronger opposition. It was the perceived failure of the BMF to adequately fight the issue of the helmet law that directly led to the formation of a new group, MAG. Ian Mutch, a founding member of MAG, explains the rationale for the creation of MAG, whilst illustrating how circumstances led a group of politically inexperienced people, motivated by a clear sense of grievance and discontent (Klandermans 1997) to establish a pressure group:

> Well, I sat around in a room with two other characters, one of whom is the editor on . . . a daily newspaper, the other of which is a lecturer at an art college in Winchester. And these two characters both had bikes and were old friends of mine, and more or less the same attitude as me, totally against helmet laws. I used to wear one perhaps half the time; especially if it was cold. But quite often I didn't want to wear one. And I'd been told it was the sensible thing to do, so I'd put it on for the sake of my parents. And also you could wear goggles with it, and goggles were part of the kit then, because they looked good. But the helmet laws were actually anathema so we had to oppose that. And we sat around, and I've still got a piece of paper somewhere where we wrote down three names, and one was SLAM, which was Stop Legislation Against Motorcyclists, the other was BUM, British Union of Motorcyclists, and the other was MAG. And then it dawned on us that none of us was capable of running this group. Because I was still at sea. The other guys, one lived at home and the other was a journalist who lived, somewhere, they both lived at home maybe at that time. So it wasn't really on. And then we heard of Dennis Howard, who'd been making the pages of Motorcycle Weekly, and there he was on this old DKW with a sign 'Helmets, yes. Compulsion, never'. He's our president. He still is. He's seventy-six. He was fifty-two when we started. And I phoned him up, I got his number from the paper, and I said, 'We've been thinking of starting a group.' And he said, 'So have I.' And it turned out we had both settled on the same name, by chance. And I went to Banbury for the vintage run. He said, 'Meet me at Banbury. I'll be in the carpark there.' And we picked him out from his voice on the phone, without knowing what he looked like. He's quite an eccentric character. And shortly after that, the Motorcycle Action Group was formed.

The helmet law was thus central to MAG's initial rationale. Whilst the BMF's formation was ostensibly to deal with the more nebulous issue of societal attitudes and bad press, MAG had a much more clearly defined early role. Ian Mutch explains:

> That was the sole issue at that time. I hadn't really seen any need to have a group, prior
> to that, because there weren't any *issues*. I was totally unaware of any threats to biking
> at all. The BMF had been in existence for at least ten years prior to that. But they had
> been formed in the wake of bad press from the rockers' era. The bust-ups with mods
> and rockers at holiday resorts. And so they'd been formed as a confederation of clubs, I
> think, partly, and largely, to redress the bad press coverage that biking was getting. And
> so they were, from the outset, a lot of clean-cut, comparatively conservative characters
> who wanted to improve the image of biking. And we didn't set-off with that objective.
> Most of our supporters then were certainly of the hairy-arsed, black, matt, open-faced
> helmet [variety], reluctantly worn, with usually a sticker on it to that effect. Riding
> Triumphs and BSAs. That was the archetypal, and in many people's minds that remains
> the archetypal, MAG member. Although the range of issues has broadened a lot more
> over the years. But that was the founding issue.

Thus, although, as is argued here, the role of the RROs is much more diverse
these days than in the 1960s and 1970s, originally the BMF and MAG were founded
to deal, respectively, with attitudes towards, and the freedoms of, the motorcyclist.
Both of these two factors are still relevant to current agendas, as the following
two quotations illustrate:

> I see it as a method of promoting motorcycling . . . and also trying to change the perceived
> attitude of a *lot* of people that bikers are somehow not as nice as what they could be, if
> you know what I mean.

> [It's about] protecting a lifestyle. Protecting *my* freedom to do what I feel I should be
> allowed to do on a motorbike and, obviously, allowing others to do the same. I don't
> like anyone to turn around in *any* situation and say, 'No, you can't do this.' Or, 'Let's
> legislate against that so they can no longer do that.' I totally hate that.

These concepts of protection and promotion are central to the philosophical
aims of the RROs, and indicate that riders' rights are both defensive and offensive
in outlook. This means that the RROs have dual functions both to defend the
motorcycling community from outside interference, yet also to take the community
to the wider society to encourage positive attitudes towards motorcyclists, whether
this is to draw in new members, prevent negative attitudes to riders or influence
politicians. This latter, as is seen elsewhere, has become an ever more important
part of the activities of the RROs since the 1980s as, increasingly, legislative
concerns have confronted the community. As one national official argues:

> Well, it says in the policy document, in the constitution and so on that the *raison d'être*
> of the BMF is to promote all aspects of motorcycling. Now, in practice, it appears that
> the core function of the BMF has become the politics, the riders' rights side of things,
> and ensuring that motorcyclists can continue to ride as they have been used to, without

interference from outside bodies. Because, if you can't achieve that, as your basic aim, then there's not much point in considering discounted ferry tickets, and encouraging touring, and encouraging social events and get-togethers, because there won't be anybody riding bikes in the first place.

Fundamentally, therefore, the organisations are primarily concerned with facilitating motorcycling, through whatever means possible, 'to get the best deal for motorcyclists.' This also involves a practical side in that the RROs perform a mundane function in the provision of services to members. This appears to be developing increasingly over the last few years to encourage riders who, as one official observes, may not necessarily appreciate the political aspects of the RROs:

> A lot of people who are fairly new to motorcycling, or they *were* in motorcycling, dropped out and they came back, the 'born-again' ones, they aren't *really* into all this legislation business, and threats about 100 break horse power and whatnot, they will only join if the BMF can *truly* offer them something tangible. . . . And then people will join the BMF and think, 'Oh, I'll join the BMF because I'll get all of these benefits. *At the same time*, the BMF will also represent me.' So, I think, we've probably got a core of people who really want to be represented, and the ones we've got to go after now are the ones who're on the 'What's in it for me? Why should I bother?'

Yet riders' rights is not merely about politics nor practical services, for the social side is also crucial, as is summed up by Neil Liversidge:

> Right, the first thing that people have got to understand about MAG is that it is not all politics. We don't want to destroy the enjoyment that people get out of motorcycling. So joining MAG is not like joining the Socialist Workers' Party where you join today and, tomorrow morning, they'll expect you to be out picketing some turkey farm somewhere. So that's the first thing people have got to get into their heads. MAG is about enjoying yourself, having a good time, getting together with loads of other motorcyclists who like doing the same things as you are, and *then* getting a bit politically involved so that you can carry on enjoying yourself, right. Therefore, MAG has got a brilliant social life. We run loads of rallies up and down the country. We run stacks of activities. We're into things that bring *practical* benefits to motorcyclists, such as discount schemes, insurance schemes and all the rest of it. So, just on a social level, it makes sense, actually, for you to be a member of MAG. Just on a level of saving yourself money, overall, with the discounts you can get, it makes *sense* for you to be a member of MAG. And *that's* where I start from.

In this way, we can see how the RROs function on a plurality of levels, from the social networks of local groups through to interaction with business and political structures (Melucci 1989). Further, the RROs also form part of the wider social movement environment through their ongoing, and expanding, provision of activities which 'range from providing "selective incentives" to members, to building consensus among current or prospective supporters, to lobbying and negotiating with authorities and to challenging cultural codes' (Tarrow 1994:4). All of this means that, as the organisations diversify, there is an increasing amount of work to be done at all structural levels, from local officers up to the national officials.

In terms of internal organisational, there are considerable similarities between the BMF and MAG. Both operate within a pyramid-type structure with local groups feeding into regional areas up to national committees based both on regional representation and national portfolio officers, for example press, research and governmental relations. As we have seen above, both organisations are also largely involved with similar activities, which are summed up by one MAG official:

> For most of its twenty-five-year history MAG was about defending riders against laws and regulations often claimed to be essential for road safety, but mostly just having the effect of discouraging motorcycling. The main tools of the job were public demonstrations and letter-writing campaigns, with information-gathering and dissemination to support those activities. As the group has developed, MAG has become more pro-active, campaigning for improvements in regulations, attitudes and facilities as well as maintaining a defensive readiness and capability – I'm beginning to sound like Peter Mandelson – and has developed an extremely effective European and international capacity . . . [For example], MAG and the other UK motorcycle organisations are placing far more emphasis on pro-actively seeking improvements in the highways and transport infrastructure. Access to bus lanes and Advanced Stop Lines at signal-controlled junctions, recognition of the beneficial role motorcycling can play in reducing traffic congestion and journey times, consultation status in local and national government, secure parking and storage, integration with public transport, preferential treatment in taxation etc.

As this indicates, therefore, there is a mixture of political and practical activities, as may be found in other social movements, although, in this instance, specifically concerned with motorcycling issues. Primarily, however, the political level tends to predominate due to the increased importance of EU legislative measures aimed at transportation issues:

> At least 90 per cent of everything we do is directly concerned with legislation which is on the go at the moment. The other 10 per cent is technical with things like the anti-theft campaign, bikes in bus lanes, you know, stuff that is actually going to be of *practical* benefit to bikers. Stuff where we're not actually having to fight against a threat. Stuff where we're being *pro-active* and going out to get something that we've never had before. But with 90 per cent of everything we do, we're fighting just to break even. Probably 90 per cent of the 90 per cent [is about the EU].

Clearly these activities carry different ramifications for different levels of the organisations. Some issues may be purely local in nature, others are national but carry implications for local areas. Further, the people who need to be addressed differ. The types of activity and target for activities, therefore, depend upon the level concerned. As such, we may argue that the RROs combine what may be called the 'old' types of collective action which are local and direct in focus and 'new' national, indirect actions (see, for example, Scott 1990; Tarrow 1994). The following two quotations indicate how this occurs:

> Problems at local pubs, such as discrimination against motorcyclists and that type of thing, really tends to be handled by the regions, that's what the regions are for, to deal with local issues. But the sort of stuff that comes to my attention tends to be pre-dominately national and European issues, though sometimes there are local issues where there are national implications, where I may get involved. [The national ones have local implications by definition], in that very often we get the regions to follow up the national issues, or EU issues, by writing to their MPs, MEPs and what have you. It's all part of raising the lobby. So it's a sort of reciprocal thing.

> I can ask every member in the country to write to a Commissioner or an MP or whatever, fine, okay, but there are only a handful of people in the country that I can actually say, 'Right, I want *you* to go and organise a meeting with this guy and give him our angle on this.' People who are actually confident to sit down with a Minister and do it. But a local group in wherever, Skegness or whatever, if we've got a national policy that says, bikes in bus lanes, more secure parking in cities, that local group in Skegness can go and see the local council and get *that* sorted out, you know what I mean? Whereas at the national level, we can put someone in with the Transport Minister and say, 'Look. Can you encourage your local councils to take up the legal target for giving them more secure parking?' We say that to the Home Office as well. So we operate on a multi-level basis and it all works very well.

One implication of this last quotation is that people who join an RRO may enjoy different types of activity, for, as Klandermans informs us, 'we have no reason to assume that someone who is motivated to take part in one kind of activity will be willing to take part in any, or every, other kind of activity' (1997:24). Consequently, although, as we shall see elsewhere, the type of activities in which an individual may get involved may sometimes be taken out of their hands due to organisational requirements, for example if they have a skill that is in particular demand, there is a tendency for members to specialise either in a particular type of role or activity:

> You tend to find amongst MAG members that different people want or enjoy different things. And you get those who are extremely politically active and aren't too interested

in the social side. All they're interested in is banging on doors and getting their message across. Conversely, you've got people who agree in principle with the political stance and the fight for riders' rights, but much more enjoy the social side and going to the rallies. And I think there's a place for both in MAG, or in any organisation come to that.

One example of specialisation, that of the letter-writing lobby, demonstrates how different levels of activity and co-ordination function within and between the RROs:

Our job is to organise the organisation in such a way that it will work with a small core of activists who can call on a larger core when necessary. And to do that you have to understand the mechanics of it. If an MEP gets six letters about a subject, that's a lot. If he gets six letters about one subject, he thinks, 'Wow,' you know. Because most of the time he gets no letters about anything. He might get one letter, which is ten pages long from somebody who's got a beef about something or another, that's a good one to choose with the [EU], isn't it, but, generally, if he gets six letters from motorcyclists on the Multi-Directive, yeah. So the mechanics of it are not actually that great. Trevor organises the letter-writers' lobby. We've got 200 guys dotted around the country who are there as a tactical weapon, where necessary. They're sent information. So there's a number of levels that the lobby takes. Firstly, within the BMF there's the Average Joe motorcyclist who's got fed-up, and who will fire off a letter to his MEP, or his MP and, basically, it will be a simple, straightforward few lines saying, 'I'm fed-up with all of this European stuff. I don't agree with this Multi-Directive and you should oppose it.' Now, the MEPs will get plenty of those letters. Then you will get the informed letters, and this is the letter-writers' lobby, a couple of hundred people who have been sent all of the necessary information by the BMF, and they will write an *informed* letter. So, then, the MEP may get only *one* informed letter, that actually goes into technical detail, backed-up by six or ten uninformed letters. On top of that, he will get a shorter technical letter from me. It's not written by me, Trevor writes it, but he'll get another one from me. So that starts to build it up. You've got the lobby going. Then, of course, on top of that, MAG are doing the same thing, they haven't got a technical letter-writers' [group], but you do get the MAG group writing lots of letters.

As these quotations indicate, whilst, as we shall see, much RRO activity is focused in Brussels, national activity continues to be central to provide the grass-roots lobbying which provides the European level with its support. As the General Secretary of the FEMA argues:

You need the co-ordinating force because, in fact, the organisations are still responsible, they still affect European policy because it's the member governments who have most of the say in European legislation, and they must be lobbied at national level. You know, from the grass-roots upwards, and it's the same with Members of the European Parliament. They really should be lobbied by national voters, motorcyclists. When I ask them to do something I always give clear instructions about what I think they should do, and then they usually do it. It's writing letters when needed, it's visiting politicians, locally in their constituency or Westminster, about the issues at the correct time. Getting out on the streets if the issue is that important.

Beneath such activities, however, lie the more mundane, everyday routines which form the basis for the activities of office-holders. Local and regional level reps must plough through, and respond to, considerable amounts of literature coming from their central office and contextualise this material for dissemination throughout their area. Further, they need to attend meetings, to arrange activities in their areas, such as the famous Egg Runs, and liaise with their national offices. Yet whilst the two RROs seem, in many ways, to be very similar in terms of activities, organisational structures and goals, many members point to differences between MAG and the BMF – dissimilarities deriving largely from what are seen as the different types of membership each organisation has. As one rider remarks:

> The two organisations are not *necessarily* very different. They *operate* differently because of the type of member we've got. There's a definite difference in the membership. Of course, there are people who are members of both organisations, yeah. But there *are* people who would join MAG and would not join the BMF, and *vice versa*.

Two riders explain such differences in more detail, and relate them both to the initial aims and structure of the organisations:

> MAG appears to come across as more of a radical group. More of a 'Let's jump up and down and make lots of noise' radical *action*, rather than 'Let's stand and talk to these people and persuade them otherwise' [group]. They're very big on demos. And bikers of a certain type like demos. They like to go out and make a lot of noise and be antisocial and that sort of thing. So it tends to attract that type of biker. It's partially to do with the way that the organisation was originally formed. The BMF, because we were originally formed from a collection of clubs, One-Make and Touring Clubs, so we are really a club-based organisation, which are people who tend to be more, 'Oh, we'll sit and have our nice little half pint of mild and discuss our trip to Bulgaria.' So those type of people were the backbone of the BMF. So that was the image. So, consequently, we attracted more of those sort of people and it's not a terribly exciting image. The image has got a lot better in the last few years, I must say, in the last two or three years. But, because of that, those people are sit-at-home. 'Let's get you to do it. You are almost our union, we'll get you to do it.' Whereas MAG people want to get more involved directly. I think it's because of the type of people. . . . The core group, the committees, the people who are active in the BMF, a lot of them came up through clubs so, consequently, you did get that [type, who] tend to be [the] more middle-aged person, who had his BSA and his BMW and . . . the original core group, I think, to some extent, are *still* those older men.

It always was perceived that the BMF was there for the BMW-riding, tourist-type people. Whereas MAG was for the scruffy oiks who rode rat bikes, or chops. Maybe that was the case at one time. Maybe it's the case that people who ride machines they've built, or modified themselves, are more aware of how the problems, the changes in the law and whatever, can affect them. Whereas people who take a bike out of the showroom, put a pair of panniers on it, aren't aware how things can change, you know, *are* changing. You know, how a change in law will affect them. Because they haven't put that work into the bike.

This perceived difference in types of member is reflected, at the level of organisation, by the idea that whereas the BMF is a conventional organisation, which walks the 'corridors of power', MAG is more radical and militant, as can be seen from its initial break away (Willetts 1982). Superficially, therefore, there would appear to be some evidence to support the notion of a split between an uncompromising, fundamentalist wing and a more pragmatic, realistic wing like that identified in the German green party, *die Grünen*, but to be found in all social movements (Yearley 1991; Scott 1990). The following quotations from members of both the BMF and MAG, make this point that the two organisations typify different aspects of the motorcycling community:

I think that there is a hard-core MAG, rabid-action group. They appeal to the younger person, who wants to see action. Who wants to get out on the streets. The BMF appeals to the more measured approach. I well know from my dealings with the press and other people in the trade in general, the BMF is seen as an establishment organisation. Which can be good and bad. Bad for the sort of young member that you're trying to attract, because he thinks you're boring, but very, very good when you're working with the Department of Transport and trying to gain special deals off the insurance companies or people in the industry.

The BMF have got skills that, on the whole, MAG don't have. They have an air of respectability that MAG has not enjoyed in the past, that would be useful for the organisation. They also have the impression of being suited and booted, where MAG doesn't have that reputation. I mean, in the past, MAG has always been associated with matt-black chops, full stop.

MAG will have a protest. They'll have a protest in London, that attracts attention and gets people to know what's going on . . . they base [their approach] more on the protest, don't they? They fight for the same things, but they go out on the street and do it.

[The BMF are] doing a good job in their own form. Taking a slightly different tack than MAG do. But they're perceived as being more *mainstream*, if you like, or *less* anarchic.

Yet, as other social movements have demonstrated, social movement organisations may move between conflict and alliance with others over time (see, for example, Klandermans 1997). Relationships with other organisations must thus be seen as dynamic, changing in differing periods and circumstances. This would appear to be the case with the RROs for, despite perceived differences, members of both organisations argue that they are becoming more alike, and that the past gulf between them is gradually closing. Ian Mutch describes the differences from the initial period after MAG was formed:

> Well, I think we are closer together. We've become more professional, and I think they recognise the enhanced image of MAG. We've all got *older*, so these demos are not as wild as they might have seemed in the early days. They're bigger, by and large. The image that we project these days is, I think, a lot *tidier* and more *disciplined* than it would have been twenty years ago. Just the runs themselves. People tend to ride crocodile fashion, two abreast. You get those kind of disciplined-looking runs. There's a lot less racing up the outside, simply because there aren't so many teenagers now, and when you're young you act like an arsehole. It's just a fact of the juvenile creature. And it was just this great mass of flapping L-plates and blue two-stroke smoke in the early '70s. And now, I was on a demo, a helmet-law demo, a Fred Hill Memorial demo, back in February where I think I counted eight brand-new Triumphs in the carpark. And there were quite a few Harleys, there were HOG members there, who you'd have thought of as pretty establishment type figures within the motorcycle hierarchy. So, yeah, our image has changed, but our principles never have.

There are two interesting implications from this statement – both an individual and an organisational one. The first is, prosaically, that the members of MAG have grown older and, thus, less militant in approach. The second point is that the organisation has, similarly, grown older and more responsible. Clearly, these two points are related. The people and the RROs have matured together as they have learnt how to operate efficiently. In this sense we can appreciate Scott's (1990) argument that organisations are pulled towards more conventional forms as they mature and become drawn into the political process. A further implication from this is that, consequently, the two organisations have become more alike in orientation. Partially, it could be that the very fact of two RROs, giving a choice to riders about where to bestow their membership and financial contributions, means that, instrumentally, each RRO has had to widen their potential appeal to enhance numbers. Alternatively, it could also be that each organisation influences the other's attitudes and approaches. One official sums this up:

> MAG is born, MAG is highly radical, polarisation between MAG and BMF. MAG evolves, grows, becomes less radical. The demands of the organisation, like the demands on the FEM, require more management practice skills, planning, strategies, all the things

Figure 9 The late Fred Hill during one of his many arrests for not wearing a helmet

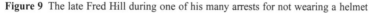

that slow you down and bog you down, to some extent. MAG starts to move towards the BMF. After the initial, 'Oh, Christ,' run away and hide in a corner reaction to their formation and the 'No Helmet' campaign etc. etc., [of] these wild men, the BMF becomes radicalised by MAG's position, and they start moving closer together.

Some of this, as is indicated above, is perceived as due to external forces, that is that threats to motorcycling, largely seen as coming from the EU, have necessitated the development of similar skills and practices. However, the new circumstances have also required the growth of mutual co-operation:

People aren't slagging the other group off as much as they used to. Both from the BMF against MAG, and MAG to the BMF. Whereas a few years ago it was a common joke, you know, if you were in MAG you didn't like the BMF. But attitudes *are* changing and they've *had* to, because of what's happening, basically, in Europe. Both organisations, or members in both organisations, and there's a lot of people in both, are beginning to realise that in order to achieve the aims, to get people aware of the positive side of biking, and the benefits and that, they've *got* to work together. It's slowly happening.

It is in this light that we can understand the feeling that the membership of the organisations are more alike than may have been the case in the past. Ian Mutch makes the comparison with the early years of MAG:

In the early days, I would never have said that it was quite as clearly class-orientated in that traditional sense, working or middle class, as people might have liked to believe. But certainly *culturally* there was a clear disparity. We had the hairies, they had the Belstaff-jacketed, BMW riders, and that was quite clear in the early days. It's *much* less clear now. I think the overlap is so total. If you look at MAG members on a demo, then we probably still get a turn-out which is unrepresentative of the organisation in total. You'll get the hairier elements that *like* to go out and demonstrate. But if you look at a lot of the people that I run into, often not at MAG-related events, who say, 'Oh, I'm a MAG member,' but they join because they want to be a part of something, because they want to help, in the same way that I join Greenpeace. I haven't got the *time* to be involved in it, I'm not in an inflatable dinghy or up a tree or anything like that, but I pay my subs every year, and I will write the occasional letter to the government or whatever. And *now*, I think we've got a lot of people in MAG who don't go to local group meetings, who don't socialise, don't go to rallies, don't go on demos, but they recognise the importance of having their long-term interests represented. And the cross-section culturally, and classwise, of MAG I would say is so broad now that you could no longer categorise the typical member in the way you could in the early '70s.

Both organisations now see themselves as catering to all sections of society and as being a microcosm of society, that is reflecting the social complexity of society itself. This is succinctly expressed by MAG's Neil Liversidge:

MAG is a broad church, absolutely. We've got people in it who are unemployed. We've got people who are, literally, chairmen of multi-national companies. We've got some very senior army officers and people in the air force. . . . We've got lawyers, doctors, you name it, we've got it in MAG. You know, there's no such thing as a 'typical' MAG member. People have this image, right, that MAG is like it was in the '70s where everybody had beards, and they all rode Brit. bikes, chops and Harleys, and it's just absolute bollocks these days, is that.

This argument is supported by dual membership, that is the numbers of riders who belong to both. Clearly, it is hard to establish exactly how many people may do this for, like many other social movements (Klandermans 1997), the RROs do not appear to hold definitive membership lists and, further, are not necessarily keen to clarify this matter, in that total membership for the RROs would then drop, as duplications would be eliminated from overall figures. Many respondents indicated, however, that they were members of both, even though active in only one, because they perceive the organisations as working for the same collective goal. The following quotation, here from a BMF member, expresses this view which is held by officers in both organisations:

> I used to be a member of MAG as well, and a lot of BMF people are members of both organisations. Because, after all, both of them are fighting for exactly what we want, although they're attacking it from different sides. So both of them should get the money because, you know, it's better than just one.

As such, members argue that there is a mutual cause and that differences have largely disappeared – factors which help draw the RROs together. What has not been so quick to disappear, however, is the *perception* of difference. As one national officer argued:

> The differences are not *great*, but people *perceive* there to be a difference. People perceive the BMF to be these middle-aged people riding BMWs. They perceive MAG as being these street-cred people who are cool and laid-back. People perceive that to be true, and *while* they perceive that to be true, some people would not join the BMF, and some people would not join MAG.

Members are aware that the two organisations are each seen as having a specific image and attracting different types of people, yet evidence suggests that this is not necessarily important enough to affect membership choices. The following quotation, from a male MAG official, illustrates this point:

> I suppose you could say I'm in the wrong group. I mean, I ride a Pan-European. I wear black leathers, with a fluorescent band which I actually bought from the BMF! I'm a member of the Institute for Advanced Motorcyclists. So, yes, perhaps I'm in the wrong group. And I don't have long hair. I do wear a suit occasionally, quite often actually. So, yeah, perhaps I'm in the wrong group. But I don't see that there's [a difference anymore]. . . . MAG was always looked upon as the more, sort of, militant of the two. I think that's gone. There are professional people in both groups. And there are more professional people in MAG than there ever was. Probably a lot to do with 'born-agains'. The divide, that social divide, or cultural divide is closed.

It is hard to uncover precisely what this perceived growing complexity of membership composition reflects. Data indicate, as is discussed here and elsewhere, that the socio-economic profile of motorcyclists is changing and thus, consequently, this can be expected to be reflected within the RROs. Partially, as we have seen above, this may be due to the perception that the organisations are growing together, and therefore an individual does not feel that they must join a specific group. However, one must also be sensitive to the role of both social networking and chance, that members may join due to association with peers who belong to a specific group (Melucci 1989; Tarrow 1994). As one Regional Rep argued, 'part of it's accidental who joins which, depending upon who they bump into.' Alternatively, it may be because one RRO is more visible in a particular locality, or that a rider sees a stand at a local or national motorcycle show. Therefore, it is hard to reach a definite conclusion. Indeed, in all probability all of these factors may be operating simultaneously. If the causes for this growing similarity are hard to demonstrate, however, the consequences are easier to see. All officials attested to a growing trend for the organisations to work together. The following two quotations, whilst acknowledging that relationships have not always been so cordial and giving potential reasons for this, indicate how this works throughout the different levels of the RROs:

> Years ago, we were so much at loggerheads with the BMF because they resented our existence. We were a challenge to them. [Interlopers]. And, I suppose, to their way of thinking, we were actually undoing their work, because we were having helmetless demos, and attracting a lot of publicity, which wasn't always bad, but they certainly feared that it must be, and so our relations were not good. More recently, we co-operate quite a lot, and we've encouraged them to join the FEM, which is the pan-European body. . . . Groups like MAG all over Europe, representing each of the European countries. And the BMF has now joined that, so they pay a percentage of the FEM costs; which is the equivalent of one ECU, which is about eighty pence, for each member that they have. So, yep, we co-operate with them. We tend now to sit on the same committees that they sit on. For example, the National Motorcycle Council, ROSPA, [the Royal Society for the Prevention of Accidents], PACTS, that's the Parliamentary Advisory Committee on Transport Safety, TAG, the Theft Action Group, that's another big issue for MAG these days; anti-theft initiatives. So we run into each other a lot, both here and in Europe.

> Well, although, in the past, there's been some negative publicity about us not getting on well, in practice the two organisations, or people from the organisations, get on fairly well ... we talk with one another. ... Now a lot of us are on E-mail, there's quite an exchange of E-mail traffic about policy and where we're going . . . in terms of dealing with our opposite numbers, no problems, certainly on a local basis. BMF and MAG work together on a lot of things. For example, bus lanes in Bristol. Now the prime mover of that was MAG, a guy called Nich Brown . . . they got together with support from the BMF. ... They did a lot of work on bus lanes. They went to committees. They set up a local forum of all the clubs, regardless of whether they were affiliated or not, and went on from there and made it a corporate approach.

Yet despite an improvement in relations, there is also a considerable amount of ongoing discomfort between the two organisations. This is not purely within the British RROs but generally across European riders'-rights groups. As the following quotation points out, there are both practical and ideological reasons behind this:

> In every country you go to, there's [organisations that are similar to] MAG and the BMF, and there's a bit of needle between them. It was worse some time back and now we're learning to live together. And in practically every country you will find this, that there are two organisations and they are rivals; either for market share of members or because their lifestyles are particularly different.

This statement is interesting in that it appears to be in accord with debates concerning competition between social movement organisations. For example, M.F. Hall (1995) informs us that organisations will compete if the potential for growth is limited due to a lack of resources or the size of market etc., with the 'winner' being that organisation with the structural flexibility to best adapt to prevailing circumstances, and that they will co-operate only if there is room for more than one organisation or if they hold distinct niches. Yet the picture that emerges from the RROs is more complex than this distinction implies. Firstly, as we have seen, the RROs do not, despite perceptions of internal difference, offer distinctive forms of organisation, aims, tactics and so on. Further, rather than always competing, it would appear from quotations above that both organisations are adapting to circumstances and, in so doing, becoming more similar in nature. This greater similarity is also supported by those arguments from members which indicate that differences in lifestyle are of declining importance. However, it is also the case that the RROs must compete for the finite resources of the motorcycling community and that this may, therefore, be the source of continuing tension.

The idea of competition for members mentioned above may thus be of some salience in that continuing rivalry may be necessitated primarily on the basis that the two RROs require a sense of difference in order to make their respective sales pitches. This idea is supported by one rider who argues, 'you are competing for members. So you want to create an artificial rift. To say that "We're different to them so join us."' This would appear to be largely financially driven. As voluntary organisations dealing with sectional interests, the potential pool for financial resources is limited; bikers are unlikely to get grants or donations from charitable bodies. As such, they are dependant upon both income from members and sales of relevant products (Klandermans 1997). The following quotation from a national BMF officer illustrates this point more fully:

> At the grass-roots . . . they're all motorcyclists, and they get a feel-good factor over meeting someone from Motorcycle Action Group. Thinking, 'Oh, he's a nice guy. Yeah, we'll work together on this project and get something done.' You can applaud that, in a way. But equally, something that I've said within the BMF, 'Let's get ourselves *clear* on what we're trying to achieve.' If you draw an analogy with the RAC and the AA, behind the scenes they no doubt talk to one another, but they never go public on it. You'll *never* see a joint RAC and AA action, campaign. They almost seem to carefully

orchestrate these things so the AA will do one and the RAC will do one. . . . Now, what they're after, they're big businesses and they're after membership. I don't know what the motivation behind the AA and RAC is, but I don't think it's particularly about the rights of the motorist; as it is the rights of the motorcyclist. They're more big businesses. They're into touring, insurance, financial services, the whole she-bang. But, nevertheless, they're in exactly the same field, that they compete with one another for members. What I've said to the BMF [is], 'You ought to get it clear what we're trying to do is compete for the hearts and minds of the same people. And it's a finite business. There's only so many motorcyclists around.' So, I've said that we shouldn't, as far as I'm concerned, continually share all of this information, and this business. It confuses, or it can confuse the market place. In that . . . I've even seen BMF people say, 'It's important that you belong to someone, either MAG or BMF, you should belong. You owe it to yourself.'

This clearly argues that there can be no quarter in a restricted area of potential activity, that is, given the finite number of British motorcyclists, organisational growth may, of necessity, in some cases be only possible at the expense of the other group. However, on the whole, the penetration of that potential market is not that significant that expansion would be at the expense of the other RRO. Although neither organisation appears to have a definitive figure for their own membership, indeed, many figures were mentioned during fieldwork, even the most optimistic numbers would put joint membership at under 200,000, including the associate members from national and one-make clubs. As such, under 20 per cent of the alleged number of motorcyclists, the problems of determining which are discussed later, are represented by a riders'-rights group. Of more concern, therefore, is not so much the fight over potential members, but over resources. If only so many motorcyclists are prepared to join an organisation, then clearly attracting those who are prepared to make a contribution becomes important. Of immediate practical consideration is how, given current numbers of members, resources – in terms of money and activists – can best be utilised. It is considerations such as these that underlie debates about a potential merger of the BMF and MAG – debates given a greater potency with the merger of the FEM and the European Motorcyclists' Association (EMA).

Two things were noticeable in respondents' attitudes to the idea of merger. Firstly, the majority of those interviewed were in favour of merging. Two MAG members explain why this would be desirable:

For the good of motorcycling, both organisations *definitely* need to be one. . . . Purely to save *awful* financial waste, and to put a lot of good minds working together instead of duplicating what they do . . . what we would get, if the two British organisations joined, is a wealth of experience of dealing with different types of people. Which would be useful. And a wealth of individuals who have always lobbied differently, but we'd have them both. It would be all there, and everything would be concentrated.

I'd like to see them merge, to be honest. To be perfectly honest, I would like to see one organisation, speaking with one voice. Because the combined resources, and the combined effort would turn the riders'-rights organisation, whatever you wanted to call it, into a much more powerful voice to speak on behalf of motorcyclists nationally. There's a *lot* of duplication of effort, and that's frustrating, but necessary when you've got two separate groups.

However, secondly, respondents did not believe the members of the other RRO would allow it. Whilst MAG members were more clearly of the opinion that a merger would not be desired by BMF members, there was also a belief that the same was true for MAG. The following quotations, from national MAG officials, explain why they think merger would be resisted by the BMF. Both explanations are grounded in the belief that this is due to entrenched attitudes within the BMF, ideas which have already received support from a BMF member earlier, yet one sees this as due to a social snobbery associated with the old differences whilst the other sees this as based on the opinions of just a few people within the BMF who hold the power to prevent change:

We've got finite resources, a finite level of interest. [Bikers] are not the most committed people in the world, they're not the most politically active, or aware and all the rest of it. There's *every* case for us being one organisation. *But*, what the BMF people will tell you is that they are different *types* of people, which is absolute crap. They're not different types of people at all, at an ordinary member level. What it is is higher echelons of the BMF have got the idea that the BMF is some sort of, I don't know, it's a social notch above MAG, if you like, and they don't want to be seen associating with the Great Unwashed. . . . We've got more waste of resources, simply because we've got this stuck-up attitude of wanting something that's a cut above the Great Unwashed in MAG, and all the other 'biker organisations' as they call them. And it's absolute bollocks.

I think we should have more co-operation. I would like to see one organisation come out of the two. We tried [merging] three years ago. It probably was a bit premature because, at that time, and to a degree now still, there's an old guard in the BMF, who really just don't like MAG at all, and they still hold a lot of influence, unfortunately. They feel that there's a need for two organisations that are completely separate, and a disparate type of people and organisations. You know, 'There's no way that we can co-operate.' And I think that that's bollocks, frankly. As I was saying earlier, bikers are bikers.

This receives support from the BMF, agreeing that BMF members would not support merger at the present time, yet, as can be seen below, there are also concerns that MAG members are not as in favour as is publicly stated:

There will reach a point in the future, no doubt, where a merger would be a valid thing. At present, the members wouldn't wear it. The BMF members have been asked, and we got a resounding, 'no'. MAG members have been asked and, whether Neil will admit it or not, MAG members have said 'no'. But it *will* change in the future.

Such arguments about continuing differences between the two memberships are hard to evaluate, especially if the statements discussed above that the two organisations are now very similar have any validity. Some respondents expressed concern that merger would merely bring different people together in unaccustomed proximity and lead to in-fighting. Consequently, although the idea of merger is welcomed on a practical level, there are doubts, largely surrounding the question of membership differences discussed earlier, which give officials pause:

> I can see, from a numbers point of view, it's maybe good to have everybody together, because it's big clout. But, on the other hand, if people want numbers, and they can say the BMF and MAG are behind them, then that's equally big clout. And maybe having two organisations battling for you is better than having one. And I think that, in Jo Public's eyes, the people who don't have much knowledge, there is still a difference. MAG is still seen as the lifestyle-biker image; which I think in some areas it probably still is. It isn't up here, but maybe in some areas it is. And the BMF is seen as the sort of BMW brigade, which I don't think it is either. But I think there still is a certain amount of that perception about. And if people want a choice between those, they should have a choice. I'm not too fussed if they don't join up. I mean, we have a lot of people who belong to both anyway. And then that's double the money in the coffers, isn't it?

This last idea is supported again by M.F. Hall (1995), who argues that working relationships with other social-movement organisations increase the resources upon which a group may draw during collective action and may, perhaps, increase one's standing when dealing with those in power. Yet this is criticised by another MAG member:

> [Some people I know in MAG have] said, 'Well, the groups, as groups, have different identities,' [but] I personally think that's bollocks, because do we have different roads to ride on? There's a BMF road, 'You ride down that.' And there's a MAG road over there, 'You ride down that,' eh?

Consequently, it ultimately comes down to whether organisational interests are prioritised over motorcyclists' interests generally. For the present, with organisational concerns dominating the agenda, activities will continue to be duplicated and resources wasted. Meanwhile, officials in Europe watch and wait:

> I believe, and I think it's personalities that stop it, I believe that what we *badly need* at the moment in the UK is a merging of the two riders' groups. We could *do* something then.

–5–

Activism and Activists

Having explored the RROs at national level, it is now necessary to examine the components that allow the organisations to carry out their work, namely the individual activists who provide the main contribution to the vast mass of work accomplished. There is a considerable amount of literature in the field identifying the steps by which individuals become politically active, for activists are not regarded in the same light as those who are quiescent. Bradley, for example, makes a three-part distinction between different types of identity formation:

> 'Passive identities' are potential identities in the sense that they derive from the sets of lived relationships . . . in which individuals are engaged, but they are not acted upon . . . 'Active identities' are those which individuals are conscious of and which provide a base for their actions. They are positive elements in an individual's self identification although we do not necessarily think of ourselves continually in terms of a single identity. . . . Politicised identities are formed through political action and provide the base for collective organisation of either a defensive or an affirmative nature (1996:25–6).

As a rough guide line, we may use this to delineate crudely between bikers who do not belong to an RRO, RRO members and RRO activists. However, it is also important to determine how individuals progress through these classifications. Klandermans, for example, looks at this process in terms of the respective obstacles confronting both those organising political activity and those who potentially may become activists. From the viewpoint of organisers he identifies four steps: 'creating mobilisation potential, forming and activating recruitment networks, stimulating the motivation to participate and removing the barriers to participation' (1997:23). From the viewpoint of the participant the four steps correlate to those of the organiser, that is one becomes part of a group potentially active, is targeted by the organisation, then motivated and overcomes problems preventing activity. Yet this account appears somewhat instrumental and lacks an understanding of the more emotive aspects to activism on the part of individuals, who seem merely adjuncts to the goals of organisers who 'seduce' them into activity. As such, we require an understanding of the common purpose and sense of group solidarity alluded to, for example, by Tarrow who argues that it:

> is participants' *recognition* of their common interests that translates the potential for movement into collective action. By mobilising consensus, movement entrepreneurs play an important role in stimulating such consensus. But leaders can only create a social movement when they tap more deep-rooted feelings of solidarity or identity (1994:5).

Therefore, we must also appreciate that collective action requires analysis of the 'processes through which individuals recognise that they share certain orientations in common and on that basis decide to act together' (Melucci 1989:30). As Melucci has argued, we need to know why people become active, not merely how they so do. This means, as Klandermans argues, that for 'all the literature on social movements, we still know very little about the backgrounds of participation' (1997:3). As such, four fundamental questions need to be addressed: namely, who joins, why they join, how they sustain motivation and the positive and negative aspects to involvement.

The first question to try to establish is that of who constitutes the membership of the RROs. Whilst MAG have not undertaken any research into the composition of membership, the BMF undertook in 1995 research that offers a statistical profile. Clearly, any conclusions drawn from the BMF results must be tentative in that, firstly, MAG membership, as is discussed above, may be different from that of the BMF and, secondly, that the sample response rate was only 28.1 per cent, that is of 10,791 questionnaires distributed to individual members only 3,030 were completed. The problem may thus be that certain characteristics typify the person who is likely to respond, rather than the typical member of the organisation. However, as this provides the most detailed data concerning membership, we may examine the research conclusions whilst bearing these reservations in mind.

What is of interest in these data is that they point to a potentially significant socio-political trend in membership. Firstly, of the sample, 86.1 per cent were over thirty years old (6 per cent over sixty years), and 74.9 per cent of the sample had held a licence for over ten years. Secondly, what is of further interest, especially given statements elsewhere about the high proportion of female activists, is that 94.5 per cent of respondents were male. Whilst social class was not specifically mentioned, 23.6 per cent recorded earnings of over £25,000 per annum, with a further 42.4 per cent earning £15,000–25,000. Data from the BMF and other sources indicate that organisational membership may also be related to size of vehicle. The AA found that although only 19 per cent of those motorcyclists interviewed were members of a club or association, this rose to 37 per cent for those with machines over 500cc (AA 1995). Whilst the BMF categories are slightly different, 75.8 per cent of the sample owned a vehicle of over 600cc. As such, it would appear, tentatively, that it is the slightly older, higher-class male rider on a larger motorcycle who would seem to be more interested in political issues. This would appear to accord with characteristics identified by other writers. Rush (1992) highlights certain factors found among those who participate politically: namely, more education than average, especially higher education, middle class, male (although this appears to be changing), middle-age, ethnic majorities and social involvement and membership of groups or organisations. Whilst the BMF research did not mention ethnicity, all respondents and riders contacted during this research were white. A further factor identified as important is that individuals identify with the particular group (Klandermans 1997). In the case of riders, this is facilitated by their existing membership of the community and, also, by virtue of length of licence and type of vehicle, may indicate a closer identification with biking among those who have ridden longest and with larger vehicles.

Figure 10 MAG demo

The next question must therefore focus on what motivates riders to join an RRO. We have already noted previously that motorcyclists have individualistic orientations. Yet this individualism has important consequences for motorcycle politics in that it provides a general predisposition towards political activism of an essentially libertarian kind, that is bikers may act collectively in order to secure the freedom of the individual. Clearly, there is a potential contradiction within this in that there are two opposing tendencies being played-out: collectivism and individualism:

> They're individuals, and I don't think they're into collective things. . . . [They have individualistic values]. It's a very big generalisation, but it's about as close as you can come to it, is that motorcyclists want to be able to do what they want, it's almost tending towards an anarchist view. They don't want anyone to tell them what to do. They just want to go out and do it, and want to be trusted to be able to make decisions for their lives. Providing it doesn't affect anyone else adversely, they just want to be left to their own devices, and they believe they *can* be trusted to do that.

As such, the intense personal, individual experience of motorcycling also carries collective, and political, ramifications, that is that the experience of freedom in one milieu may drive one to pursue the same elsewhere. As one rider succinctly remarks, 'if you're looking for one word that sums up biker politics, or biker attitudes, it's "freedom".' Another rider explains more fully:

> It's a physical freedom that intuitively translates to a political freedom. It translates if you're willing to *do* something about it. There's a condition to it, really, of recognising that it's something that's worth doing and that it's something that won't always be there if you get Safety Nazis in the way, and you get bureaucrats in the way, and people who sit in grey buildings and wear grey suits and live grey lives and have grey wives and write with grey pens on grey bits of paper. They just don't see any of the colour of it.

Therefore, for riders, displaying certain attitudes to their motorcycles, this means that when threatened by the trends of the EU to harmonise standards across Europe, they may be brought into direct political conflict with legislating bodies who seek to impose limitations on an individual's freedom to express themselves through their bike. Two quotations make such links directly. The first stresses how the EU challenges the whole ethos of riding, whilst the second stresses how, being the kind of people they are, riders will tend to respond to perceived attacks:

> That's another *big* issue, type approval. Because that challenged the whole *philosophy*, the whole *culture* of biking, as a form of self-expression. Now most people outside biking will just see a bike as a nasty thing, they won't see it as an *art* form. And yet, certainly post-Easy Rider, increasingly, the motorcycle is an instrument of self-expression. This has become very much a reality. Custom bikes, I mean, everybody wants to be different from everybody else. Everybody wants a unique custom. And what type approval challenged was that whole philosophy. And this is the Germanic philosophy as well. 'Here is the machine. It has been designed by people much cleverer than you. You will not change one nut or bolt on it. Either cosmetically or mechanically.' And that sort of thinking is anathema to us.

> I think bikers, having always had this terrible public image of being the Wild Bunch and, you know, dirty, hairy, greasy bikers on chops and Hell's Angels and all this crap,

they were an ideal target. And I don't think anybody really had *any* idea that bikers, *because* of what they do, they are pretty highly individualistic. They do have, the majority of them, a lot of personality and character just because they do what they do and they enjoy it. And I don't think [the politicians] knew what they'd taken on. I mean, and these days, biking is *not* a cheap form of transport, and a lot of people are into their custom leathers, and matching helmets and Goldwings and good for them . . .! And these people are intelligent people and I don't know what [the politicians] thought they were doing, but really, most bikers are intelligent, they've got a certain amount of grit, if you like . . . and they will fight for what they want.

Whilst this may help explain a general propensity towards potential political engagement, however, we must also examine the specific factors which draw people into activism. For activists, the motivation for *enrolling* new members is instrument- ally tied to money, for without financial backing rider's rights cannot be fought. As one Regional Director argues, 'A lot of people say, "Oh, why do I need to join? Why should I?" But, to me, we can't keep up with Europe unless we've got some money to do it with. And that's a sad fact, but it's true.' Yet we still need to understand why people join. Four main areas were mentioned by respondents: joining because they merely happened to be in a certain place at a certain time, for social reasons and, the most commonly-given reasons, either due to specific issues or for the general feeling that motorcycling was under attack. The first of these reasons is explained in the following quotations:

I joined in 1982, because I was at a concert in Cornwall, it was a 'Girlschool' concert. It was a very good concert and somebody threw a membership form at me. So I thought, 'This is what I've been waiting for.' So I joined. . . . The BMF wasn't established at that time in that area and, I suppose, if someone had presented me with a BMF form and told me their aims, I would have joined the BMF.

I was down at the BMF Show in 1988 or '89, and some bearded, hairy nutty came up to me clutching one of the old, tabloid-style *MAG News*. 'Do you want one of these, mate?' 'Oh, all right then. Thank you very much.' Tucked that in my pocket. Took it home and read it. Thought, 'Yeah.' ['But you were at the BMF Rally, so how did you end up joining MAG?']. Well, because MAG came up to me and gave me some literature in an entertaining and flamboyant way. And I took it back and read it and thought, 'Yeah, this looks a bit canny. I'll send the form off.' Sent my tenner.

In these, we can see the role circumstances played in becoming a member, for whilst both indicate that they were interested in the issues involved, they had not previously acted to develop this interest. This would seem to support the idea that, rather than there being people who are either interested or not, there is a greater pool of potential sympathy that must be effectively tapped in order to maximise grass-roots support. Yet it is also interesting to note, especially given comments made elsewhere about the particularistic characters of the two RROs, that rather than the decision being made to join a specific organisation, it was mere chance that brought these riders to join their particular RRO and that, if circumstances had been different, they might easily have become members of the other. There are two possible consequences of this. Firstly, it may help explain those comments in the chapter above about people who feel they fit the characteristics of the other organisation. Secondly, it may possibly mean that members of an organisation may be as much 'made' as 'born' in that, if allegiance is initially to a cause rather than to an approach, particular characteristics or attitudes of an RRO member may be, at least partially, due to socialisation within the group.

The second reason given was to participate in the social aspects of the motorcycling community. The following quotations refer to two aspects of membership. The formal one makes them a member of an RRO, but there is also an informal membership, conferring rights to participate in a social group to which they want to belong: to be a biker:

And here I am, there's a friendly group called 'bikers'. There's a Motorcycle Club with *lots* of people in it, all different walks of life. It's good fun. We can all mingle. You can forget you're a policeman: you're a *motorcyclist*. It's the social aspect of it that drew me.

[MAG] looked like something where I could meet other bikers. I could almost have a pass to get into my first few rallies and stuff. Because I'd read the magazines, I'd seen these rallies. I wanted to go, but I didn't know if I *could*. I didn't *know* what the scene was like. So getting involved with MAG, where they appeared quite happy to let me in with a 200, and then an old 250 Suzuki, it was fine. They were little bikes, but nobody cared. I thought, 'Oh, this is cool. Nobody cares what I ride, so that's fine. I can get in.'

The two most popular explanations for membership, however, relate specifically to political aspects. The first explanation relates to how a specific issue may be the catalyst that finally goads a biker into active participation. To some extent this bears similarities to the first reason given above, that is that an individual may be predisposed towards membership, but needs a direct push, whether from an individual or an issue, to take the initiative. As such, a sense of grievance may provide the means for drawing a group together (Klandermans 1997). For contemporary bikers the crucial years appear to have come in the late 1980s when legislative proposals, and particularly that of leg protectors, were seen as requiring more direct opposition. Many respondents, therefore, identified this period as providing the trigger leading them towards active participation. The following quotations, from MAG's Director of Transport Policy Development (and Vice-Chair) and from its former Director of Research and Government Relations respectively, both make references to this specific threat:

> [In] 1988/9, Peter Bottomley said, 'It's not a question of *if* you get leg-protectors, just a question of *when*.' MAG membership practically doubled overnight, I was one of that intake.

> I thought it was time I started putting something back. I'd spent years riding around and I was aware of the issues that were going on. Then the leg protector thing came along, and the 400cc issue thing came along and I thought, 'Well, you know, I'm not just going to sit here and let this happen to me,' so I joined Bath MAG and became a Rep a few months later when the Rep there stood down.

For others, it would appear, however, it is not a specific issue that finally motivates people to membership, but the growing, or sudden, realisation of the totality of threat about which an individual was not previously aware. It would appear, from the following quotations, that it is customarily a specific person or event that brings the individual to 'enlightenment'. One rider spoke of how their local postman, a MAG Rep, had persuaded them to go along to meetings and how 'I got to understand more about what was happening, to the legislation and that sort of thing, and the threats that were being posed to me and my ability to ride my motorcycle.' Another rider relates how, in the early 1990s, she became a member after winning the Miss Federation competition at a BMF Rally. Friends from her club, which was affiliated to the BMF, had pestered her to enter and, given that the winner won a year's free insurance, she agreed to enter, and won. As a result of her 'victory' she was required to attend events such as the Bike Show and General Council (GC) meetings. At one GC meeting, there was a discussion about proposed legislation:

> And I was *stunned* by what was going on. I thought, 'Why don't I *know* about this? This is *terrible*. This can't go on. This is *really* bad.' And it was *then* that I thought, 'I don't want to drop out anymore. I want to keep involved with this.' Because you *know* what's happening, and you *know* what's going on and I felt that before you were kept in the dark. I mean, fair enough, now the BMF magazine tries to keep you more posted about what's happening. You can write to Trevor Magner and people send you stuff. But, at the time, I was just *stunned* that I knew *nothing* about all this that was coming in to threaten bikes. And I thought, 'That's it. I want to stay in with this. I want to find out what's going on and do something about it.' And that was really it.

For another rider, an Assistant Regional Director, it was witnessing the sacrifices that others were prepared to make for riders' rights that persuaded him that he had to become a full member – a variant on the most commonly given motivation identified by Klandermans of 'if I don't do it nobody else will', that is 'if others can do it, so can I' (1997:69):

> I was . . . a member through the various clubs I was in, but I still wasn't a *full* member. And then I met Trevor Magner, and it suddenly dawned on me that there was a guy here who could be earning a lot more money in industry. Obviously, he loved motorcycling, or else he would never stick with the job he's got. What he was doing, you know, even becoming a full member wasn't really doing as much as he was. But at least I'd be doing as much as *I* could.

However, it is not the case that the social and the political are mutually exclusive, for reasons for joining may intertwine the two. This is summed up by one national BMF official:

> I'm quite concerned to help where I can and try and do something. If I've got the energy, and the ability, I like to help. Then when Jim said to me that you might not be able to ride a motorbike in ten years time, if someone doesn't do something we're going to be legislated off the road. And I thought, 'Hang on a minute. How so? Explain.' It took him a year to persuade me to join as an individual member, but I finally joined because I thought, 'Yeah. He's got a point.' So it's a case of I enjoy riding the bikes, I enjoy the people that ride bikes, I've had a *brilliant* social life since I started riding a bike and I don't want to lose that. I don't want to lose that at all. And I don't see why any of us should.

Yet, as Rush (1992) informs us, there is clearly a difference between the passivity of paid-up membership and the activism of holding office, being prepared to take on a position within an organisation and give up one's free time and energy in addition to a cash contribution. As such, we need to understand what compels some individuals to undertake voluntary duties. In many ways this reflects reasons for joining in the first place. As such, some officers became active merely by virtue of being in a certain place at a certain time:

> Well, it was the usual case. [It was] the time of year when they decide they need a Rep, they vote for a Rep. The chap who was doing it had stood down and somebody nominated me and I said, 'Yeah, right.'

> If you stand up and have an idea. 'Oh, you've had an idea! In that case you're in charge of implementing it.' Someone says, 'Let's have a bike show.' 'What a good idea. You're bike show organiser.'

These two quotations support Klanderman's (1997) work on union members, wherein two commonly identified reasons were being asked to volunteer or actively putting oneself forward. Yet, for most, activism springs from the desire to continue riding their motorcycles, and ensure that this is still viable for future generations:

> I wanted to keep riding my bike. I enjoy it. Still enjoy it. I just don't really enjoy a car. I don't want to be forced into a car.

> I think [I became active] mainly because of [my son] Philip. I mean, when he was six months old he was sitting on Daddy's bike. And the thought that when he's older it would be difficult for him to obtain something that he wants, I mean, I won't stop him having a bike. They say they're dangerous, but it's just as dangerous getting on a bus these days. And I don't want to see people like Philip not being able to obtain a bike when they're older. I think that's one of the main issues, it's the thought that in ten years they'll legislate us off the road. And that's not a long time, if you think about it. So I want my son to be able to ride a bike. And I've got visions of me riding my bike when I'm getting on a bit and all! There's a lot of older bikers on the road now and, I mean, I just don't want it to be so expensive none of us can afford it. I mean, you've only got to look at insurance from that point of view.

This is tied into a fear of what legislation may do to change the nature of motorcycling if it is not fought, as can be seen above. As this rider continues, 'I probably got involved with the BMF mainly because I think the biking fraternity, about five years ago, had to get more political because it was going to affect us all.'

Once again, we can use the example of the issue of leg protectors to indicate how political issues can lead people to activism. Neil Liversidge explains more fully the type of opposition that leg protectors called forth and, in so doing, transformed him from member to activist:

> I joined MAG in 1981 when I first got a motorcycle on the road, because, obviously, being politically aware as a person, through my involvement with the Labour Party and everything else, I knew that certain things were being mooted by politicians that would affect me as a motorcyclist. So, I've just got this theory that if you don't get involved in politics you end up being governed by your inferiors. And I don't *like* being governed by my inferiors, as some past bosses of mine would no doubt tell you! So I took the decision, at that point, to join MAG but, I've got to say, back in 1981, MAG was a shambles, and my involvement between '81 and '88 simply consisted of going on a few demos. But the real turning-point, if you like, was, I think, probably late '87, early '88, I read in the *Financial Times* of all papers that Peter Bottomley, who was the then Secretary of State for Transport, if not Secretary of State he was certainly a Transport Minister, had decreed that within a certain period of time, all bikes were going to be fitted with compulsory leg protectors; which was an idea that I didn't fancy at all, because I'd seen reports on leg protectors when they'd been tried in the late '60s on Norton Commandos, along with chest supports and everything else. And it seemed to me that here was an idiot who'd never ridden a bike, who was deciding that bikes were going to be modified in a particular way that, one, I thought would make them look ugly anyway,

two, I didn't want on any bike of mine and, three, which I thought would be positively bloody dangerous, and I certainly wouldn't even be prepared to ride a bike with leg protectors, such as they're proposing, on. And I knew that, if they were going to decree that these were going be fitted to all bikes, and I wasn't prepared to do ouwt about it, I either had to stop riding bikes, which I wasn't prepared to do, *or* I had to stop the legislation. Now, by this time, MAG had got its act together, and the publicity material that was coming out was a lot better. It was obviously an organisation which had pulled itself together, so I thought, 'Well, yeah. They can probably make a difference.'

In a sense, therefore, and quite obviously, the fundamental reason any activist becomes involved is both to help themselves, and help others. However, there is also a feeling that work needs to be done to improve the image of motorcyclists within society. Three quotations pick up on this theme. The first comes from a rider who joined in the 1960s, when the image of a motorcyclist was at a low point, and the last two from people who became active within the last decade:

About '68 when the BMF was only eight years old, I became aware of it and I joined it because I thought we needed to get together . . . it was clear to me that motorcycles were *so* unpopular, and *so* looked down upon that they could do with all the help they could get.

[People are active] because they enjoy it. Yeah, they enjoy it and, plus, it's a real *buzz* when people realise you're not the hardened criminals that people think you are. When they realise you're nice people anyway, just *normal* Joe Bloggses, who care about things, as well as caring about the bikes and things you ride.

We do it because we want to, and also to demonstrate to people out there, by a photograph and a little write-up in the newspaper, that motorcyclists are friendly, happy chaps and chapesses.

However, riders also argue that their activism also springs from other, intangible, factors. Most commonly identified are the dislike for injustice, mentioned above, and/or an oppositional character. The following quotations come from the BMF's Government Relations Executive, Trevor Magner, and MAG's Ian Mutch:

Perhaps it sounds immodest to say, maybe I've got a strong sense of what's right and wrong, and I get *offended* when I see oppression, and I felt that motorcycling was getting a bad deal. And, in many respects at that time, when I started getting involved, I rather admired the way that MAG operated with their demos, and the fact that they went into the streets and showed that they weren't going to be walked over, and the issue that was mainly alive at the time, was the helmet law. But when I became really active, it was shortly after there was an attempt to introduce a tax on ownership of vehicles, about '80, '81, that was when there was an attempt to do that, and a local MAG group was being set up, so I decided to go along and see what it was like. And then they started formulating the Transport Act 1981, that was that nice Kenneth Clarke! Motorcyclists' faces were one of the stepping stones that he used to progress to his elevated position in the cabinet. And I started writing letters, and started seeing the replies from the government, and from him, which *dripped* arrogance, and basically, when confronted with that, instead of backing off, I just got more mad. So I got more involved. ... I think it's basically people trying to force their *will* on us, or *ignore* us, ignore the powered two-wheeler, as we now tend to refer to the generic term for motorcycles and related machinery, as a legitimate and practical mode of transport. And being ignored just tends to wind me up and, consequently, the more I'm ignored the louder I shout.

In the early days [of the anti-helmet law campaign], it was almost, not exactly gratuitous rebellion, I was genuinely, and still am, very *angry* and *insulted* that anyone should tell me how to dress. ... But I would continue to do that anyway. If somebody ... had a crystal ball, and said 'You will *never* repeal that law,' I would go on just the same, arguing against it indefinitely. But then, I enjoy arguing. I was chairman of the Debating Society at school. So I'll argue with no real object in mind at all.

Yet this anti-authoritarian attitude is not a negative one in activists, for it provides a key motivation for their political involvement. Further, the above quotations indicate that, not only does there need to be a sense of injustice but also that individuals 'must become convinced that they have the power to change their condition' (Klandermans 1997:18). As he argues, activists are thus those 'who demonstrate the strength of mind to go against the force of habit, and to act on their hopes for a better future' (1997:3). Clearly, this also relates to those quotations above that allude to riders being drawn into activism by virtue of being present at a meeting or making suggestions, in the sense that it is those who see an organisation not operating efficiently or effectively, and make this known, that can talk themselves into a post. The first quotation, from a BMF official, refers to how this operated in 1977, whilst the second, from a former MAG official, refers to the early 1990s:

I wrote to the BMF and said, 'I've been a member for twelve months, also a member of MAG. MAG seem to do far more than the BMF. Why is this? You know, you really ought to get your act together.' And I remember the General Secretary phoned me up and said 'Very interesting letter, Jeff. Could you come along to our next Press and Publicity meeting,' or Publicity Committee or something or other. I said, 'Yeah, okay.' And so I did. Went down to London. Went to this first meeting one evening. Shot my mouth off, as always, 'This is what the BMF should do, and this is what the BMF should do. Why doesn't the BMF do this?' Blah, blah, blah. The then Chairman of the BMF ... said, 'Well, would you like to be our Press Officer?' So I said, 'Well, I'll have a crack. I've never done it before.'

So there was a form, so I filled it in, sent it away and joined up. And went along to the local group, which was tiny, and realised that if I said anything, they listened. Straight from the beginning . . . and I was also rather amazed that there were a lot of people who couldn't see *obvious* things that we should do; either to forward ourselves, or to forward the aims. And when I voiced something, they'd say, 'Oh, that's a good idea.' 'It's not. It's just obvious. Why have you not thought of it?' But couldn't become active, couldn't hold a position – handed-out literature, did things, went on rallies and stuff – but didn't really want to get fully active while I was doing my degree. But I ended-up getting sucked into it anyway. Just because being on the periphery as a member, but not holding a position, I could see events going horribly wrong, that shouldn't have been done that way. But when I tried being too vocal about specifics, it was, like, 'Well, stand for a position.'

This is not to imply that individuals do not actively seek a greater commitment and level of involvement. Responses from activists appear to suggest that people who become participants are those who have a considerable degree of motivation and commitment generally. As such, as Klandermans argues, commitment 'is both antecedent and consequent to ongoing participation. The more committed to a movement someone is, the more likely it is that he or she will continue to participate, and the longer an individual participates, the more committed he or she becomes' (1997:29). The FEMA's Simon Milward, in speaking of how he talked himself into a job, demonstrates this quality:

So in 1986 I sat down. I used to do a bit of wood-carving, and I was busy carving the MAG logo with a slogan underneath. . . . And I thought, 'Why am I sat here doing this wood-carving when I could actually be working for the organisation?' So I stopped it. Still haven't finished it. It is still being used as a bread-board in my house in Exeter. So I wrote to the MAG National Committee and said, 'What do I have to do?' There wasn't a lot of guidance so I just got with the job. There was no [local] MAG group so I became the Rep. In the Exeter area at that time, well, there was virtually no members all. Then when I became County Rep and then South-West Regional Rep I suppose there was a few hundred in the local area. In the South-West region, the most members that we had when I was still working as a Regional Rep on a voluntary basis, with a normal job, was about 1,200 members. It was one of the biggest regions, apart from Yorkshire MAG, which was also very big. . . . I was always late for my normal work, and when I had two weeks holiday, I was trying to make the decision to give-up the job, as the Yorkshire Rep had done, Dave Ramsden; he gave up his job and was working full-time for his region in Yorkshire. But I didn't have the courage to make that decision on my own, and I returned to work after the two weeks holiday, I was ten minutes late, and the boss gave me a written warning and I said, 'Well, let's call it quits now.' So we did.

The individuals mentioned above all demonstrate considerable amounts of motivation for their activism. Yet if motivation thus seems to come from a mixture of a response to the structural constraints facing motorcyclists and individual orientations, the rewards activism brings, and which help sustain motivation over time, are clearly personal and subjective. Office holders speak of a sense of achievement that comes from their activities:

> 'Motorcyclists working for Motorcyclists' – a BMF phrase. It doesn't matter *who* you are, what job you do, you're all together. If you can help your fellow motorcyclist, by lobbying Parliament, by encouraging good behaviour, then you've achieved something.

> I enjoy it. The best thing is to see results, and to see things happen. You know, when you've co-ordinated the lobby from the national organisations, and you see politicians change their view, and you've put pressure on a government and it changes its position. Or you present facts to the Commission, or Parliament members, and they change their position and they vote with you. It's nice to see that work. To see that political process work. I mean, there's a lot of criticism of the EU as being undemocratic but, really, you just need to present the facts and press the right buttons, and it's nice to see that *change*. It's nice to get *results*. That's what I like doing.

The sense of achievement activism brings, that through one's actions one can bring about change, consequently provides office holders with a sense of enpowerment. One Local Rep speaks of how belonging to an RRO can foster a growing sense of confidence within members:

> It's quite nice if you can see them begin to gain in confidence in themselves within the group environment, to start to work towards sticking in their oar as we're going along. They're more prepared to pipe up and say, 'Hang on a minute. That's a pretty good idea, but have you thought about this?' or 'Why don't you try doing it that way?' Then you know you've got a potential active member on your hands because they will actually start to develop from that point onwards.

As such, we can understand how activism can provide intrinsic rewards that encourage a more positive self-image whilst, at the same time, indicating the 'affective commitment' (Bauman 1992) generated by interactions within the organisation. The consequences, therefore, of activism may be that the feelings of accomplishment enhance a sense of self-worth:

> [At least I've] *taken* an action. *Done* something about it. It is a strange thing. I mean, sometimes. . . . I do think '*Why* on earth am I doing it?' Wouldn't I be better [off] just putting my feet up and not bothering to do *any* of this at all, and surviving reasonably well on my pension. But that's not in my nature. I'd want to be doing something . . . [It

gives you a feeling of] self-worth. You're being valued. You're doing something. I'm never one to sit.

It must be borne in mind that there are negative aspects to activism also. One problem is that activists, as a small proportional number of both the motorcycling community and RRO membership, can feel overburdened by their duties. The following quotations refer to a feeling that the workload is high for people who are trying to fulfil a post in their spare time, although whilst the pressure on the individual can be intense this can, at least, be partially mitigated by the help of others:

Sometimes you can feel a bit like a one-man band. You know, it can be a bit of a solitary position, because although being a Rep you're not necessarily the boss, you're the focus of the information. You tend to find that the groups will assume that, as the Rep, you are the boss, so you tend to find yourself stuck out the front with all the responsibility and trying to persuade other people to kick in behind you.

It's difficult because, I mean, I've got a family, I've got a job that does demand long and irregular hours, and it does occasionally get very difficult to fit everything in. I'm lucky that I've got some good friends, members in the local area of MAG, that I can delegate to or they can take some of the work.

However, it is not merely time and effort that are volunteered. It can also be onerous financially:

I'm not wealthy, and haven't been. But I put a lot of my personal finances into MAG. And people occasionally said, 'Ooh, put a claim form in.' But I was putting so much money in that I didn't have the heart to claim it. And, anyway, if I was claiming money from the region, I had to go out there to get the money *back into* the region. I had to put more time in to organise more events, or more fund-raising, to get the money back in, so I was increasing my workload even *more*, so I couldn't be bothered.

Whilst, clearly, the problem of workloads is intense for part-time volunteers, it is not necessarily the case that the pressure is less for full-time officials. Although paid officials comment that volunteers tend to assume by doing the job on a full-time basis they have an 'easier' time of it and that, by being paid officers, are at least being remunerated for work that others do voluntarily, this is not seen to be completely the case. Firstly, RROs, by relying on membership fees and the money from services and events, are not financially in a very strong position and thus cannot afford to pay highly. Secondly, due to the reliance on a relatively small number of volunteers for the majority of RRO duties, the workloads of paid officials are both punishing and, as volunteers largely carry out their duties in the evenings

Figure 11 August 1995. Police road blocks keep thousands of bikers from a good night out

and weekends, of a twenty-four-hour, seven-day-a-week nature. As such, full-time officials work both during the working day and then during 'leisure' periods also. Two full-timers make these points:

> I suppose, if you're *good* at this job, the job generates more and more work. ... Also, when you're on a fixed fee as well, you're doing all of this work and, unlike making widgets, buttons [or whatever], you just work and work more and there's no extra money in it. In fact, there's less satisfaction because you end up working so hard, you get cheesed-off instead of feeling good about it.

> There's just not time to have any sort of life outside it, really, because most of the people we work with, in the countries and stuff, are voluntary, so they do most of their work in the evenings and, therefore, we have to be available in the evenings as well, some of the time, or most of the time, in order to get the work done.

Clearly, the demands of a position, whether paid or unpaid, can lead to considerable tensions and personal problems. As Klandermans informs us, 'stressful experiences, burnout, attractive alternatives, changed life stage, or simply lost motivation, all account for resignation' (1997:102). All activists had either experienced such difficulties personally, or knew of those who had. As indicated below, the major hindrance is that activism encroaches on other aspects of one's life, whether that is leisure, family or work time:

> I looked at last year, and from March until November, I had *one* weekend that was *mine*. Every other weekend I'd devoted to MAG. And, you know, I couldn't really do anything for myself, and *that* I started to resent a little bit. I've got a couple of bikes out in the garage that've been waiting for some sort of partial restoration *since* I became a MAG Rep. They haven't been *touched*. I was really starting to miss sitting out till four o'clock in the morning, with a light in the garage, getting covered in oil. You know I really *missed* that.

> You do get knackered after a while. Yeah, you do. All of your personal life, and your free time, tends to get taken up. If you're doing your job properly, then you don't have a lot of free time, and after a while you need a break.

> On average, I probably put in about twenty-five hours a week into MAG; on top of my work [and family].

> I get frustrated from time-to-time and it takes a lot of time and energy I could be spending on developing [my] career, social life etc.

This can be particularly hard for personal relationships, either getting or keeping one:

> Up to now, in my life, my partner has been, you know, if it's a long-term partner, she's had to be involved in the riders'-rights movement, because there's just not time to have any sort of life outside it, really.

> . . . there was no way I could even have attempted to hold down a personal relationship, unless I had somebody who was *so* forgiving, that they wanted to spend *absolutely no* quality time with me. I tried one or two, which went abysmally wrong. Unfortunately, I found that, yeah, the person that I was actually trying to get a relationship off the deck with *was* very understanding, but *that* then annoyed me, because they were giving everything to me. They were quite *happy* to not see me for two or three weeks, and just the odd phone call. Or we'd agree to go out for dinner, or we'd agree to do something, and then I'd have to phone up and cancel. 'I'm sorry. I've got to go to do something. I've got to go and see this group. I've got to go and say something, there's something on.' Or when she could never get through, because the phone used to ring from, like six o'clock until eleven, half eleven, I'd just be on the phone all the time; which also started to piss off the people I was living with, because nobody could get in contact with them.

Such factors act as demotivating forces, undermining individuals' will and drive:

> . . . sometimes you can be working far too long hours over a number of weeks or months, and you might feel very demotivated.

I think, at the moment, yeah, I'm definitely feeling a bit stale about it and, probably, having a break and going back to it afresh is a good idea.

Periodic bouts of inertia or lack of motivation are understandable for people who are giving up significant amounts of time and effort for a particular cause. Those who manage to sustain activism over time are those who keep a strict control over allocation of time. Many, however, are unable to do this, and thus there is a tendency for new activists to initially be very enthusiastic, and then fade away as they realise that such levels of commitment are unsustainable. The following quotations highlight these points:

Well, some people seem to stick at it for an *awful* long time; many, many years. Others, like me, tend to do it when you can. There is a high turnover. It's always a problem with keeping continuity. There are some groups who are fortunate, where they've had a Rep and a constant core of members for a very long time. But, generally, most of the groups I know, there's a fairly high turnover of Reps. Once every year, every couple of years, people just don't have the time after a while, they've got other things that need doing, that they decide to do.

I would say you've got a hardened core of people who have found an acceptable level between their personal and their public lives, and can absorb the minor peaks and troughs. But there are a lot of people who come and go.

The problems all identified above are not, however, restricted merely to the RROs. The stress, frustration, social problems or whatever are seen elsewhere and, once again, Klandermans (1997) provides a useful discussion on such matters. Where the biker activists do seem to diverge from the literature is that no respondents argued that participation was no longer rewarding or that their commitment to riders' rights had waned. Rather, this tendency for people to undertake posts or activities for short periods of time would appear to be best explained as 'burn-out', when, after periods of intense commitment, activists cease all involvement. As Klandermans argues:

Activist[s] are by definition the more committed members of a movement who feel a moral obligation to actively support the movement. In this way this makes them more vulnerable to burnout than other supporters. If on the top of that they are part of a movement culture which conveys the message that no periods of low motivation can be permitted, the already existing susceptibility to burnout is easily carried through. Indeed, Gomes and Maslach suggest that unreasonably high standards of unwavering commitment often backfires, leading eventually to complete withdrawal and that by living a more flexible life activists can increase their overall effectiveness and function as role models for other activists and enjoy their lives more along the way (1997:104).

As we shall see in the following discussion, these points find many resonances among riders'-rights activists; perhaps the only exception being, as will be seen, that the RROs themselves are not as demanding as the movement culture type described above. There is, however, an awareness that some individuals are susceptible to burn-out. As one officer informs us:

> People get burnt out. There are people who are very keen, and they spend virtually every waking moment [on it], and they just get burnt out. Some people get to the stage where they can't delegate. They have to do everything theirself. And people like that last about two years.

This can be exacerbated for those with familial commitments:

> People do get burnt out. If you're very active, doing what you do, being a Rep, or on a committee, it can take over your life. It's all very well for people, perhaps, like me, who's got a husband who's very understanding, who gets involved with it, who doesn't mind the fact that he doesn't have a clean shirt or a meal. He just looks after himself. He doesn't look at me as that sort of person. But, sometimes, if you have a husband, wife, who expects you to put the shelves up, or 'What are we going to do about this?' Or, 'We need that room decorated.' And you're out doing BMF stuff again, they resent it. And so, consequently, you either do very little work, you just have to ration what you do. Or if you're fully involved, people get so burnt out so quickly, and their families get fed up with it, so they don't do it anymore.

Clearly, this is a problem for any political group that relies on a limited number of people to act as volunteers, in that, whilst officers realise the risks, the pressure of work to be done and limited manpower makes it difficult not to take all that a person may, in the short-term, be able to give. That this problem is recognised by national officers is indicated in the following comments:

> We're always saying to people, 'Delegate,' but it's not always easy when there's a limited pool of people who will actually do something.

> There have been BMF Directors in the past who have done too much, they've been totally overloaded, and they've been given more work to do because there was no alternative, in the full knowledge that there was a cost involved in this. In other words, that person's skills are going to be available to us short-term because we're going to overload them. 'But, hey, there's nobody else to do it. It's got to be done.' But once it *has* been done it will become easier all round. In other words, there's a price to be paid, yeah? [So individuals pay it]. The organisation exists for a reason. People become part of that organisation and, I mean, I don't separate myself from this, in order to achieve your objective, having first made sure that the objective is worthwhile, not just any old thing, then pressure is put on people to achieve that objective. That's all there is to it.

And somebody has to do that. Somebody has to sometimes be the bad guy to say to someone, 'You've got to do it anyway. You'll have to stay up all night if necessary.'

One ex-Regional Rep describes how burn-out can occur from a mixture of too much to do, too few activists and a high degree of commitment:

I handled eighteen months of not getting the same enthusiasm out of my Reps as *I* was putting in. And I was going, 'Well, why not? *Why* aren't you as keyed-up as I am? Why *won't* you put as much time in as I will? Why will you get grumpy with me when I say there's another event on this weekend and I'll need your support at it,' or whatever. And that was really starting to bug me. I mean, I tried for as long as I could to put it out of my mind. . . . B[ut] I *couldn't* let things lie. I *couldn't* let things be half done. They had to be done right or there was just no bloody point starting them in the first place. So I was just taking on too much. I *wholly* recognise the fact that I was burnt out. ... There wasn't [enough of me]. And I was annoyed that there wasn't enough of me. I was annoyed that I wasn't then doing enough of what I should have done for everything. I expected *more* from other activists that would have made it easier. I expected *more* ability to be booked up for a rally, make sure the stand was going to be there, and simply phone a respective Rep, even if it was only within two weeks notice, and say, 'We've got this rally this weekend. You've got to take the stand down.' 'I can't. I'm going out.' So I just had to do them all. And a lot of them, I found, if I would get a Rep to go and do a rally, I couldn't quite leave it, so I would pop in at some point over the weekend, and realise that it was going *abysmally.* That nobody was being approached. Yes, the stand was there, the presence was there. But I'd look around the car park and there would not be one leaflet on any bike. And I'd go, 'Why not? We've got a big car park here full of bikes. They all ride. They're *easy targets.* Why haven't you noticed that? Why haven't you done that? . . .' I was killing myself, quite happily, and I was destroying a lot of the region because my managerial skills weren't *good* enough. I'd see the boundary level, the line whereby attempting to coerce people became pissing them off. . . . But then I'd be annoyed that I couldn't push it a little bit further before I pissed them off.

The problem would seem to be, therefore, that there is a failure to encourage more activists from among members:

If you actually look at the number of volunteers there is with the BMF, there's very few. If you consider that there's something in the region of about 130,000 cards issued, but, realistically, there's probably between 70 and 80,000 members of the BMF. Of that number, there's nearly 14,000 individual members thereabouts. If you count the number of volunteers that work on a regular basis, I'm not including the marshals at the BMF Rally or whatever, I'm talking about the Reps, Committee members, there's probably less than 150. So the percentage of actually *active* people is very, very small.

On the other hand, however, it is appreciated that it is a matter of choice whether or not to become actively involved or not and, for those who do not wish to participate, their membership fee is of equal value. Thus, whilst members' time is desired, for those who cannot provide this, their money is sufficient:

> You've got to be quite honest and say you don't *care* whether or not they become active. It would be *nice* if they did, if everybody that you joined up became active, but, at the end of the day, they're not going to. If you get 5 per cent of them becoming active that's enough, you know, for now. It's never enough, but it's good, as long as you get the money out of the rest of them, and their names out of the rest of them so that they can be kept aware of what we're doing. They can be kept aware of what's happening on the scene. Maybe something that will happen will get them angry enough to become active *but*, at the end of the day, their £15 is supplying those of us who *do* want to work for them the money to do it.

One of the more immediately felt problems is that of the general lack of commitment from motorcyclists to become involved with riders'-rights issues, that the 'number of people willing to *commit* themselves is remarkably small.' As one national MAG official argues:

> The downside is the lack of support from other bikers. Right now, I suppose we represent about one or one and a half per cent, at most, of the total number of bikers in this country – 15,000 members, there's a million people riding bikes. And that's dispiriting. Obviously, it would be unrealistic to expect *everybody* with a motorcycle licence, there's six million, I was told, with licences, and about one million registered motorcycles. And I wouldn't expect all of the guys commuting on Honda 50s to be that much into the biker lifestyle that they would want to join us, although we'd like them. But let's say there's 100,000, at least, *serious* bikers, it might be more than that now, actually, because the sales area of great growth is the enthusiasts' market, it's not the commuter market, and I think it would be realistic to assume that we might get, say, 20 per cent of *that* group. But we haven't achieved that yet.

As such, activists perceive the average rider as either unwilling or unable to see that there are any potentially threatening changes ahead that could affect them. As one Rep maintains, 'You've got to make them aware. A lot of people *aren't* aware of what's happening. They think if they just continue riding it will go away, or they've got a modern bike, it doesn't matter.' This can carry important ramifications for those who are prepared to be active. As one ex-activist argues, 'What made me angry was the apathy. There's a lot of apathy from bikers who don't understand what *power* politicians have.' This can have a demoralising effect on activists:

> If motorcycling is to carry on, people have got to get more interested And it *appals* me that motorcyclists don't want to know. . . . Sometimes when you're talking to them

you're talking to a brick wall. Because you say to them, you know, 'Join the BMF.' I mean, I'm a firm believer, I would like to see every motorcyclist a member of the BMF, or a member of MAG, one or the other. I don't [mind which]. They're both doing good work in different ways.

You learn quite a lot about human psychology and what makes people react, and sometimes that's quite depressing. Because you realise that there's only a very small minority that you can appeal to, in pursuit of membership specifically, on an ethical ground. 'Do this because it's the right thing to do. Because people are taking away your rights. Because they're threatening your future.' That *appeal* can only succeed with a very small proportion of people. And to appeal to a much *bigger* group of people you've got to show them a much more *tangible* benefit to membership. And so we introduced a number of tangible benefits, like insurance schemes, discounts on data-tag kits and tyres. Discounts on rallies, and discounts in bike shops, and all that kind of thing, which you *feel* shouldn't be necessary. And you almost feel a little disappointed or ashamed in having to promote these things. But it's a fact of life, you do.

This unwillingness to participate is held to be due to the fact that the majority of riders fail to appreciate the gravity of the threats confronting them. Yet this is not a problem that is seen as specific to motorcyclists, but is viewed merely as a reflection of general attitudes in society. Two comments make this point in different ways. The first alludes to the difficulty of involving anybody in political activity, the second argues that the number of committed motorcyclists is similar, proportionately, to the numbers of politically active people in the population in general:

It's difficult to mobilise *anyone*. If someone doesn't physically feel anything's under threat they're not going to react. So motorcyclists today haven't really noticed that there's any difference to their motorcycling activities than there was ten years ago, or ten years before that. So why should they worry? There's not any change. They're not affected by driving licence regulations and what have you. They're not going to be affected by any of these new things that come in after the Multi-Directive because they're not retrospective to start with, and by the time they *might* be affected by something it's too bloody late anyway! And they'll accept it like they did with the helmet law. So that's human nature, it's not motorcycling. You tell me any pressure group that can mobilise all of the people in their sphere of interest.

[It's] easier than you might think [to mobilise bikers], actually. Because whereas our membership might seem to be a small proportion of the total motorcycling population in the country, it's like comparing the number of Labour Party members with the number of Labour Party voters. And I don't know what the figures are now, but when Labour was polling about thirteen million votes, they only had 300,000 members. So, in proportion, our membership is probably roughly the same, *pro rata*.

More optimistically, however, it is believed that in the last decade, which has witnessed increasing amounts of anti-motorcycle legislation and, concomitantly, a significant rise in the motorcycle lobby, motorcyclists have become *more* aware of the issues threatening the community:

> I would say, now, very few motorcyclists don't know that there's something happening. They'll have varying degrees of knowledge, depending on how interested or active they are. Where in 1985, or prior to that, if you mentioned some political aspect, they'd say, 'I wouldn't know. I wouldn't have a clue.' And I certainly wouldn't have at that time. No knowledge of it whatsoever.

To conclude, therefore, we have seen why people join the riders'-rights movements, what motivates activists and how this may be sustained or lost over time. However, the issue of burn-out among activists, and the small numbers prepared for such intensity of involvement are both reasons that underlie current programmes in both organisations to become less dependant upon voluntary workers and move towards greater professionalisation. It is this trend which we shall examine in the next chapter.

-6-

Voluntarism and Professionalisation

All of the riders'-rights organisations, both national and international, are almost overwhelmingly voluntary in structure. However, unlike other groups whose members may or may not be personally affected by the issues for which they campaign (for example, Amnesty International), all members of the riders'-rights groups are motorcyclists, and thus are individually affected by the issues upon which the organisations are active. Yet, clearly, as we have noted elsewhere, there is a vast difference between being a member of such an organisation and being active, that is choosing to volunteer for specific duties within the organisation as opposed to merely paying one's fees and reading the relevant literature or attending occasional events. In this chapter, we shall explore the dynamics of voluntary activism for the involved individuals, and the consequences of voluntarism for the organisations. It shall be seen that, as with other pressure groups, such as Greenpeace, riders' rights are now making the move towards increased professionalism in a bid to consolidate their positions, that is both to enhance organisational efficiency and the achievement of interest-group goals within the larger socio-political sphere. This process is currently under way, yet is fraught with practical problems that could, perhaps, lead to the sorts of tensions that have been identified between factions in other social movements between pragmatists and radicals (Willetts 1982; Yearley 1991).

There are, as we have seen, many reasons for joining an RRO, for they function on a variety of levels. As such, being a member will mean different things to different people. Yet most people become active due to a belief in the ideals held by their organisation for, whilst it is true that one can get 'sucked in' to activism for pragmatic reasons, (such as making a suggestion, being at a meeting), in the last instance people choose to take on roles because they either actively want to, or do not actively *not* want to. As such, loyalty and commitment to the cause of riders' rights is the fundamental motivation behind activism (Willetts 1982). For those who become intensely active, the major reason given is that they feel that they wish to contribute, to put something back into motorcycling to repay what they have taken out. As one BMF member maintains, 'It's corny, but everybody says that they've had so much fun out of biking they feel they've got to put a bit back in. And that really *is* one of the things that drives us all. That we feel we *can* put something back in, so let's do it.'

Figure 12 After a ride across rural Warwickshire, bikers touch base despite the ban

However, as we shall see, it is not sufficient merely to be willing and enthusiastic. As riders'-rights organisations grow and become more complex structurally, administrative and bureaucratic tasks often require considerable specialist skills. As motorcyclists come from highly diffuse social settings, this means that, usually, somewhere, someone can be identified with the relevant skills for a specific job. Thus selection for activism is by no means necessarily random, but based upon the assessment of an individual's qualities by other office-holders (Klandermans 1997). Many respondents refer to how they were identified by more experienced activists and brought on to increased participation:

> The Director for Government Relations would occasionally ask me to do little jobs for him, and the one that brought me to his attention was when I went to a meeting of the Historic Vehicles Clubs committee which, at the time, was changing its form, into the Federation of Historic Vehicle Clubs, mainly in response to perceived threats from Europe on the older vehicles; such as, having to bring them up to modern spec. And it was quite a formative experience in two respects. One was that I wrote a fairly comprehensive report, which I think goes back to my scientific training, where I tend to have a respect for facts and accuracy when I write reports. Although it doesn't stop me putting opinions down, but I stick to the basic facts as a basis. And then, the other thing was, one of the MEPs, the MEP for Dorset, one Brian Cassidy, gave a talk on what the European Union was about and that quite interested me, and it really got me started on my interest in European Union politics and how things work. But the result of that was that I came to the BMF's attention as, perhaps, a potential officer at a higher level.

Here we can see that both an *actual* skill, learnt at work, and a *potential* skill, that is, an as-yet unformed interest in European politics, identify this rider as good material for activism. Indeed, it is one of the skills necessary in officers that they have this ability to identify, in others, skills the organisation needs. As Steve Bergman, the ex-Chairman of the BMF, argues, 'In the first instance you recognise skills within your volunteers, and you direct your volunteers in the direction that their skills are good for.' The ability to draw out those skills and use them in tandem with others, is what enables a national officer to steer the organisation. MAG's Neil Liversidge elaborates:

> But you've got to be able to give a lead and, really, I've made the National Chairman's job a leadership job, and I don't make any excuse for that, and I don't make any bones about that. I look upon it more in the way that you would chair a company that, you know, somebody has ultimately got to be responsible for everything, right. It's a bit like being a conductor in front of an orchestra. I'm not the best trombone player, I'm not the best drummer, I'm not the best clarinet player, and all the rest of it. *But* the conductor's got to understand what sort of sound he wants to come out of the trombone, he knows how a trombone works, he knows what sort of sound should come out of a clarinet, he knows when he wants one to play or be quiet, he knows when he wants another to play or be quiet. And, yeah, while there are people on the NC who can all do their individual jobs better than I could do their jobs, it's *my* job to see that they all work at the same speed, and that MAG advances on a broad front, right, and that we don't have people running off willy-nilly here and there, and the whole thing becomes disorganised and disorientated. So *that* is my job really.

As is implied by this quotation, 'people' skills are important in an activist if they are to motivate others. Two quotations illustrate more explicitly how such skills are drawn upon. The first comes from a male MAG Regional Rep, and the second from a female MAG Group Secretary:

> There's a lot of crossover. A tremendous amount of what I do at work is communication. A lot of which is personal communication, really, but it's got to be fairly well-defined, unambiguous, painting-by-numbers, particularly if you've got people working for you and you say, 'I'd like you to do this.' And then you go back and say, 'Yeah, you've done well there.' Or 'You've done that bit very well, but you could have done that bit slightly better.' So there's a lot of motivation stuff as well. For example, I occasionally have to go off to meetings and speak through microphones and even try and inspire people, which is a frightening prospect!

> In nursing, you're the one, *you* are the one that has to draw out other people. No doubt about it. If you're any good at your job at all you have to be able to bring people's confidences out, their worries, their fears. Talk to them, make them feel better, make them feel comfortable, relaxed, this sort of thing. And it's the same in any situation, I

think. If you can make people feel comfortable and relaxed, they're *much* more likely to be responsive. And it's the same in a MAG meeting. If people feel relaxed, that's no-one's going to laugh at them . . . then they'll come out with it.

Here we can see how often the skills needed by the riders'-rights organisations are those an activist has acquired from their occupational training and experience. As Steve Bergman argues, it may be that, such are their skills, they may be put to use in areas requiring these work skills in preference to other areas of interest:

In the past, you would get people volunteering to work for the BMF and, no doubt, it's no different for MAG, because they wanted to get involved in riders' rights. My answer to them is, 'Well, I suppose you do. Unfortunately, your expertise lies in finance and we want you to go on the Finance Committee.' So, in the first instance, you actually use the skills of your volunteers appropriately, okay?

This may mean that, despite ones original intention on becoming active, organisational needs pull people into areas of necessity:

For me, when I first got involved with the BMF . . . I was concerned about the future of motorcycling, but I also thought, 'Here's a chance. I'll do some lobbying. I'll get involved in that.' But because I have other skills the BMF can use, I've sort of gone in a slightly different direction. . . . But I don't mind that because I'm still contributing to the whole. So I really don't mind. It's finding a niche somewhere, because there are other people who can do the lobbying.

Tod Booth, former Marketing Director with the BMF, gives us an illustration of how this works in practice:

I do this because somebody else will do that bit. But I can fund them. They can say, 'I've got to go to Brussels because I have a meeting with some MEPs.' And I'll say, 'Good. We've sold this much membership, we've sold this much regalia, we've sold this much advertising in the magazine. We've brought in all this money. There you go. You go and do it.'

Many, as we can see below, are happy to oblige in order to further group goals:

As an administrator, I've got a natural inclination to sort of buzz information about. It's just the way I am, and I like organising things. So I've got a perfect opportunity to use all these skills, which I'm quite happy with, in that sort of environment. And I like the people. I mean, they're a really nice bunch of people. And, at the end of the day, if we can keep an eye on what's going on legislation-wise, it keeps me on the road, and everybody else I know on the road as well.

It's almost a symbiotic relationship. I mean, I've got a range of experiences and skills which are relevant, valuable, useful, to the organisation. I'm able to use and practise those skills. I'm able to have some self-respect or status, authority. . . . I *get* from the organisation. I *give* to the organisation. In a very new way for me.

The symbiotic aspect of this relationship may also be viewed in terms of the skills one can *acquire* through activism. As Willetts (1982) argues, social movement leaders, of necessity, become specialists, acquiring knowledge of their subject and learning new skills. The following quotation, from a relatively new Local Rep., shows us how one can acquire practical skills, whilst the second, from a Regional Rep., shows how this may tie into the political:

But the presentational skills, I'd never before in my life had to give a presentation to anybody. So standing up in a group, and being a Rep and having to do a sort of, like, mini-presentation. I was terrified the first time I did it. 'Oh my God! What have I let myself in for?' So doing that was really good, because it gave me some focus on what I was supposed to be doing with actually building a presentation. And that I have been able to translate that back into the working environment. And some of the IT stuff, as well, was useful. It gave me a broader view of what was actually happening. The guy actually did quite a bit on the Web, which I hadn't really come up against at that point in time. So that was quite useful.

I haven't actually found any other uses for knowledge of the Maastricht Treaty, apart for the implications for riders' rights. I don't know, I was able to do a talk on it to the TUC, and say, 'Well, these are the additional powers the Commission would get. And they are that big [indicates a lot]. And here are the additional powers that the Parliament would get and they are that big [indicates not a lot]. So the democratic deficit, if it's like that at the moment [indicates not a lot], is now like that [indicates a lot].'

The literature clearly argues that belonging to a group or being active within it are only part of the process of becoming fully politically engaged, and that political socialisation from the movement is central. Thus, whilst individuals may have a sense of grievance which acts as a motivation to join a group, the availability of educative mechanisms is also necessary to translate this into political actions (see, for example, Parkin 1971; Gallie 1983). Rush (1992), for example, argues that whilst we learn throughout life, whenever we join a new group we acquire new knowledge. Knowledge may be transmitted formally, with deliberate instruction, or may be informally acquired through the process of experience, for example learning how to act within the new group, carrying out one's duties or whatever. This new knowledge, however, transforms the perception of the individual thus socialised. 'The more politicised a person, the more she or he will be inclined to interpret and define every situation, relation or network of relations in terms of their political dimensions. Political consciousness, then, is central to an activist's identity' (Klandermans 1997:112). Further, this is crucial also for an activist's sense of self in that 'the construction of identity is a *political process*. It is framed by changing political movements, practices and discourses which promote awareness' (Bradley 1996:212). Various respondents indicated that they gained considerable political knowledge from their involvement in riders' rights. Three quotations highlight this:

> The understanding of how the political animal works is useful. It's useful in any set-up. And I've got a greater understanding of how the European Parliament works through MAG than I would ever have got through my social life or possibly work, which helps to lay a basis.

> It's made me an awful lot more aware of the various political systems that we have to get involved with and that rule our lives, and some of the drawbacks of the way they go about it, yes. Before I was active with MAG I hadn't got a clue about how Brussels and that work. But now I'm frightened fartless about the way it works! Because we've got so little control, the general public who it *affects*, have got so little control over it.

> It's certainly taught me a lot about how things work in the European Union. . . . We seem to think that because we're an island just off the mainland that we're not part of Europe. And I think it should be recognised that we *are*, and I've tended to see how things work in Europe. I mean, for example, the way the [Conservative Party] talks, there's this amorphous mass called 'Europe' that's trying to force its will on us. . . . [But] half of the *nonsense* that we get thrown at us is supported by national governments and they put it through the European Union so that they can blame *them* and they don't get the blame themselves. And, certainly, being involved in this has taught me a lot about Europe and it shows that a united Europe, as such, is *not* a bad thing. A lot of the way it's *run* is a bad thing because, of the main institutions that run it, only *one* is democratically elected, and that one is the one that's got the least power; although it's getting more. And that's *wrong*, but the principle's okay.

Thus, although working voluntarily within an RRO may seem somewhat like a 'busman's holiday', people are largely happy to do it for several reasons. Firstly, they get a sense of self-worth from using their skills, perhaps in an environment different from that in which they first acquired them, in order to further a cause in which they believe; secondly, in a reciprocal way, they can learn new skills from activism; and thirdly, and most importantly, perhaps, they are able to gain political socialisation which carries benefits for their understanding of the wider world around them. Yet there is a lighter side to this in that people are willing to use their skills because they are doing it in convivial company. As Steve Bergman informs us, it is the mix of work and play that enables the organisations to function:

> If someone goes to work nine to five, fiddling round with accounts, how do you persuade that person to come in at the weekend and do it for us for nothing? [They do it because they like their bike], right. And if the people they're working with are great, and they get to go out and party with them occasionally, and they have great fun, and suddenly it's good fun. It's still this task they do from Monday to Friday but they're working with these people and it's *fun*. And, you know, when one of them has a party they invite everybody else, and they all go along. And suddenly you get this team-thing going, and they're all working well together. And they know you're taking notice of what they're saying.

As such, it is not 'work' in the same sense as the use of those skills in an occupational setting would be, that is that by drawing upon occupational skills in pursuance of a private enthusiasm, people may be using their expertise in more fulfilling ways than they do during regular working hours. As Sharon Nash, Chairman and former Finance and Administration Director of the BMF, informs us:

> They say it's different to doing it at work. Maybe it's even that there isn't the same sort of pressure because you *are* a volunteer, and no-one's bossing you around. Management meetings are a bit different, they're slightly more formal, but whenever I chair committee meetings, I'm *so* aware that these people are volunteers. So if they want to sit around and discuss bikey things, or want to keep digressing, I will allow it to a certain extent. I mean, there is a limit and you've got to say, 'I'm really sorry. I know this is going to bore . . . you all, but can we just go back and look at these figures again?' And they go, 'Oh, you're such a bully!' and that's okay. Because it's a chance for us all to sit around and have a chat, because we're all like-minded people. You know what it's like. Wherever you meet another biker, whether you've just bumped into them by accident, at work or whatever it is, you get on with them. You start talking bikes. And that's what we do. We all get together and start talking bikes and bikey things and we do a bit of accounts while we're there.

Good leaders, therefore, are ones who understand the problems of working voluntarily that, as one MAG official observes, 'I have to remind myself that the people who work for us are volunteers. You've got to bear that in mind all the time doing this, that the people who are working with you at the regional level are giving up their spare time, and that puts it into perspective for me, that these people are volunteers, they'll do as much as they can.' Therefore, it would appear that the RROs are managing to avoid the potential alienation members may suffer when faced by poor officials (Willetts 1982). Yet there are times when it becomes hard to function with volunteers. The difficulty can lie in officials' demand for effort from people, knowing that workers are only doing a job voluntarily, and that organisations are existing largely on good will. Again, Steve Bergman:

> A large part of the job is about allowing them to operate. Recognising what people can do. Allowing them to operate. It's about complimenting them. It's about bollocking them as well. It's . . . when this department needs something, and this department's been working really *hard*, and they really *do* need some time off, being the person who goes to them and says, 'Sorry, but you're going to have to do some more. The other department needs such-and-such by such-and-such. I know you're really busy. I'm sorry to have to ask you this, but we need that by tomorrow.'

Whilst we have discussed the many positive ways in which riders'-rights organisations draw upon the skills and expertise of their membership, there is also negative sides to this in that, in addition to the over-reliance on particular people with the necessary skills mentioned above (Willetts 1982), even when enthusiasm for the task may be very apparent, that alone is not enough to sustain an organisation. Organisations also require organisational expertise and resources:

> I mean, the willing band of enthusiasts is great. And I'm probably going to slip into the heading of boring old fart now, but coming from outside, with activists' skills and experience, and looking at the FEM and, not riders' rights generally because, in Britain, I think both BMF and MAG are quite *sophisticated* organisations but, elsewhere, generally, looking at riders' rights, I mean, it seemed there was some naive belief that enthusiasm would carry all before it.

> [They can be] brimming with enthusiasm but not having a great deal of direction. And that's not necessarily anybody's fault, but it's down to the bureaucracy within the BMF and the fact that you have to move at a snail's pace, in relation to a voluntary organisation, you move at a snail's pace, whereas with your day job, you can move with the speed of a whippet.

A further problem is that organisations which must rely on volunteers may then tend to end up, should no more experienced person be found for a position, with officers who are willing, but not able, or, as one official argued, 'if you volunteer, you can have a job in the BMF.' Another national official argues:

You've got people there that are trying to do a job, and they're trying to put their best efforts in, there's no doubt about that, but they don't know what they're doing. You can have experience, I've got experience in [my area], but I could quite easily be a dustman and [still have got the job]. Within the BMF system, because of the fact that I was unopposed in my election, because there are no rules to say that you should produce a CV, and I firmly believe that if you're becoming a director of a company you should produce your *professional* CV, because you don't have to *do that*, you have to give them information but you don't have to give them your CV, anybody can be elected to any post, and they *are*.

Figure 13 BMF Show 1998

This therefore means that organisations are currently not necessarily operating at maximum efficiency. The same activist continues:

> If you need to take legal advice, you take legal advice through the solicitors. You do not take legal advice from a bunch of volunteers, some of which *may* be qualified, some of which may *not* be. If you're taking legal advice, you make sure you *pay* for it.

The consequences of this are that people who are untrained may make mistakes which may act detrimentally upon the organisation, particularly if done in public. Another officer remarks:

> The media's always out to get whatever it can to be sensational, but sometimes you read things that someone from MAG has said and you think, 'Oh my God, you've just undone about ten years work,' you know. And other times you think, 'Yeah, good on you.' Everybody's their own worst enemy. You can build something up and shoot it down just as quickly.

The implications of the above are that voluntary organisations run the risk of being counterproductive in their actions, that, as Willetts (1982) argues, the combination of a voluntary organisation without an effective bureaucracy means there may be no strong, central authority to enforce decisions. The following quotation shows how, it is felt, this lack of focus needs to be addressed:

> The BMF, in its *working* capacity, must be 98 per cent or even higher, voluntary-run. The directors are volunteers, the representatives out in the field. Very difficult to co-ordinate actions, when you've got a set-up like that, with minimal full-time staff. And so, you can end up with people going off at tangents. [It's too decentralised to often effectively operate national activities] or focus on national activities. I think, taking a leaf out of the BT days, now that I've left BT, you realise that even though you used to complain about the firm, just how well organised it was. Despite all of the, sort of, sniping outside. . . . No wonder BT's very profitable. But a lot of the lessons from there you can apply to a voluntary organisation. You *must have* structures in place. You *must* know reporting structures, who is doing what. Regular reports from the field going to a central point, where they collate things, get feedback, detect patterns to where bus lanes might be used, if parking is or is not a problem, and get some direction to all of this. And so the BMF needs a clear structure. Everyone who is a volunteer for the BMF needs a job description so they know what they're supposed to do, and they know the constraints within those jobs. And, in that way, I think you *can* get more focus, and you *can* understand what you're trying to achieve.

The various problems associated with operating exclusively with volunteers has thus led both of the riders'-rights groups to move towards a more professional type of organisation and an increase in full-time paid employees. Neither British organisation, at the time of writing, employs more than ten full-timers, which surprises the many members who think that all Reps, Directors and so on are paid for the work that they do. The drive towards increasing paid employees is linked directly to the needs to sustain an efficient organisational structure. Thus, as Ware (1986) has argued, we can see how the demands for efficiency and effectiveness may pull a movement towards greater institutionalisation. The following quotation indicates how this drive is proceeding:

> You see, at the moment we've got six full-timers. We've got three administrative staff, which you've *got* to have, otherwise you just can't get the turnaround on memberships, and if people don't *feel* they're getting a professional organisation then that will provide a reason for them to drop out. And, indeed, for years, when the secretary was out trying to make a living dispatching in a van, and then you come home and try and do the memberships, and a week would pass, and the paperwork would pile up and you couldn't cope. And you'd get in part-timers, and all that sort of carry on. Well, fortunately, now we've got three full-timers at the office on administration. We've got me on Public Relations and *MAG News*, we've got a Financial Projects Officer, who also helps with the PR side of things, and we've got a Research Officer full-time. So the main areas are covered. The administration, the PR, and Research, which is essential, because for so long we just didn't have the facts at our fingertips and that's a problem which we're now addressing.

Moves are thus afoot to bring in increasing numbers of people who can work for riders' rights as a full-time profession. This may be partially due to the increasing complexity and accompanying specialisation of society generally, that is that as we require ever more sophisticated levels of information to function and, as no one person can be an expert on everything, we need to break down tasks into smaller, more tightly focused areas of expertise in order to increase efficacy. As such, there is a tendency increasingly to draw on the knowledge of experts (Tarrow 1994):

> You bring in as many volunteers as you can, but you just get the work done. As you sort the organisation out, and then start running it, albeit with volunteers, on a company style, a professional style, and you get the organisation straightened out, then you bring in the paid people to continue. And that has been the plan in putting the BMF straight. It's a simple plan of, you know, 'Well, okay, let's have a Chief Executive and pay him.' It is a company with three quarters of a million pounds turnover. It *should* have a Chief Executive. It *should* have a paid Finance Officer. If the people you've got haven't got the skills then send them away and get them trained. And if it costs money, we'll save some money somewhere else. And we've been on a long-term goal, for the last few years, we've been doing training. To start with, at the headquarters, we've sent away, one after the other, more and more people on training courses. Trevor's been away on training courses, Jeff's been on them, and we continue to train them. Presently, we've just appointed a volunteer assistant to Trevor, and the goal is, within the next two years, that that post will be paid as well. The same with Marketing. Marketing would either be out-of-house or paid. There is not enough people who are prepared to put their hands in their pockets and join a riders'-rights organisation to run it. So we need to make money elsewhere, it's as simple as that.

The need to professionalise is clearly linked in the following quotation to the rights of the members, whose subscription fees finance the organisations:

> Another bit of the Chairman's job, you see, is making sure that we employ the right people. Time was when anyone could get a job in MAG just by being the right friend of the right person, right. *Now*, the people MAG employs are competent people. If they're not competent people, they'll be sacked. I don't make any bones about that, you know what I mean? The point of being a socialist is not to employ idiots. I mean, people get their wages paid out of members' money.

Money, as alluded two in both of the previous quotations, one from the BMF and the other from MAG, continues to be a problem although, as has been seen, it is hoped that moves to expand the services to members will increase the funds available in order to professionalise and, through that, achieve organisational goals. The evidence for the necessity to provide long-term financial security can amply be seen from the following remarks from Simon Milward and Bob Tomlins of FEMA. Without the work of these two men in Brussels, the work of the motorcycle lobby in the EU would not be achievable and yet, as examples of the dependency upon voluntary activism, both men initially undertook much of their lobbying work without financial remuneration:

When I went full-time for MAG, I was not offered any remuneration by the National Committee. So I wrote to all the members in the Southwest Region asking them to donate some money to me by standing order from their bank each month, and I was able to be sustained through that. And after six months the National Committee decided to pay me. Well, it's like with any voluntary organisation, I've always felt, it's always up to you to create the environment where you can do what you want. There was no procedure whereby we would take on people working full-time, and it always seemed like it was up to that person to take the initiative themselves.

I've ridden bikes virtually all of my life, felt that I'd got a range of experience and skills that were relevant, was quite happy to drop down several gears and work in support of someone. Everything seemed to be right. So I did that. The only problem was the FEM didn't have the money to pay me. So I . . . effectively [worked] for them voluntarily. I [was] unemployed and working for them in a voluntary capacity. [Then in November 1996] they agreed to a series of changes . . . [which brought] us to the point where I [was] actually going to be directly employed, properly paid, by the FEM.

Whilst these remarks demonstrate considerable commitment to the cause of motorcycling, they provide, perhaps, cause for wondering how the European lobby has managed to achieve the success it has given its reliance on such individually inspired motivation. It would appear that, in the past, individuals have had to create a niche for themselves as, and when, they see one, rather than there being a coherent organisational drive to identify structural needs. Further, as was seen earlier, whilst the organisations' strengths lie in the enthusiasm of their members, it may also be a weakness, in the long-term, to rely so heavily on the commitment of a few, if activists have to sacrifice their personal lives to an organisation and then burn out. The push to professionalism, therefore, may be directly linked to possibilities for future political success.

This is not to say that the amateur and voluntary status of rights' rights organisations is necessarily a detrimental thing. As we shall see later, the 'amateur' status of the lobby is what provides much of its appeal and power within the EU and, further, as we saw earlier, the ability to draw talented people informally and quickly through the ranks into positions suiting their skills may be seen positively, as opposed to the need to advertise and interview people for formal positions. Further, it may be that, should professional administrators and bureaucrats be increasingly employed they may be chosen for occupational skills rather than a commitment to motorcycling, which might then imply their loyalties would be to the *organisations* rather than the *goals of the organisations* themselves. It may be that such 'company' employees would thus lack the passion that inspires the volunteers. The literature attests that there are considerable dangers in the drive to professionalisation. The increased use of professional employees may tend both to lead to a sense of distance between leadership and rank-and-file (Scott 1990) and/or to a declining number of grass-roots activists (Tarrow 1994). Further, whilst there are drawbacks to the lack of a centralised bureaucracy, as was addressed earlier, it could well be that *should* this develop, it will lead to a lessening flexibility within the RROs which would undermine the ability to respond with speed to any crises (Willetts 1982). Perhaps a more telling point is that professionalisation indicates a political decision about the allocation of financial resources, which may lead to divisions between leaders and rank-and-file members. Klandermans, in a discussion of Amnesty International in The Netherlands, makes some interesting points:

> The opinions on how to proceed were divided. On the one hand, two thirds of the paid staff wanted to professionalise the organisation and spend a larger proportion of the resources to hire more staff or reduce the number of volunteers to make more time available to paid staff for other activities than supervising volunteers. Not surprisingly, the volunteers were less convinced – only two-fifths were in favour of that opinion. On the other hand, the majority of the volunteers and a substantial number of the paid staff preferred to keep more volunteers in order to be able to spend more resources on the external goals of the organisation (1997:133).

Consequently, either to professionalise or not, both avenues have their draw-backs. All of this, however, is still very much in the future. Until the financial positions of the RROs are secured, both organisations will continue to rely on the small number of volunteers that carry the rest of Britain's riders pillion.

Part III
The European Lobby

–7–

Legislation

As Melucci has observed, people do not 'act in a void' but in an 'already structured context' (1989:4). As such, we must ask why a social movement emerges when and where it does. Central to this must be an understanding of the ways in which the state itself may generate movement activity (Tarrow 1994). The apparent growth in the RROs and the drive towards professionalisation may be seen as a direct result of the increased threats to motorcycling posed by legislative moves since the 1970s. Given the age of most riders, which we shall discuss later, the only legislation of note to have affected motorcycling during their biking history would have been the introduction of compulsory helmet use in 1973, probably just before they had started riding. Trends within the legislative process towards increased intervention have thus been directly experienced by the current generation of riders. Much of the organised response witnessed within the riders'-rights movement, therefore, is based upon how proposed legislation has been perceived by individuals. Thus, in accordance with much of the literature on politicisation, we may agree that a sense of grievance may be an initial stage in the process whereby individuals become politicised (Gallie 1983).

Many riders attest to the increasingly nature of political interference. One 38-year-old MAG member comments on his first days on a bike:

> . . . at the time, when I first rode a bike, it was very shortly after the helmet law was introduced. Which was annoying at the time, because my brother rode for a couple of years without a helmet, but I didn't think too much of it. 'What the hell. It's only a helmet.' But I was, not naive, but I didn't have the same intolerance to people telling me what to do. I didn't have any *notion* that there was a problem, that things were changing, that I was going to be told what to ride and what not to ride back in the early days. I just got on the bike and rode it. I think there were less changes, less legalities afoot.

However, the situation began to change in the early 1980s, particularly after 1981 which saw the introduction of the two-part test, restrictions on the use of provisional licences, and capacity and power-to-weight ratio restrictions. It was from this period, and intensifying into the late 1980s and 1990s that the nature of the RROs began to change. Steve Bergman, formerly Chairman of the BMF comments:

> ... the fight is based on a different thing. The BMF or, rather, the Federation of National and One-Make Clubs, as it originally was, got together because there was a lot of bad press about motorcycling. There wasn't anybody passing *laws*, it was just that all of these newspapers were suddenly, you know, writing stories about death-squad motorcyclists who go out on a Saturday night and kill themselves, and it's terrible. They got together because of *that*, so it was more of a sort of *social* threat, you know. We've changed now, and we're not dealing with a social threat or a law based on someone's narrow-minded view of what their perception of motorcyclists is, and 'I don't want these people in my pub.' We're not *doing that* any more.

A 36-year-old from MAG concurs that there has been a definite change, and points to its cause:

> Europe's definitely come to the fore in the last few years, I think, because Europe itself has become more of an issue altogether, with heading for single currency and all this sort of thing. I mean, when I first joined MAG, Europe wasn't really an issue particularly, it was more the UK government and this kind of thing, helmet laws and such like.

As we can see from the above quotations, it is the EU that is the focus for much of these perceptions of change. As Mazey and Richardson argue, it since the early 1980s that 'growing numbers of organised interests ... have come to recognise the increasing importance of Economic Community [*sic*] legislation' (1993a:191). Motorcyclists, particularly activists within the RROs, are aware of how all-encompassing the EU has become, as the BMF's Government Relations Executive informs us:

> It's changing, because the members of Europe are getting more cohesive. Originally, when it started, it was a number of different communities. There was the Euratom, there was the coal and steel community, and there was the economic community, and the economic community tended to swallow the others up. And then it tended to get more close-knit as more members joined, as well. You know, we're talking about in *depth* as well as *width*. And, as they did that, it started to change its form, and there was always a sort of agreement that any laws from this pan-European organisation would be mandatory upon the member governments, who would have to obey them. But, I think, that at the beginning that nobody thought that that would happen, and then you got things like the Single European Act, which made it the European Community rather than the European Economic Community, and then the Maastricht Treaty, the Treaty of Union, which made it the European Union, rather than the Economic Community.

Consequently, the nature of trends in Europe has been towards increasing homogeneity. As MAG's Vice-Chair informs us:

> . . . the nature and extent of the threat of official interference has grown tremendously since 1988–89. At home, there have been restrictions on public gatherings, increasingly complex learner-testing and taxation arrangements. The greatest change has come from the increasing influence of European and other international regulatory bodies. The EU programmes to bring about commonality in areas such as construction and use, licensing and testing, vehicle and equipment design characteristics, emissions, taxation, road safety, vehicle disposal, design protection etc., have necessitated changes to UK regulations. The United Nations, OECD and other supra-national bodies have similar agendas in pursuit of global markets.

In a situation wherein the EU is expanding and consolidating its position, there are fears that the growing trend towards increasing amounts of legislation will, by institutional necessity, continue without abatement into the future. Yet the difficulties facing the RROs are not experienced solely by motorcyclists, but are ones facing all European citizens. As such, motorcyclists are aware that they are merely caught up in legislative imperatives aimed elsewhere. These trends are crucially bound up with the idea of harmonisation in the EU. As one MEP informs us, this would appear, theoretically, to be a positive step for Europe:

> The rationale was that for all products, including motorbikes, there should be a single market across Europe. In principle that is a very good, very commendable thing, because if the whole market is 350 million people, then the conditions for getting better products and better confidence in investment etc., the conditions are better for European industry to thrive. If you've got fifteen member states, and each has got different regulations and rules about what the bikes must be, then the home market is the one country in which you are manufacturing. If you've got common standards right across Europe, the home market is Europe-wide. Japan's got a home market something like the size of the European market, and used that with its innovation and everything else, but was able to call on its home market to sustain its development programme and its research programme. And rather than ban their very good bikes, we need to create the conditions of the single market so that the European manufacturers produce goods as good, if not better. We don't want to ban their good ones, we want to get better ones.

Another MEP elaborates on how harmonisation more nearly affects motorcycles:

> The reason all these type-approval directives have been brought forward is to stop individual member states creating technical barriers to trade. If a motorcycle manufacturer in the United Kingdom conforms with European type approval, then the Germans or the French or the Spaniards can't stop British manufacturers selling their bikes abroad. And, of course, that applies too to companies like Harley Davidson, Yamaha and so on. There just have to be one set of technical requirements now which are Europe-wide

instead of fifteen different sets. And the other thing is that, if your vehicle conforms with the European Directive, even though you may have customised it, the French or the Germans can't stop you driving your UK-registered vehicle on their roads. And this has all come about because of the Single Market and the fact that more and more people are now wanting to take their customised vehicles abroad.

In this drive for harmonisation, motorcyclists are aware that the philosophy and aims of legislative trends lie elsewhere. As Steve Bergman observes, 'We're dealing with a Commission who really don't care if you ride a motorcycle or not, the Commission aren't *anti*-motorcycling, they're not anti-car, they're not 'anti' anything. They're just going down the road of harmonisation.' MAG's Ian Mutch agrees that harmonisation is not 'anti-motorcycling' as such and, therefore, may contain a mixture of good and bad aspects:

Brussels has become the fountain of legislation these days, and sometimes we're caught in the crossfire of objectives which are not directly aimed at us. For example, the rabid attempt to harmonise everything, sometimes for trade reasons, gives us problems. For example, in one country there will be a noise limit for motorcycles, and in another country there will be a different noise limit; particularly Austria and Germany have very severe limits. So if you're going to sustain a variety of different requirements for manufacturers to meet you don't really have a single market. So, in pursuit of the single market, so that manufacturers, say, from outside Europe, can say, 'Right. This is for the European market. It will meet the requirements of each country,' you have to have a degree of harmonisation. So often the impetus comes from, if not a benign, certainly not an anti-motorcycling stance necessarily. But perhaps an unsympathetic one. People just haven't *thought* about what they're doing.

Clearly, the basis for such ideas lies fundamentally in the growing importance of the EU to the lives of Europeans generally but, in this process, riders do feel that they have had to deal with this development earlier than other sectors of the population:

I think Europe as a whole has become much more the issue for *everyday life*, and therefore it's become more of an issue for bikes as well. I think it became more of an issue for bikes *before* it came to the public's attention as a whole, but, I mean, I think, I would *hope*, because of our publicity and what have you, our runs and things, I mean, we hand our leaflets to folk explaining what it's all about, and they actually do read them. . . . And I would hope we've brought it to the attention of a few car drivers what's heading their way.

In this sense, motorcycling merely reflects wider society and thus motorcyclists are confronting just one part of a mainstream political trend. Yet this quotation also captures the idea that riders can establish links with non-riders in a positive way. This is achieved by drawing attention to the particular restrictions faced by motorcyclists and, through this, engendering empathy with the public who may face such restrictions in the future. In this way, legislation is a way of focusing on both motorcyclists' difference from others, and their potential similarity. Two quotations emphasise how the EU can be used positively in dealing with the public:

> I usually end up having a pile of papers on the stand, because they're the things people ask questions about. Even if they're not bikers. I mean, they'll ask how Europe works because they'll see, Trevor does a lovely sort of table with everything in boxes on how Europe works. And you get some people look at that and think, 'Oh God. I didn't know it was *that* complicated.'

> It begins to really wake people when you get them to a point whereby you can really have a discussion with them. And they say, 'Well, what are you all getting hot under the collar about?' And you start to put these ideas through to them, and they go, 'Yeah. That could be us. If they're doing it to motorcycle tyres, why can't they do it to car tyres? They're reducing decibels on this, they can do it on cars as well.' The penny drops.

Yet whilst European legislation is of growing importance in all areas of social life, by implication the scope of the task facing legislators, trying to establish laws

Figure 14 The FEMA's Simon Milward tries to mix business with pleasure

to encompass such differing sets of circumstances, means there is a great possibility for error. One crucial factor alluded to by many riders is that there is a lack of detailed thought among legislators, which presents a logistical problem in trying to introduce uniformity across a number of very disparate and different countries. The specific problems for RROs are twofold: firstly, that complex legislation calls for technical expertise in order to be able to understand fully the ramifications of proposals and, secondly, they must thus be able to make informed decisions about what that legislation may mean in detailed circumstances. Yet, as Steve Bergman illustrates for us, whilst also indicating how much more simple legislation was in the past, it is hard for such legislation to be sensitive for all potential scenarios:

> The whole lot's changed. The things that the riders' rights were fighting in the past were very straightforward, very simple to understand the laws, the helmet law, riding in sidecars, very simple to understand, really there's nothing technical there at all. The European thing is all based on harmonisation . . . and the MOT standard is a simple [example], we need a European-wide, if we're allowed free movement, we need a European-wide standard. And that standard may be no standard, the middle ground or a very technical ground. But, nonetheless, it's fundamental, if you live in the UK, you should be able to buy a bike in France, ride it over, and carry on riding it. At present, you cannot do that. And, in moving towards harmonisation, and I *agree* with that, I should be able to buy a bike anywhere I want and just ride it, what's the problem? you know. But presently, I can't. So, I agree in principle with the harmonisation. But, obviously, when you get to these things you're into seriously technical subjects, and it's wading through all of those technicalities, having the *people* who can wade through those technicalities and advise us on what we should be doing, you know, it's beyond me to sit and read a 500-page document and make any sense out of it, especially when it's written in French. So the difference is also, it's those laws and the fight is based on a different thing. The Commission are . . . just going down the road of harmonisation. 'Oh, we need a harmonised law on paint. It would be a good thing not to have cellulose paint any more. It's going to be water-based, because that's environmentally friendly. So we'll put a Directive together that by 1998 everyone's going to be using this when they're spraying cars, a water-based paint.' That's an excellent idea. And the MEPs will [say], 'Yeah, we'll go for that. That's excellent.' So we get the documents and we say, 'Well, when you say "cars", do you mean cars, or do you mean all vehicles, or what? And what about people who may have some specialist role, and in doing a specialised thing they may need to use something that's non-water based?' I mean, this is off the top of my head. And then we'll say to them, 'If it's proven that you may need to use a spirit-based [paint] for this particular thing, would you put in something in the law which will allow, under certain circumstances, certain things to be used,' and so on.

If, as has been alluded to above, the construction of machinery and the types of work one may be allowed to carry out on one's bike may be affected by moves towards greater harmonisation, it is also the case that the ways in which one rides are also potentially affected. Again, the following quotation from a MAG Scottish Group Secretary, not only draws attention to differing riding practices and circumstances across Europe, but also to how attempts to make them uniform would fail to deal with the complexities of European life and experience:

> I can understand the European ties are maybe good for industry and this kind of thing, but also this business of standardising and, 'You must all have your bananas straight,' this kind of *rubbish* I just think is *so* ridiculous. And, for me, it totally detracts from what might be the real benefits, it really does. And the business of bikes is a prime example of that, really. I mean, I've been to Europe, I've been to France and what have you, and you see all of these people tearing about on these huge off-road bikes and all the rest of it and, yeah, it's loony, absolutely loony. I mean, the circular road that goes around Paris is just *mayhem*. But I don't feel that, perhaps, just because a country has a problem the rest of Europe should be penalised for that. And that's what they're trying to do. I think it's a completely different situation in each country. I mean, we've just been to Greece, very nice. But there we were, in this lovely part of Greece, and there were mopeds and bikes *everywhere*, no helmets. Chugging along, no-one's doing much more than thirty miles an hour, because it's such a lovely day, you know, and they're chugging along. And when they get out of towns they do put helmets on, that's what they seem to do. The police are wandering around, big sports bikes, no helmets and shades, cruising the streets. And it was great. And, in that situation, you *don't* need helmets, it's *not* unsafe, you know. And then you go to Athens, where they're still riding with no helmets and it's absolute mayhem. I mean, the number of near-misses we saw just driving through just had you on the edge of your seat. And I think they're so interested in putting a blanket across, which means they have to cater to the worst situation in Europe for everybody, but they forget that different areas have different problems and *that's* what should be addressed. I think that they're just approaching it from entirely the wrong angle. And they ought to understand the situation before they start trying to make these blanket laws and what have you, and they obviously *don't*.

One of the potential reasons for a lack of sensitivity in legislative procedures may be that, in a complex modern society which requires specialisation of knowledge, we entrust law-making to people who both do not necessarily have the technical expertise necessary in a particular area, and who, consequently, must rely on the skills of others in order to reach decisions (Mazey and Richardson 1993b). As Giddens (1990) argues, we must trust the knowledge and experience of others, yet this contains risks. Clearly, we must all, at some time or another, rely on the skills of others in areas where we have no expertise ourselves, whether it be trusting our bank to look after our money, the garage to mend our motorcycle, our solicitor on legal matters, our doctor on health matters and so on. Also as clearly, sometimes our trust may be misplaced. Within the context of legislative proceedings we are in a double-risk scenario, in that we are trusting law-makers who are trusting in the expertise of their advisers, officials who do not necessarily have sufficient specialist knowledge themselves (Mazey and Richardson 1993b). Further, however, this situation assumes both that governmental officials understand complex issues and are also capable of suspending ideological imperatives in order to pursue what is objectively determined, where possible, as the correct course of action. Yet there are certain difficulties within this. Firstly, some research data are hard to interpret, particularly for the non-specialist; secondly, they may fail to give conclusive evidence; but thirdly, even if such data are produced, political goals may intervene.

This issue is particularly important for motorcyclists where much of the legislation proposed is highly technical, whether decibel levels, emissions or whatever. The experience of riders'-rights activists would appear to agree with Giddens's arguments in that a considerable amount of scepticism is displayed in these regards. Indeed, it would appear that there is a deep feeling that legislators find it easier to retreat into a position in which simplistic attitudes towards motorcycles and motorcyclists are assumed, rather than engage with the complexity of technical research data. The following quotation raises various points, which will be dealt with below. What is of particular interest at the moment, however, are the views that refer to both anti-biking feeling among legislators, and a tendency to make simplistic, knee-jerk decisions on the part of inexperienced people merely in order to be seen to be 'doing something':

[Legislation has] accelerated dramatically in the last three, four, five years as the EU seems to have acquired more and more power. And some of it *is* directly anti-bike and, as I say, we're caught in the crossfire some of the time, but take the 100 break horse power issue, that was specifically a motorcycling safety-based initiative. And, again, it was based on the assumption that if a bike is very powerful it will therefore be going very fast all of the time, and your chances of having a bad accident will be that much greater. And that was advanced by somebody that, I think, *probably* has a downer on bikes anyway. Martin Bangemann's sons both ride bikes and perhaps that makes him very anxious, and it's become a bit of a hobby-horse of his, and he's promoted that issue to the point of irrationality. There are other issues that we should perhaps mention at this point. There was the leg protector issue which, *again*, like the helmet issue, was a very simplistic, red-herring of a solution to a problem. 'Bikers get a lot of leg issues,' which is true. 'Here is something which offers an *element* of protection, we *think*, therefore we must have a law compelling everybody to have them.' And you make this quantum leap from the *recognition* of a problem, to the *identification* of something which *might* provide a possible solution, to the *conclusion* that there must be a law compelling its enforcement. And it's that quantum leap that's skipped over with such speed by those who are not part of the movement, or part of the experience which they're affecting. If you said a lot of people die from heart attacks, it's the country's biggest killer, and a lot of people are overweight, and that increases the chances of them *having* a heart attack, therefore we must have a law *compelling* people to conform to a certain weight for their height and build, then there would be *outrage*. But if you could *possibly* enforce it, which, of course, you couldn't, the savings to the Health Service . . . would be *infinitely* more valuable, and the consequences infinitely greater to society, but the political practicality would rule it out.

Therefore, despite an awareness, discussed earlier, that motorcyclists are merely part of an ongoing political process, there is also a belief that riders are more likely to be targeted for legislative proposals. There are two aspects to this. This first is that whilst motorcyclists are merely part of legislative trends confronting all vehicle drivers, and thus not being singled out for attention, it is also the case that motorcycling is, in reality, being discriminated against unintentionally in the sense that it is often ignored, that is that legislation for cars is merely *assumed* to be relevant and appropriate for motorcycles as well. It is commonly believed among riders that 'transport policy has traditionally ignored motorcycling – except for the purposes of restricting it – or at least assumed that anything done with cars in mind will suit bikes.' This blindness to the specific circumstances of motorcycles is captured in the following quotation:

> There's the legislative [issues], which effect everyone anyway, when you look at what comes out of Europe, whether it's straight cucumbers or whatever it happens to be. But motorcyclists tend to feel these things much closer. Ones on anti-tampering of machines. The car world has had this for some time. Things are built into cars so that you can't mess around with the fuel injection. Well, you can do, but they're not designed for home maintenance. And that doesn't cause a problem to most motorists, they're just not bothered. A car is a car. It gets them from A to B. For some reason the motorcyclist feels much, well, not for some reason, it's obvious, feels much closer to the machine. He's *part* of the machine. He sits *on* it, not *in* it. And so there's that affinity there with what makes the bike tick.

In this sense, motorcyclists are discriminated against by omission. The second factor which riders believe separates motorcyclists from other citizens is that it is felt that the restrictions currently being faced by motorcyclists are ones which are, or may become, experienced by other sections of society. Thus whilst riders appreciate that, as was argued earlier, legislative trends, and their underlying political motivations, have a momentum of their own, there is also a suspicion that they are a 'testing ground' for legislation to be applied more widely at some later date. Further, it is believed that the reason that motorcyclists have been targeted for legislation earlier than other groups is simply by virtue of the fact that they constitute only a minority of the electorate, and thus can safely be experimented on without severe consequences for representatives' majorities:

> As I see it, the problems that society are facing are truly horrendous, truly horrendous, and politicians are increasingly under pressure to *do* something to make the world a safer place, a nicer place, however they describe it. [So they're going to make us] the scapegoats. . . . But that's been a trend, isn't it, increasingly.

> My personal view is, I sometimes get the impression this legislation is tried out on us, before it gets as far as the motoring industry proper, sort of thing, with the cars and things, and I just get this sneaking suspicion that if they can get it through us without too much rumpus then, you know, they'll just wield it out on the car drivers, and the car drivers won't be fussed either way. They'll just sort of stick their hands in their pockets and get on with it. So, I sometimes wonder whether or not we're a bit of a litmus paper for these guys. My personal inclination is that it all smacks a bit of Big Brother tactics. 'Let's try it out on something small and if they squeak too loudly, we might rethink it before we try it out on the big picture' sort of thing.

> I think, initially, we were perceived as a soft target. 'We can do this and we're not going to upset *that* many people.' Putting it in a blunt term, it's about pure voters. 'If we introduce a biking law we're only going to upset 14 per cent. That's acceptable.' They look at it as an acceptable damage thing. It goes back to that [perception] which classed us as social misfits.

Whilst, as another rider argues, 'the social acceptability of motorcycles and their riders has often been either the catalyst, or the excuse, for regulation,' this may also be seen as resulting from motorcyclists' difference, that is that they are a target because they do not conform to the norm. As discussed previously, therefore, there is a feeling that riders are attacked because of their individualistic characteristics:

> There's no doubt about it, [the EU] are trying to remove motorcycling from the face of the planet. They do *not* want to have motorcycles. People who ride motorcycles stand out from the crowd. They're individuals. And the EU does not like that. The EU is run by, and on behalf of, big companies. And big companies want everybody to act like nice, little consumers. They don't want them to think for themselves too hard. They want everybody to act the same. So what I think the EU is doing, is making motorcycling as unattractive as possible.

This idea of attempts to make them conform is central to riders' understandings of the motivations behind legislative proposals, in that many feel that they are being subjected to unwanted intrusion by a 'nanny state' seeking to protect them from themselves. As one rider maintains:

> Motorcycling *is* dangerous, but *my* view is that they're only dangerous because there's so many bloody cars on the road and a huge majority, as far as I know, of people with

influence see it the other way round; that bikes are dangerous *inherently* and so they want to protect us from ourselves. So, like leg protectors, that was brought on by TRRL, [Transport and Road Research Laboratory] a chap in there, said 'These will be good for you. These won't break your legs,' which is a motorcycle accident problem. With the European lot it's, again, civil servants who are trying to save us from ourselves, *or* are trying to price us off the market or make it very difficult for people to ride them, as far as I can see. . . . Quite literally they are doing it for what *they* think is our own benefit. Out of an ill-informed stance. . . . The people making the decisions see that as protecting us from ourselves.

This is seen as interfering with an individual's right to make their own decisions, that is it interferes with riders' rights to choose their own behaviour. Anti-motorcycle legislation is thus understood as an attack on lifestyle – politics is intruding on cultural expression:

I think it's almost impossible to separate the two because if people weren't trying to interfere with the lifestyle there wouldn't be any point in defending it. You see, the kind of things which really attack the lifestyle . . . [are] things like the helmet law, like type approval, like anti-tampering, which is another form of type approval. The anti-tampering proposals from Europe would have threatened the whole home maintenance, they still do threaten the whole philosophy of home maintenance. The right of a biker to pull his engine to bits and make it go better has been something which has only really been challenged very recently. And, to the typical motorist, who doesn't really care what's under the bonnet so long as it makes his car go, it probably seems a strange thing that you should *want* to pull the engine to bits and do things to it. So we're up against a pretty unsympathetic bunch of characters in Europe, those who would interfere with us in that respect. So because that *is* part of the lifestyle, it's not so *physically* apparent as whether you wear a helmet of not, or whether you have a fluorescent waistcoat on or not, it is still pretty fundamental to the whole ethos. So . . . you can't separate the challenge to the lifestyle from the legislative interference.

Legislation, therefore, is crucially bound up with the issues of civil rights and freedom of expression, for attempts to standardise legislature and practice across the EU are seen as wrong *morally*, in that they neglect to take into account, and ride rough-shod over, the wishes of the motorcycling electorate:

The whole philosophy of motorcycling is being *challenged* because, from a road safety perspective, there are people who are saying, the same kind of mentality which, in '73, dictated that there should be a helmet law because, what they were saying, 'This is an unacceptably dangerous way of behaving.' Riding a motorcycle without a helmet. Even though the law made no difference to the accident statistics whatsoever, but they didn't *know* that, or they certainly pretended not to. And the natural extension of that logic is to advance the idea that motorcycling itself is too dangerous and, therefore, unacceptable and, therefore, should be banned. And we've now seen that specific proposal come from Sweden, where a prominent road safety campaigner has enshrined that notion in what he calls the 'zero vision'; which is a vision of no accidents whatsoever. And since motorcyclists are involved in, well, varying estimates, anywhere from thirty times more fatal accidents per mile travelled, or ten times as many, depending on how you juggle the statistics, and what your estimates of mileage are. Whichever way you look at it, yes, it is still a lot more dangerous. And whether or not it is the fault of the other party, primarily, or not, may be viewed as secondary to the fact that you are more likely to sustain a serious or fatal injury on a motorcycle. So we have to defend philosophically, ultimately, the fact that we *like* doing it, we *know* it's more dangerous, but we just enjoy it . . . that you're prepared to accept a level of risk which other people are not prepared for *you* to accept, and it's *that* conflict of philosophy which is the *core* of the arguments that we have.

I'm a great believer in freedom of choice, within limits. And I just feel this whole business of standardising this, that and the other, and not being able to do this, that and the other for *no* good reason. I mean, if people were really crashing and dying because their bikes were over 1100cc or whatever, and it was a major problem, you could make a good case for doing something about it. But just trying to limit brake horse power just because people *feel* like it, basically, to me is totally wrong, totally wrong. I just don't see any justification for it at all. And decibel limits and this sort of thing as well. I think people get carried away. They get onto a good idea, or what they think is a good idea, and they just get carried away with it. And they get blinkers on and they just go for it. And you have to try and make them *stop*, and try and see the wider picture of what they're actually doing and how it affects people.

As these quotations indicate, such arguments are crucially reflective of new social-movements literature, which defines contemporary pressure-group activity as bound up with civil rights and autonomy. This means that whilst, superficially, riders' rights seem primarily preoccupied with the '*political* issue of democratic control over technology' (Bauman 1991:276), such as challenging the role of experts and technocrats (Garner 1996) and fighting 'encroaching political power' (Touraine 1992:143), it is also a struggle to extend equal rights into a new area (M.J. Smith 1995; Hall & Held 1990). Therefore, if the RROs are seeking inclusion into the political process, through integration into mainstream politics (Scott 1990; Mayer 1995; Garner 1996), this is being fought in order to preserve individual autonomy from 'overwhelming social forces' (Bocock 1992:126). It is in this way that we can understand Melucci's comment that democracy 'in complex societies requires conditions which enable individuals and social groups to affirm themselves and to be recognised for what they are or wish to be' (1989:172). The right to ride is not merely a cultural issue concerning individual rights, however, for, as we saw earlier, personal and cultural demands are also political demands (Scott

Figure 15 Every biker's best friend. Simon Milward explains biker opposition to the 100bhp limit to Martin Bangemann (centre). The BMF's Trevor Magner (back right) checks his dilithium crystals

1990:23). The pursuit of freedom is thus about individual choice and the rights to self-realisation (Bauman 1992).

Consequently, it may be argued that the infringement of riders' rights to personal autonomy are inherently involved within the whole issue of rider politicisation. It is through the perception of such legislative infringements that riders are drawn into political activity, and RROs into greater political activity. As one rider informs us:

> [The] regulation and restriction of options open to riders is at the root of all riders'-rights organisations. Many motorcycle organisations were formed for other reasons – sporting, touring, marque, locality etc. – but most have had to respond to, or at least have been affected by, attempts by various public authorities to regulate their activities in some way.

This has the consequence of drawing the RROs together in defence of riding. The European Union, therefore, is partially responsible for the recent better accord between the RROs nationally, in that, as was mentioned earlier, 'people aren't slagging the other group off as much as they used to.' Further, as is argued below by Steve Bergman, much of this potential for coherent activity has additionally been facilitated by the fact that the EU presents a simple, if internally complex, target that ensures that the lobby knows where to aim:

> It's become easier. It's given us a single target. It's become easier. We've got a single target and we've got a unified force to do that. We've got a unified force. Forget MAG, forget BMF, forget [FEMA], you've got a unified force, and that is riders'-rights organisations. And we've got a single target. It's become *easier* since it went to Europe . . . because of the way the Commission and the Parliament is structured in Europe.

As a result of statements such as these we may conclude that, as Bauman (1992) argues, the state has a declining role in policy-making. Instead, the national 'centralised states' (Tarrow 1994:89) are being replaced by the centralised transnational state of the EU. Thus, we may agree with Klandermans that central to movement participation and political conflict are 'collectively defined grievances that produce a 'we' feeling and causal attributions that denote a 'they' which is held responsible for the collective grievances' (1997:41), and that the EU can be seen as having acted as the originator of grievance. Yet, simultaneously, if the EU presents an easily identifiable target, another advantage for challengers is that one can argue that it is the EU, more than any other factor, which accounts for the growth in size and sophistication of the riders'-rights organisations. As Neil Liversidge argues:

> Licensing laws were starting to be tightened up in the early '80s, you know, when they stopped people riding 250s, forced people onto 125s, brought in a one-year ban for anyone who hadn't passed their test in two years. Bottomley came up with the leg protectors thing. Leg protectors just keep on having life breathed back into them by things like the Multi-Directive and all the rest of it. But the fight is a lot more sophisticated these days than it ever was before. But as the politicians, and the bureaucrats have realised, I think they thought that if they raised the debate to such an elevated level, and they transported it overseas to Brussels, Strasbourg or whatever, then out of this great, grey cloud all the thunderbolts of legislation would drop and nobody would be able to do ouwt about them. But what we've done is we've elevated our campaigning to their level, and we can match them on their own ground. We've got an office in Brussels to do it. We've got people out there who know what they're on about. And we've got our foot in the door with the MEPs as well. So they can carry on raising the stakes as much as they like and we'll meet them. We'll raise them and see them. If they want to play poker with us, we'll raise them and see them every time.

–8–

The European Riders'-Rights Movement

Within the field of European pressure groups and social movements the most significant political factor since the early 1980s, along with changes in Eastern Europe, has been the growing influence that the European Union has gained over the lives of all citizens living in member states. In this regard, the Single European Act (SEA) is of particular importance for, as Mazey and Richardson (1993a) argue, the reform of the decision-making process that occurred in its wake has led to an increase in pressure groups and professional lobbyists attempting to influence political decisions taken in the EU. This has led to changes in the ways in which lobbying occurs in that, whilst prior to the SEA, groups sought access to political structures largely at local and regional levels, now it is increasingly necessary to be based in Brussels in order to monitor what proposals are under discussion and to gain access to the relevant individuals and committees whose decisions affect legislative outcomes. Clearly, as M.J. Smith argues (1995), groups have tended to move to Brussels as their interests become part of EU agenda. Yet it was not sufficient merely that national groups make this transition, for it has also entailed the development of closer co-operation with other European organisations with similar concerns, that is to form 'Eurogroups'. In the last chapter, we saw how EU legislation made RROs increasingly aware of the need for a response to such changes. In this chapter, we will explore how the riders'-rights organisations have made this transformation, before going on to examine how the lobby has developed since its inception.

The riders'-rights organisations realised how important the EU was to their interests comparatively early. The first organisation, the FEM, was established in 1988 at a demonstration in Strasbourg; its purpose being to defend and further riders' rights in the European Union. In attendance at the first gathering were FFMC of France, Kühle Wampe of Germany and MAG UK's Ian Mutch. MAG Austria, MOTO-E of Greece, Gacchi Bleu of Italy, LMI of Luxembourg and MAG Holland were also at the demonstration, but apparently did not know of the important meeting being held in a field. Initially, the FEM was based in Yorkshire, where it stayed until 1991 when it moved to Charleroi in Belgium but, in 1992, realising the need to have more effective access to the EU, it moved to Brussels, under its first General Secretary, Frank Pearson. All of the above-named organisations, in addition to MAG Belgium, ABATE Denmark, ANDDB France, Biker Union Germany, MAG Ireland, FNM Portugal and, later, the BMF, were to become member organisations of the FEM. Motorcyclists were thus quick to attempt union with their European counterparts and realise the necessity of being at the centre of the EU, but also to establish an organisational structure to carry out both administrative and lobbying activities.

In April 1992, Pearson returned to England and Simon Milward, at that time MAG UK's European Liaison Officer volunteered to replace him. This was confirmed by the FEM Committee and Milward has continued in office from that time, assisted by Christina Gésios of MAG Belgium and, later, MAG UK's Bob Tomlins. Together, these three constituted the Secretariat who carried out the main business of the FEM. Other people helped on a part-time, voluntary basis. The main policy business of the FEM was carried out by the FEM Committee. In addition, there was a Finances and General Purposes Committee (FGPC) which was made up of the Secretariat and two other people elected from national organisations. As national organisations had to be able to finance trips to Committee meetings, these additional members were usually appointed dependant upon either proximity to Brussels or the financial standing of their organisation. This Committee considered finance, administration and any constitutional proposals to go to the Committee as a whole. The FEM Committee normally met three times and the FGPC three or four times yearly. Each member organisation had two delegates on the FEM Committee: the chair or president and one other, usually the European Liaison Officer. To qualify for membership, a national RRO was required to contribute a minimum affiliation fee which was equivalent to one thousand members, thus ensuring that all organisations had a valid constituency and rights to representation. Organisations were also required to represent all riders from throughout their respective countries, that is regional associations would not qualify for FEM membership. The aim was a democratic federation:

> FEM [was] a broad-based . . . alliance open to national motorcycle groups across Europe. Democracy [was] on a one-nation, one-vote basis. This . . . ensured protection for smaller organisations and countries from domination by richer partners, but at the expense of bigger organisations who [had] to make a greater financial contribution, often for a relatively smaller share of the vote.

Clearly, to maintain its presence in Brussels and undertake its lobbying activities required both considerable financial support and expertise and knowledge of EU processes and procedures (M.J. Smith 1995). Materially, whilst the FEM progressed considerably in its first decade, initially, resources were very limited; thus impeding chances of fulfilling organisational aims. Bob Tomlins talks about the situation that confronted him when he joined the FEM office in August 1994:

> When I first came into the FEM, [Simon] was living in the office, sleeping in the back
> room of the little garret we had, this little attic set-up . . . [and] two of the phone lines
> had been cut off. Now, you know, one thing that is absolutely crucial to an international
> organisation, a lobbying organisation, an organisation that is trying to change people's
> minds is the ability to *talk* to people and the phone is *absolutely essential*. But we had
> two phone lines cut off because we couldn't pay the bills!

By 1997, however, changes in controlling accounting and increases in income
meant that the FEM had attained greater financial security although, as with the
national organisations, money continued to be a major problem in carrying out
activities. By that time, the FEM had an annual income of around £70,000, with
about 65 per cent of revenue coming directly from motorcyclists – mostly from
affiliation fees of member organisations, but also from donations and fund-raising
activities from members and the FEM's own activities and marketed goods. The
next largest contribution came from industry, from manufacturers and specialist
aftermarket companies; this contributed approximately another 20 per cent. In the
years 1995–97, the remaining 15 per cent was generated by work carried out for
the European Commission into rider training around the community. As such, the
constraints upon performance had become somewhat easier although, clearly, as
with many other organisations, financial considerations were always of concern.

In terms of expertise, this, of necessity, largely arose out of experience as, unlike
other organisations, the FEM's personnel came from its own population, European

Figure 16 Luxembourg bhp demo 1993

motorcyclists, rather than being staffed by professional lobbyists or those from other pressure groups; the arrival of Bob Tomlins, with years of British and European trade-union experience, being fortuitous rather than planned. Lack of financial support meant that much of the FEM's performance was critically bound up with Simon Milward, its General Secretary. It was Milward's responsibility to deal with the European governmental institutions. This entailed research into prospective legislative proposals and the co-ordination of the lobby (with instructions about what should be done, when things should be done and whom should be lobbied). He had also to deal with officials and representatives, again knowing who, when and how to deal with them. Given the cumbersome nature of European government and 'the unpredictability of the EU policy agenda' (Mazey and Richardson 1993a:206) this work was both complex and continual. He comments:

> I think that's very important. To be well-targeted. and well-co-ordinated. You have to know the process. Which Committees are doing what and have the timing right. It's quite a task. I mean, sometimes you hear about a Directive going through, and then you dig into it a bit more, and research it, and you find out that it's really quite important, and you're quite late in starting on the lobby. There's various newspapers and publications by the European Community which you can look in, but there's a whole stack of them, and if you spent your time reading all of them then you wouldn't get any lobby work done.

Milward was also responsible, however, for liaison with member organisations. Firstly, and, perhaps, above all, FEM had to co-ordinate the activities of the European lobby. This required considerable attention, given that different countries have different methods of action. For example:

> Well, that's one of the nice things about the Germans, because if you give the Germans an instruction to do then they do it very well, although they might not have done it before. I mean, when I say, 'Send a letter to all these people,' you know, the Germans are very well organised and they do it with individually-addressed letters, and they all arrive here in a nice little bundle and I can go and put them in the pigeon-holes. The French way, of course, is just to get out on the streets. So they have these different ways of doing things. . . . We're quite specific in what we want national organisations to do, and how important it is that everybody does it.

Further, Milward had to deal with queries from national organisations, visit them in the member countries, attending their events and showing the official face of FEM. This meant that he sometimes might spend two or three weeks away from Brussels at any one given time. Milward, therefore, had a punishing workload. As

Tomlins comments:

> He's a guy who quit working in the traditional sense a long time ago, still a very young man, to work for riders' right and has, literally, dedicated his life to it. . . . I mean, Simon is a workaholic. I mean, God knows, he must work, on average, at least twelve to fourteen hours a day, he works mostly seven days a week. I mean, if I want to get hold of him at ten o'clock at night, someone will phone me up and I want to talk to Simon, I'll probably get him in the office at ten o'clock at night, most nights.

Like many primarily voluntary organisations, under-resourced and under-staffed, therefore, much had been dependant upon Milward's preparedness to dedicate his own energies to the FEM. One national MAG officer clearly links the success of the FEM to Milward's personal commitment:

> FEM was formed to organise a European bikers' voice in Brussels. The personal achievements and sacrifices of the FEM staff, particularly the General Secretary, Simon Milward, in bringing together riders'-rights organisations . . . to present a common, effective, persuasive lobby in Brussels cannot be overstated.

Yet, until 1997 there was also another international RRO, namely the European Motorcyclists' Association. Theories about the background to the setting up of EMA differ. Whereas the FEM was usually seen, in Britain at least, as a MAG UK organisation, largely due to the facts that different organisations that happen to be called MAG exist in different countries even though they are separate organisations and, also, that the first two General Secretaries have happened to come from MAG UK, the EMA was commonly accredited as being a BMF organisation, set up and dominated by that organisation. This idea was encouraged by the fact that the BMF did not affiliate to the FEM until 1994, when it joined as a result of pressure from its membership. This belief in the essential differences of the two organisations was held generally among the members of the BMF:

> Our Chairman of the time set up a meeting with some of the Nordic organisations and we ended-up with EMA being formed, or EMU as it was then, the European Motor-cyclists' Union. . . . And that seemed to be the way to go, because a lot of the organisations seemed to be more like-minded. They seemed to be run more on BMF lines. SMC in Sweden, for example, NMCU in Norway, are very much run on BMF lines, rather than on MAG lines; not that I'm saying there's very much difference between BMF and MAG. We've got fundamentally the same aims, but perhaps different approaches of achieving them.

This belief resulted, for some time, in a sense of division between two 'sides' within the European organisations, a feeling that gradually diminished:

> . . . working through people like EMA and FEM. . . . We're not so antagonistic as we used to be with them, because there used to be a more MAG-oriented FEM so,

consequently, because we were the BMF on one side, MAG on the other, we didn't talk to the FEM. We were with the FIM, which aren't really concerned with road-riding, it's more racing. So we had problems with that. It was a case of, 'Oh, the FEM are just going to work with MAG.' But now it appears that everybody works together a lot more harmoniously.

Yet, according to both EMA and FEM leadership, it was not actually the case that the BMF set up the EMA. Both accredit the driving impetus for the establishment of EMA to the Scandinavian riders'-rights organisations, specifically the Norwegians, who realised that they needed to be in Europe and who, along with the BMF, formed EMA in December 1992. Yet it was not merely the desire to be in Europe that lay behind the move, for, clearly, the FEM already had a presence in Brussels by that time. The founding of yet another European riders'-rights group, seen by many UK riders as wasteful and divisive, was based on a desire to avoid what was seen as the radicalism and 'lifestyle' image of the FEM, as can be seen from the following quotations, from the EMA's Don Lewis and the FEM's Simon Milward respectively:

> Because, at that time, [FEM was] a very radical organisation. Having demos and that kind of thing. And the *culture*, if you like, of the people in EMA is that we'd rather not be associated with that kind of thing, if you know what I mean. And, also, why you're at it, why was MAG set up when the BMF existed? It caters for a particular sort of person with a particular outlook. And the people join one or the other depending on what they want to do.

> I think the main moves for forming EMA came from the Scandinavian organisations, who perceived the FEM as being too close to the Hell's Angels and only doing demos against the helmet law; which was all total rubbish. And we've had quite a hard job to dispel that.

Whether or not such differences actually existed is not the point, however. What is, is that the *perception* that they did directly influenced the relationship between the two. Yet the EMA did not, and could not, replicate the FEM. Although it represented around 200,000 riders, the EMA was a much smaller organisation, with only eight affiliates, mainly northern European but with an Italian group also, and an income of about £7,500–8,000 annually. They had no paid staff, and organisational work, such as running the office, writing letters or whatever, was carried out by the Chairman, Don Lewis, from his house in Hampshire. Further, unlike the FEM, which allowed more than one organisation from any given country to affiliate, EMA only allowed one national organisation from any country to join, in order not to import antagonism. As Lewis argued:

> . . . we said that if we had a national organisation, with national coverage, in a particular country then we can represent the motorcyclists in that country. And we [did] not, therefore, import national rivalries into what we [hoped was] going to be a very friendly [inter]national organisation.

Yet whilst such an aim might have seemed laudable in theory, in practice it was perceived somewhat differently by those outside the EMA:

> You know, the thing I really like about the FEM is that it's an *inclusive* organisation. FIM and, to a lesser extent, EMA, are *exclusive* organisations. They have rules designed to *keep people out*. To keep motorcyclists out. They can find many reasons for not allowing a *bona fide* riders' organisation from being able to affiliate to them. The FEM's the other way round.

A further two other differences, apart from ones purely of organisational structure, characterised the EMA in distinction from the FEM. The first lay in its method of operation and the second in its relationship with the FIM, the International Federation of Motorcyclists. In relation to the first, organisationally, the EMA was purely a co-ordinating office, doing no lobbying itself. Each member country was responsible for its own national and international activities. This way of working may account for the perceived lack of activity seen as coming from the EMA, for, as one Local Rep quipped, on being asked for an opinion about the activities of the EMA, 'I've never experienced their inactivity.' Yet much of this approach may have been simply due to lack of resources and a lack of physical presence in Brussels, rather than organisational philosophy. For whatever reason, however, many activists, like the one below, felt that the EMA was not making a full contribution to the rights of motorcyclists. 'We don't feel that EMA organisations are paying their way, in terms of resources put into the riders'-rights movement, or in terms of effort put into lobbying on a European basis.'

It is also possible that the second factor of difference, the relationship with the FIM, may also have been partially responsible for the invisibility of EMA's activities. This relationship appears to have stemmed largely from the BMF's earlier relationship with that organisation, which survived into the EMA period:

> The BMF has got a relationship with FIM, the international organisation, via ACU. Now perhaps I should explain the complexities of that. FIM, in its rules, is only allowed to have *one* national federation in each country, and it tends to have sporting organisations because its main function is sport, although it has a lesser function of dealing with road-riding issues; like touring and politics, in the wider sense, EU lobbying-type politics. In the case of the UK, that member is the ACU, the Auto Cycle Union, which is purely a sporting federation. Consequently, we have an arrangement with the ACU that on

Figure 17 Simon Milward at the 1996 Euro Demo

certain panels of FIM the BMF can represent motorcyclists, because it's outside the remit of ACU.

The EMA applied for affiliation to the FIM in Dublin in 1993, where their supplication was voted upon by the Annual Congress. Whilst initially the future seemed promising, this was not to last:

> We decided that the FIM is the recognised world authority on motorcycling and though it did little about the road-riding motorcyclist, the fact that it was FIM gave it entrée to various organisations, and respect. So we thought we could join FIM as an associate member, which we did, and we stayed in it for two years. And we were anticipating that the FIM would recognise our worth, as they did, initially. Our very first full meeting of EMA, the president of the FIM came along to sort of give us his blessing. And we were anticipating a *useful* association. *They* had 200,000 members, that showed that they had the grassroots support, if you like, of the riders, *we* had a certain experience in political lobbying and that kind of thing, because we [were] drawing on the experience of the national organisations. There is no national organisation, to my knowledge, that hasn't got some political experience, it's usually the reason that all of the clubs coalesce, or join, or support a national organisation. But it didn't seem to work out. I don't know [why not]. You don't get very much for it. But EMA had a seat . . . on the Road Safety and Public Policy panel while we were members. But it was generally agreed that EMA, we were losing our identity. Because we were affiliated to the FIM, people said, 'Oh,

yeah, well, EMA, it's an offshoot of the FIM,' and, consequently, I think, we lost out in the longer term. So, at the end of 1995, we separated from FIM, we didn't renew our associate membership, with full understanding on either sides of why it was happening. . . . But we, I think, were possibly naive. The FIM, I think, was possibly a bit soggy and didn't grasp the opportunity that we offered. We were willing to do all of the work. . . . They could have had an operative arm, if you like, within the FIM, but they decided, I don't know why, they sort of went off the boil, and the association was there, and we were sort of saying, 'Well, we're not getting anywhere.' And then it came home to us that people just thought us part of the soggy, old FIM.

Attitudes towards the FIM are generally ambivalent. Firstly, there is a feeling that the FIM does not have any real responsibility towards road-riding motorcyclists as that it not its remit:

It looks after the sporting side. It is an authority in its own right. It should have, over the years, looked after the interests of road-riding motorcyclists more than it has, I think that's acknowledged, but its main *impetus* and its main *income* comes from sport. . . . There's no money in politics, you know. There's money in TV, selling TV rights and things like that.

What you see is road riders very seriously prejudiced by . . . the FIM, because of the sport domination. The sport interest has dominated. It's where the *dosh is*. It's where the *glamour* is. It's where all the *buzz* is. That's where the adrenaline flows.

Yet this is compounded by a feeling of disgruntlement that the FIM gets the money and excitement but does not put back into the motorcycling what it takes out. Consequently, riders'-rights organisations, both national and European, can be seen to have sprung up in the vacuum left by the FIM's failure to represent the, perhaps, less profitable aspects of motorcycling:

We've not only proved ourselves, we've taken their space. That's what we've done. And that's why we're treated seriously now. I mean, like many things, what happened in FIM, in my opinion, was everyone concentrated on the sports side, they allowed the road riders to go off and do their own thing, but they never *formally relinquished* that responsibility. They still want to be 'Mr Motorcycling'. They want to be the voice of *all* motorcyclists. But what we did, I mean, because *they* didn't do the work, *we* came into existence, *we* responded to the need, *we* filled the vacuum, *we* took their space. And they went through a number of years of trying to push us out, to get that space back, and they've realised they *can't* now. We *exist*. . . . We are the *voice* and the *force* of motorcycling in Europe.

However, it would appear that, not only has the FIM come to accept the RROs, but that it may also be prepared to work more closely with them. As such, there appears to be a feeling of optimism and excitement about future collaboration. Much of this is seen as coming from changes within the FIM itself:

> There are certainly key people who think that the International Federation of Motor-cyclists should be what its name says. The International Federation for *all* Motorcyclists, not just sports motorcyclists. And, I mean, I said our relationship is getting very much better. It's very much down to people like Ed Youngblood and Rob Rasor, from the American Motorcyclists' Association, an organisation that's both sport *and* road riding, properly balanced, with equal weight, you know, a really healthy relationship between the two. And the resources that they're able to put into road-riding issues come, to a very large extent, from the money that's generated by the sport. From my point of view, if we can become one European road-riding organisation, and we can sort out our relationship with the FIM, so that we get enough money to pay the bills, to be able to employ a very small team of people on very moderate rates, we don't have to raffle bikes, and run festivals and motorcycling and the like, but we can get on and deal with the real work, then *that* has to be an objective worth securing.

This feeling that riders' rights should be taking more positive steps to ensure its future was, by 1997, also focusing on the relationship between the FEM and EMA. Many queried the necessity of having two organisations. This was best expressed in June 1997 by the FEM's Bob Tomlins:

> My trade-union background says to me, in any interest group, whether it's workers in the workplace, or motorcyclists on the road, the adage that 'united we stand, divided we fall', is *still* the truism. And we are weaker because EMA exists. EMA exists with a predominance of Scandinavian organisations. But the fact that they're not part of the whole, at a European level, makes us both weaker. And to try and dress it up in terms of, 'Well, there are bikers and motorcyclists' and that, is a load of crap, in my view. Bringing EMA and FEM together, in one way or another, utilising in the most effective way our very limited resources, is crucial. And I know Simon's committed to it. I'm *totally* committed to it. If, at the end, in nine years time, when I'm sixty or sixty-five, whenever I retire or whatever, I see there being effectively one European road-riding riders'-rights organisation, I will think that we've moved forward. *Dramatically*, and *massively*, and *practically*.

Much of the growing desire for merger, as can be seen above, sprang from a perceived awareness of the waste of resources resultant upon the functioning of two organisations. Repeatedly, riders argued that a merger of the two associations was necessary 'purely to save awful financial waste, and to put a lot of good minds working together, instead of duplicating what they do.' Interestingly, initial possibilities for such a goal opened up as a result of a conference hosted by the

FIM in Luxembourg in April 1997. Simon Milward explains:

> . . . all the FEM organisations and the EMA organisations were there, along with riders
> from the States and Australia and stuff. And it was specifically to discuss riders'-rights
> issues. And it was the first time that the FEM members had actually got together with
> the EMA members and, as well as in the meetings, both groups were able to present the
> work they were doing in a way that was not kind of influenced by anybody's own
> personal views; very open. And both members saw that the other members were really
> very much the same as themselves, with the same aims and views, and even methods of
> working.

Following overtures from the EMA to discuss a proposed merger, representatives
from each organisation met in July 1997 at a meeting hosted by the BMF in
England. This meeting saw agreement on some aspects of amalgamation: namely,
the continuance of the FEM's Secretariat in the same role for the new organisation
with, finances allowing, a fourth member to join the team from the EMA in 1998;
the membership fee base; voting system and the new name. These principles were
then circulated to all members of each organisation and a working group comprising
members of both the FEM and EMA was established to draw up a draft constitution.
By the end of November 1997 both organisations had ratified the merger and agreed
that, from the 1 January 1998, there would be one international riders'-rights
organisation to represent all of Europe's bikers – the Federation of European
Motorcyclists' Associations. From start to finish, therefore, the merger was
accomplished in five months, a speed which may have caused resentments that
might take time to dissipate. The impetus for this is seen as coming from the British:

> They were forcing the pace. In fact, a few organisations got quite upset with them over
> it. But I think the other organisations saw the *sense* in the amalgamation. The Brits had
> the view, especially the BMF because they were paying to belong to both, they
> desperately wanted one organisation to save money and effectiveness. I think it was the
> *energy* with which the Brits wanted this to happen. The others felt as it they were being
> a little bit rail-roaded. Whereas, they would have liked more discussion on, for example,
> the voting, the weights of the votes. Quite a few didn't see the point of changing the
> name but, of course, unless we did change the name, then we probably wouldn't have
> brought the EMA members on board. Because they obviously wanted to see a change
> in order for EMA to get recognised so, in some ways, it was a bit political.

As this statement hints, it was clear, from before the amalgamation, that it
probably was not be a 'marriage of equals' in that, both organisationally and
politically, the FEM far outweighed the EMA. As one national MAG officer stated

during the negotiating period:

> The influence and impact of EMA is arguably much less than that of the FEM. It is notable that in negotiations over the proposed merger, the majority of parties to the negotiation have supported an organisational structure and methodology that is, to all extents and purposes, that developed by the FEM.

The reality, therefore, was potentially more what may be called a 'graft' rather than a merger, with the FEM dominating the new RRO. Organisationally, the MAG official quoted above has been proved correct in his assessment. The FEMA is run by the Secretariat, FEMA Committee and Financial and General Purposes Committee, as before, although with a slightly different constitutional base and a revised voting system. Yet the philosophical aims behind the changes remain those that characterised the FEM's previous existence, that is a commitment to equalise differences of size and financial importance between the national organisations in such a way that smaller organisations cannot be overpowered by their more dominant colleagues. More importantly, whilst the numbers of members represented by the FEMA has now doubled to around 400,000, the organisation has not significantly increased its financial income due to the membership fee structure which has an upper limit on dues. As Simon Milward explains:

> . . . when they joined, the members wanted to put a ceiling on the maximum fee payable, so an organisation joins on the basis of a maximum of 10,000 members. That's what they pay for even if they have, like the Swedish, fifty-odd thousand. And then, in FEM, the minimum fee payable was based on 1,000 members and, when we amalgamated, they reduced that to 500. So while we've substantially increased the number of riders we represent, it really hasn't had the same sort of proportional increase in the revenue from organisations.

Clearly, this may affect the organisation's potential effectiveness in its activities unless it can enforce some unpalatable financial decisions in the near future. In the meantime, the Secretariat have been focusing on attempts to meld the two former organisations into a single unit that can maximise its potentiality in order to fight for riders' rights. Again, Milward explains:

> . . . we are still striving to live happily ever after. Obviously, it's increased the workload for us all. Increased also the effectiveness in some ways, because we're able now to deal directly with former EMA members and help *them* develop, and they help *us* develop as well. . . . Increasingly, what we're doing at meetings now is to kind of train, cross-fertilise information and good practice that works in one country and hasn't been thought of, perhaps, in other organisations. And so we're trying to exchange information a lot more on a more formal basis to help all organisations improve and grow. . . . Having

FEM and EMA together means that we now, potentially, have the maximum number of rider's rights organisations in membership in Europe, so all that's left to do now is to improve the effectiveness of everybody. And we're at that stage now, we can really sit down and examine what are the best mechanisms throughout the organisations in Europe, and how we can cross-fertilise those ideas. And we can really start *in earnest* to make the movement as effective as possible, because now we can deal with everybody under one roof, and we haven't got a separate group. I mean, talking with my old FEM hat on, I always thought it was terrible that we couldn't really work with the EMA members, and it seemed such a waste because they were big organisations. But now we can, and so we have the challenge of actually making that process work, and becoming more effective.

To conclude, therefore, the last decade has seen considerable organisational maturation among riders'-rights activists as they have come to respond to the challenge set by the dynamics of the EU and its growing role in European affairs. In the next chapter, we shall focus more narrowly on the activities, strengths and weaknesses of that response.

–9–

The Lobby

As we have already seen, to a large extent the lobby, as characterised by the FEMA, came into existence due to the increase in legislative proposals from the 1980s. It is in this sense that we can understand the BMF's Research Officer, Steven Prower's comment that 'motorcyclists are organised because they feel threatened, and they *very rightly* feel threatened.' Already, by this time, proposals being made in the British Parliament were alerting motorcyclists to potential restrictions. As Ian Mutch, MAG's Public Relations Officer, informs us:

> We had the biggest demonstration MAG had ever held in '88, which we called Riders' Rights Day. The first time we ever got co-operation from the BMF, they joined in on that, which was against leg protectors. Now, Peter Bottomley was Transport Minister at that time, Roads Minister, and he was promoting the idea of them being compulsory, but he back-pedalled on it *very* quickly. But he *definitely* did say he wanted these contraptions made compulsory as quickly as possible. This pulled everybody out of the woodwork who had not been traditional MAG supporters in the past. From the vintage to the boy racers, the cafe racers. You see, on that occasion we got a lot of publicity for over 25,000 bikers in Hyde Park. Not as much as we'd have liked, but we got BBC TV coverage, which wasn't bad. And my feeling is that senior people in the government felt that Bottomley had stuck his neck out too far in promoting these things. I mean, there may be other reasons why he was then moved out of the Ministry of Transport, but he was, and I like to think that we played a part in that. And that was a bit of a watershed for us. Partly because it pulled a lot more people into the game.

Initially, as we have seen, the national RROs had not paid much attention to the EU, concentrating on issues and events within the UK. However, the organis-ations were quick to realise that legislation proposals being made within the EU at the same time would affect riders, and thus required their attention. As the BMF's Government Relations Executive, Trevor Magner argues:

> Traditionally, we hadn't been too concerned about what was going on in Europe because it didn't directly affect us. But when the EC Driving Licence Directive was first drafted and came up, in '87, '88, round about that time. When that first came up we realised that it *would* affect us, and that it was something that national governments would have to go along with.

Consequently, we can understand developments in the late 1980s as due to an increase in potential threat. Yet, as was argued earlier, this threat may also be seen as an 'opportunity' in that it created the conditions for the mobilisation of the lobby. As Tarrow argues, decisions 'to take collective action usually occur in social networks in response to political opportunities. Both challenge and response are nested in a complex social and policy system . . . and experiences of contention and conflict become the resources of both challengers and their opponents' (1994:25). However, at first the two organisations plotted very different routes into the European dimension. Magner continues:

> BMF and MAG became wise to all this, and it was BMF that first sent people over to Europe ... went over to Brussels and had a meeting with the Commission about it. So BMF was first into Europe, and they were totally misled, as it happens. But then, MAG were also concerned and had been liaising with BMF on that before BMF people went over, and started sending people over themselves. Then the way the two things went was that BMF was saying 'Well, why reinvent the wheel? Why not use what's already there with FIM?' which has been around for a long time but had tended to get away from road-riding aspects, only having touring as an interest, and not doing a great deal in terms of politicking, rider's rights issues. So there was a suggestion that we should work through them, whereas MAG tended to look around at other European organis-ations, with a view to setting up a new organisation. A pan-European [organisation]. And that, really, is why we sort of started going separate ways.

The expansion of the motorcycle lobby into Europe was a shock, for both the lobby and the politicians. Simon Milward recalls, 'a number of people have said, "When we first saw you, we thought, 'What the bloody hell's this walking into Parliament?'"' But, in many ways, the greatest shock lay in store for the lobby itself. There was a steep learning curve due to the complexities of the way European government functions.

Proposals for EU legislation take a long and tortuous route. Legislative proposals are formed by the Commission. The Parliament then comments and can propose amendments at the first reading, most of which work is done by committees, with committee opinions likely to be endorsed by Parliament as a whole. Next, however, Parliament's position is sent to the Council of Ministers which decides which of Parliament's amendments, if any, they wish to accept. There, a 'common position' is reached which all member states can support. This is the second stage. These conclusions then return to Parliament for a second reading. Parliament can resubmit amendments which the Council might have taken out, but they can only resubmit amendments which were voted on at first and had been passed. If they were rejected first-time round then they cannot be resubmitted. Neither can Parliament put in new amendments at this stage: all it can do is resubmit. Results then go back to the Council, and the Council of Ministers decide whether or not to accept the

Figure 18 Roger Barton MEP doing his famous Elvis Presley impersonation at the 1996 Euro Demo

Parliament's amendments. If they do not, then the 'conciliation procedure' starts to reconcile the sides. In the conciliation are representatives from the relevant committee, made up of representatives from the political groupings in that committee. One of the Vice-Presidents of the Parliament being, in a sense, a co-chair with whatever Minister is responsible for the issue, will chair the meeting. The member-state representatives are usually civil servants, because of the detailed nature of matters. It is not customary for ministers to fly over for such meetings. The civil servants may be permanently based in Brussels for a particular member state, or can be flown in from the home states. They represent the fifteen member states of the Council. At meetings of the conciliation committee, there is a delegation from the European Parliament which meets the representatives of the fifteen member states in order, basically, to haggle over those aspects on which the Council are prepared, or not prepared, to give way. At this point acceptance, rejection or compromise may be reached. Rejection would lead to no legislation at all, after all of the work involved. Thus compromise is a likely solution.

To a certain extent, the peculiarities of the EU are something that can be taken advantage of, due to the way the Commission and the Parliament are structured in Europe:

> The Parliament has very little powers. We, as a lobby, take advantage of what powers it *does* have to oppose the Commission. And we also, we go the opposite way as well, the

European Parliament wants more power, and if they can find something to have a go at the Commission about, they'll more likely take it on board. And that's what's happened with riders' rights.

This relationship can be reciprocal in that, as one officer comments, 'we've been very closely tied with the European Parliament, and their desire to *enhance* their power, and they've often been using the motorcycle issues in order to do so.' In this way, we may see how a lobby may create political opportunities for MEPs in that politicians 'are unlikely to be persuaded to make policy changes that are not in their interest. Reform is most likely when challenges from outside the polity provide a political incentive for elites within it to advance their own policies and careers' (Tarrow 1994:98).

Yet if merely learning how to plot ones way through the morass that is EU legislature sounds complicated, it must also be borne in mind that, at the moment, the EU is also quite young and thus still evolving. In this sense the current instability is yet another opportunity for the lobby, in that the lack of rigid structures may make it easier to mount challenges against the system (Tarrow 1994). Trevor Magner gives an example of how changes resultant upon the Maastricht Treaty made redundant all previous procedures, whilst also indicating the bureaucratic, and time-consuming, nature of EU activities:

Before Maastricht came into effect, I think it was November '93, but before Maastricht came into effect, everything was on the basis of the Single European Act. Now, the European Parliament had an option, when it was given a reading of a Directive, where they could do three things. They could accept it as it was; they could write amendments, where there was no guarantee that the Council of Ministers, at the end of the day, would actually take any notice of those amendments, or they could reject it in its entirety. And that was all you could do. So, if you were really 'anti' it, you could reject it. Now, on the 100 brake horse power issue, that was voted on in October, under Single European Act rules, and there was an absolute majority, you had to have an absolute majority, which is half of the house, or half of the number of MEPs, regardless of how many turn up at the time, and it was something like 270. They got this absolute majority, and the Directive should have been *dead*, but what happened a few weeks later was somebody said, 'Well, seeing that the Maastricht treaty has now come into effect, it's all going to have to be considered again under Maastricht rules.' So it had to go back to them and be voted on under Maastricht rules, where you had a slightly different emphasis, where you had a middle course that if you did reject something, or you moved amendments, with an absolute majority, you could have a conciliation committee, where members of the Parliament and members of the Council of Ministers would sit around a table and discuss it, and then the Parliament could have the final veto if they didn't agree. But that was the sort of thing where we'd got it all done and dusted, and then some bright spark says, 'Well, because you haven't completed the business while the Single European Act is still in effect, you've got to go back and do it again.' It is *that* sort of thing that you get. But we *learn* the changes of rules quickly, and we adapt, and that is why the motorcycle lobby has been successful.

Bob Tomlins talks about what it feels like to be part of this new 'game':

What we've got is no history, no precedent, no agreed albeit unwritten rules on when you pull the stumps within the European Union. It's all *new*. The rules are being made as we're going along. And Simon's enthusiasm, Simon's drive and, indeed, Simon's lack of appropriate political experience outside of riders' rights were, in that sense, a strength. . . . Simon didn't have that *baggage* with him, Simon pushed on and *we* wrote *new* rules of the games. And *that* is important, and, I mean, our influence in this *evolving*, I mean, it's still almost embryonic, you know, developing political organisation and structure. The dynamism of it isn't *channelled* and *controlled* into distinct lines. Very fluid. And for us to work in that sort of environment, for me, I find it quite exciting.

Riders'-rights activists have thus had to learn how this game works. As two officers comment:

Having to learn the machinations of how Europe works is just like a degree in itself, just about! But, yeah, you try, and you get the basics of it so that you've got an idea, when you're talking to people, that you know how the European Commission or Parliament works roughly. And who does what, and how the voting system works, which is absolutely *disgusting* and this sort of thing. And, yeah, you learn because you want to reach an endpoint, and to get there you have to.

If you're going to play a game it helps to know how the rules work. And one of the reasons that the motorcycle lobby has been successful in Europe is we know how to play the game.

This has meant that, in a comparatively short period of time, a very complex and dynamic set of circumstances has needed to be assimilated. Bob Tomlins, with a wealth of trade-union experience, assesses the political expertise of the motorcycle lobby:

The thing that amazes me, is that I actually think we've got a very *sophisticated* constituency. I *really* do. I am *amazed*. I don't do it often, I mean, Si's our leader, and he's the person that MAG groups want to go and talk to them, but I know quite a few and that, and I, from time to time, two or three times a year, I'll be speaking to a local group on riders' rights. I mean, the thing that always amazes me is that you can have conversations on, in my view, very sophisticated political levels. You can talk to them about the pressures that exist, you can talk to them how Roger Barton's going to be inside the European Parliament and the politics of the Parliament post-Maastricht and, I mean, what I, from my lifetime of political and trade-union experience, recognise as being highly sophisticated political analysis and understanding. And it's there. I actually find that the rank-and-file riders'-rights activist, I would say, is more *aware*, more *in tune*, more *conscious* of what are the issues and what's the machinery that we've got to move inside, than the rank-and-file trade-union member. A *lot* more. . . . I think the average biker *knows* that what he or she is going to be allowed to ride, *if* they're even going to be allowed to ride, is going to be *determined* in the European Union, in Brussels and Strasbourg, and in the United Nations, in Geneva and New York.

This does not mean that the lobby has been without its problems. The first, clearly, as has been alluded to elsewhere, is that the fact of representing a minority makes it hard to apply the pressure necessary to bring about change, or to prevent change:

What lobby group really is effective? We've got no money, we can't suddenly go on strike or withdraw our labour. If we all stopped riding bikes tomorrow the Government would be delighted, I would have thought! So, I know people are irritated because they feel that perhaps we should be achieving more, but I'm buggered if I know how, considering that we are just a group representing motorcyclists. We're not a big organisation at all. And you listen to the same flannel from politicians as all the other pressure groups do. And we're just not important. We only are a small percentage of voters, so why on earth is any politician going to risk his neck supporting us? I try and be realistic. Some other people might say that's being negative, but although I try and set high targets, I don't like to set impossible ones.

The major problem, however, is perceived to be the attitudes of politicians, which have needed to be fought to win recognition that the lobby is a valid political pressure group. One officer refers to attitudes he has encountered:

I don't know, it just seems to be blind prejudice. I don't really fully understand it, but they've got this *fixation* that 'If we encourage motorcycling, there's going to be an increase in casualties and we don't want to be seen to be responsible for increasing casualties.' Then they get onto the sort of environmental side of things and say, 'Oh, motorcycles are polluting because they haven't got catalytic converters.' And you say, 'Well, hang on a minute. Catalytic converters are horribly polluting until they warm up. Plus they increase fuel consumption. They use a lot of resources, in terms of precious metals. And they increase CO_2 emissions, which is the greenhouse gas.' And then they'll say, 'Well. We want to see electric vehicles used.' And I said, 'Well, how do you think electricity's generated? You know, it doesn't fall out of the sky! So what you're doing is trading in a bit of pollution in a city centre for acid rain on Sweden and Germany, but it's all right because they're foreigners so it can go over there, I suppose.' I mean, that seems to be the attitude. So you come up against this entrenched attitude of they don't want to know. Now, the sort of argument I'm using is that racial, religious, sexual intolerance is socially unacceptable, so why shouldn't [intolerance against] the mode of transport people choose to use be equally unacceptable?

This means that riders'-rights organisations initially work with a greater handicap than other areas of political lobbying. This necessitates that activists need to be more thoughtful in their approach to ensure a fair hearing:

> A reasoned argument plays a much bigger part than it does in other political areas, in riders' rights. I mean, you've actually got to *convince* people. You're actually working from a handicapped position. You start off, you go along and you talk to someone about motorcycling, and you are, almost by definition, a Hell's Angel or somebody who is, at best, anarchic, at worst, destructive. And you can only combat that by being *reasonable*, and *making* arguments, and *convincing* people and, importantly, living with what you've said previously. You've got to go back and say, 'I told you it was right.' The ability to say that. So, in that sense, it's a far more consensual area of political of activity.

The lobby, therefore has needed to counteract potentially negative assumptions among those in power and not alienate those from whom they required support by 'playing down their differences' (Tarrow 1994:10), that is, being reasoned, responsible and respectable. As riders have learnt, and Klandermans observes, 'credibility always counts' (1997:50). Much of this, as is suggested above, has to do with appearance, but it is an area, as an MEP suggests, that has become less of a problem in the EU due to Milward's continued presence:

> . . . when I went to this rally, it was interesting from a number of points of view, not the least of which was the fact that some people who I met in a pub before the rally said, 'I know we don't serve our own cause best because we do look fiercesome figures in our helmets and our leathers.' And then, after the rally, a lady came up to me and said, 'I'm a biker but I'm also a grannie.' And Simon has done a lot to make it quite clear to people that bikers aren't yobos. Although they do have a bit of a reputation for being yobos. Because people do look quite fiercesome, and, of course, to people of a certain generation, there is the [Marlon Brando in *The Wild Ones*] aspect of things. And of course, some of the people that you see wear studs and tattoos and all that sort of thing, just like football. . . . But I don't think that that was a particular problem as far as non-Brits were concerned. And, of course, Simon being around all of the time and Roger Barton himself also being a biker, Members of the European Parliament didn't have any particular hang-up about it.

Clearly, this carries the implication that, as with the biking community more generally, it may merely have been a lack of familiarity with riders that may have presented initial problems, but that these have dwindled due to the presence and activities of the international RROs. Such a conclusion is borne out by Roger Barton, MEP:

> [MEPs have come round] in stages. None of us go through many revolutions in our lives, although there's a lot of evolution, and, hopefully, part of that was my appearing

in 'classy' white leathers and I think a colleague's comment was, 'Elvis is not dead, he's just put a lot of weight on.' And, hopefully, that was *one* contribution. And then the systematic argument, in the absence of arguments coming from constituents on other issues, and there was a vacuum there for them to make a real impression, which they did very successfully. And we're now going to be having a celebratory ride annually in Strasbourg, which the local club will provide more than a hundred bikes for. We'll take people out to a wine village or whatever. And it's all helping to shift attitudes, and to see people as people, rather than as objects of Hollywood's creation, you know, nuisances or whatever. And, you know, that's a continuing process. When there was a lobby of Parliament, Westminster, around this issue, I put John Prescott, who was not Deputy Leader of the Party at that time, on the back of a Triumph and we rode down Parliament Square. We went into the Grand Committee Room in Parliament and MPs came up to me afterwards and said, 'We were really frightened that they were going to start smashing things about, or whatever, when we heard that bikers were going to be lobbying us by their thousands.' And we said, 'Why did you think that?' 'But some of them were solicitors, and doctors, and ordinary people and that.' And I said, 'Yeah. And this is a shock to you?' 'Yeah, yeah. Oh, and they were brilliant. They knew what they were talking about.' Well, fine. If that's helped to get people thinking more positively then I'm happy.

As can be seen, much of the acceptance gained has come from the kinds of activities in which the FEMA has engaged. The following quotation, from an MEP, again alludes to the combination of Milward and FEMA's activities:

Simon Milward suddenly became a figure in the European Parliament, and he's always around now. . . . Simon is a very noticeable person, and the others are slightly less noticeable. Less colourful, shall we say. Simon's been around and is well-known not just to British MEPs, but non-British ones too. And Simon organised a demonstration on the question of decibels which persuaded the Parliament. I mean, it was the Parliament that actually said that you could allow bikes to go up to whatever it is. And Simon organised a noise demonstration which satisfied Members of the European Parliament that it wasn't objectionable.

In this way, the lobby has achieved a major objective for social movements: inclusion within the polity. This is crucial because groups 'that are viewed positively by policy makers are more likely to get access than those who are viewed negatively' (Klandermans 1997:171). One particular aspect of FEMA's activities may be held to be especially relevant to its success in the EU, that is the mass lobbying of members by constituents. For many non-British MEPs, FEMA tactics were unfamiliar. An MEP, explains why:

The British are more sophisticated lobbyists than other countries. I suppose because it's more part of our democratic system. Members of Parliament, and Members of the

European Parliament, are used to being lobbied by their constituents. Every time you get a letter from a constituent it is a form of lobby. Other countries haven't quite got the same approach; although the French are beginning to get it. Lobbying is considered to be an Anglo-Saxon technique.

Roger Barton illustrates how this has been used by the riders'-rights movement in the EU:

How [did] the Parliament respond? The first reaction was *shock*. In the UK, it's quite common for MPs to be lobbied by individual constituents. Where you have a national list, PR representation, press, all the other member states, the idea of an individual, rather than a company or a well-developed special-interest group or whatever, the idea of individuals lobbying their elected Members is a complete culture shock. So, initially, they were *amazed* and *astounded* to be receiving letters from individuals, all being co-ordinated and encouraged by their bikers'-rights groups getting together. So the 'common enemy' syndrome of that proposal actually motivated people into doing things that was not normal for them, although it was quite normal in the UK. And, often, Simon Milward and myself would sit down and we'd say, 'We really ought to be trying to get letters in on this particular point at this time.' Simon would have a meeting with his Executive Members from different countries. They would discuss that and maybe change it, whatever. They would send that message on. People would write to MEPs, their individual letters to their individual MEPs in different countries, who would then come back to me and say, 'How should I respond to these letters?' And that's not a *trick* of the democratic process, that's actually activating it. And it's not *manipulating* it, it's saying it *belongs* to the citizen to take part in it.

It is this idea of belonging that is central to an understanding of the success of the motorcycle lobby in Europe, for the primary characteristic of the lobby is that it is carried out by ordinary people crucially affected by European proposals, that is that the lobby is 'a lobby of ordinary people'. This sets it apart from other lobbies in Europe which rely on professionals. As an MEP says, 'it's a very effective and, I think, quite a sophisticated lobby, in the sense that they're not the usual sort of lobby smoothie.' One Regional Rep., talking in July 1997, reflects on the reasons for that effectiveness:

I think it's because we *do* the thing, and we *live* the thing that we're fighting for. And for a lot of other single-issue groups, pressure groups, lobbying groups, whatever, they have an idea about it, and they think, 'Yeah, that would be good. And that would affect a bit of my life in some way or another.' But it's not something that's *integral* to what they do every single day. It's a difficult thing to express, but there's big ideas, like freedom, and freedom is something that you feel every time that you get out on a bike. And you know it. And you know that in society it's not there, at all. And you can tell the difference, almost *instinctively*. I don't think that *gut feeling* applies in *any* other pressure group I can think of. I'll give you an example, let's say the Red Cross, which I'm a member of, that has a campaign against land-mines. And they can do all sorts of new stunts. They can get Princess Diana to go and walk through a mine-field . . . and all the photographers go snip, snip, snip, snip, snip. 'Yes, that's a very good idea. Let's not have any land-mines.' And there's still hundreds of thousands of land-mines everywhere. And the new Labour Government has said, 'Well, yes. We're going to abolish land-mines, except for the ones that are tactically necessary.' Which, presumably, still blow people's legs off. And that hasn't worked. Part of that is that the people doing that campaigning are not, themselves at daily threat of having *their* legs blown-off by land-mines. And the people that *are* under daily threat of having their legs blown-off by land-mines aren't in the best position to fight for it.

It is this connectedness to the subject of the lobby that has led bikers to learn the confusing complexities of the EU which were discussed earlier:

'MEPs and whatnot, I do think they underestimated us. I think they saw it as like a cheap target and, maybe, [saw us as] people who wouldn't know how to fight it, how to react. And, yeah, I think they did totally underestimate us. If you care about something enough, and most bikers *do*, then even if they don't want to actively get in there, like I did at first, they'll join MAG or the BMF or whatever, even with just a bit of their dosh. But they will *find out* how to fight it, and *learn* how, I mean, we didn't know, so you learn how to lobby and how to present cases to MPs and pressure them to actually do something.

Another quotation shows how this operates in practice:

. . . the thing that makes me *reasonably* relaxed about it, is that we have, without *any* doubt, established ourselves as *the most effective* lobbying group in Brussels. Because we are one of the *few* lobbying groups that it is not *professional*. We *act* professionally, I believe, we operate professionally, I think we present ourselves well, nobody can complain about us as being coarse or crude, rank amateurs, or anything like that. *But* we, actually, are *not* a very specific, professional, interest group, and we don't employ professional lobbyists to represent our points. I think, to a large extent, they do [find that refreshing]. I mean, I think Simon is quite wonderful for us, because he is a *biker*. He *looks* a biker. And he goes in and he talks to people and, I mean, you can almost *sense* the initial sort of pulling back in revulsion. And 'This Hell's Angel, he's going to pull a chicken out from under his shirt and bite its head off,' and all this crap. But they *then* see he's such a *gentle* man. He's reasoned, he talks, he's considerate, he's caring. And, in many ways, they sort of switch back on. They switch off in reaction, they switch back on, and they *stay* switched back on. Whereas, the suit turns up and it's probably the same suit they listened to yesterday making a case for whatever. Use of certain chemicals in agriculture or whatever it is. And they don't feel *threatened* by them, and they never switch *on* in the first place, it's just *grey*.

Yet the democratic nature of the lobby, with its roots in individual members in the nation states, is also one of the reasons that MEPs have responded to it, in that, unlike dealing with professional interest groups, the media or whatever, it represents their own voters:

> . . . they're getting support from their constituents. I think, you know, that they like to be seen to be doing what their constituents ask and, also, at the same time, it's happened on motorcycle legislation so far, with the motorcycle lobby, it's a solid grass-roots lobby coming from voters, and them sticking up for us, it increases their democratic credentials, and the longer they hold out for the citizens, for the voters, then the more they increase their credibility with those voters. And it also makes them feel good as well.

As such, overall, we can see that the success of the lobby is due to a combination of people and practices that have enabled it to gain entrance and acceptance within the EU. Bikers, therefore, are becoming 'respectable':

> I think we've shown ourselves to be a responsible lobby, in that we play by the rules, we do work within the law, within the constraints. It's not a case of saying, 'Well, if you're not going to go along with it we're just going to have some massive demo where we're going to flout the laws and just show you.' I mean, it's not anarchistic. So I think we tend to be positive in that effect in terms of attitudes we engender towards us.

> . . . we know people in the organisations and are learning how to communicate better with the people in power, to get them to appreciate our points of view. I assume that's what it is. The years of lobbying through the system and a lot more personal contact. We've now got some very good members who spend a lot of time talking to politicians, to policy makers, and they're not now dismissed as being mindless loonies, they're being accepted as having serious points of view, and are being listened to.

This last point is a significant one, that the motorcycle lobby is now in a position where its opinions are listened to and solicited:

> And what I said a moment ago about we've put down markers and they think long and hard before they mindlessly include the motorcyclist now, is very relevant. I mean, road-worthiness testing is a good example, you know. We picked-up that they're looking to introduce, and it's coming at us from a number of angles, a European MOT system. If that was to become a German-based system then that would be horrendous, absolutely horrendous. Now, we go along to the DG7, to the Commission, and we start laying down all our concerns, you know. Two things happen. The first thing is the Commission say, 'Fine. Okay. Right, we take these points. Yes, we understand. Absolutely. Correctly. You write us the words and we'll put it in the first draft Directive . . .' So, probably for the first time *ever* we're actually going to have legislation affecting motorcycles where key areas, negative areas, we will actually have written the initial words. So we're

negotiating from our position. And *that*, I think, is an indication of the sort of change that *has* occurred, and is occurring. . . . We don't have to bang and scream on doors because doors are open now.

Such an opinion would support M.J. Smith's (1995) arguments that it is those groups that are well-informed and respectable, and who are willing to discuss issues quietly with civil servants rather than try and embarrass governments, which are most likely to influence policies. It is such groups that may be called 'insider groups' – those seen as legitimate by governments and who have access to the consultation process. Further, success means that riders will no longer be seen as the 'easy targets' that they once were, and it is in that sense that we can understand the following comment:

> The main success of the lobby is [in] that legislation that people do not propose. . . . The reason the motorcycle lobby is respected, which is another way of putting 'feared', is because it's energetic, and because it fights to the end, regardless. . . . And the reason that the motorcyclists' lobby *is* almost feared in both Britain and now in Europe, is because motorcyclists have an interest which is organised and which actually *does* do something to look after itself.

Figure 19 The British contingent at the 1996 Euro Demo

The Lobby

This view gains support from the following illustration from an MEP:

> One thing that has happened as a result of the super-bike campaign, and total victory for the bikers on that, is that the Commission now will *never again* make proposals without at least taking full account of the views of the bikers'-rights organisations. Ironically, the bikers'-rights organisations have matured *considerably* in their European dimension, as a result, and I now *regularly* meet with national representatives from many of the member states who're saying, 'How can we advance it further? We want to get into safety issues. We want to get into training. We want to understand good practice. We want to develop it *positively*, rather than be on the defensive.' So maybe the award for maximum contribution to the development of bikers'-rights culture should go to Martin Bangemann, who had put up the stupid proposal in the first place to ban super bikes. Unwittingly, he unified them in a way that nobody had managed to achieve before.

These gains, however, must not be taken for granted. He continues:

> I don't think it's a coincidence that all three main political parties of the UK fought the last General Election on very positive statements on biking issues. And *that* is a testimony to the activity of bikers'-rights people. And it will bear fruit for a long time. It won't be guaranteed and be there for ever, it will require eternal vigilance, as usual. But, that's where it's all going, and they need to keep that momentum.

In some ways, planning the future will be more difficult than in the past, for now that the RROs have won gains, they have something to lose. Acceptance within the system, and ensuring its continuance, may thus require that they must play more by the rules:

> . . . we've had some success and riders are going to expect a similar level of success all the way through, and I don't think that that's necessarily going to be possible. But now, having got to the situation where we *are* being consulted, and at least people are listening to us if not agreeing with us, we've got to be very careful how we go now. We've got to be *less extreme* than we were when we were trying to get in, haven't we? But that's going to piss most of our members off, because they're going to think we're not being pro-active enough. But if we push too hard *now* we could end up being shoved back out the door. So, again, I can't say yes or no, it's such a balancing act, and we could completely cock it up without even realising it.

One point raised here finds much resonance among riders'-rights activists, namely the need to take a more dynamic approach to the future. It is felt that, too often in the past, RROs have merely responded to events and that, hopefully, now with the greater acceptance accorded the organisations, steps can be taken to promote, rather than merely defend, motorcycling. As Bob Tomlins states, 'Our role has always been a reactive one. I mean, riders' rights, generally, is a reactive activity. Legislators, policy makers, decide to do something against motorcyclists, in our perception. We respond to that and try and change it.' He continues:

> . . . what is constant, I find, is the need to actually *analyse* the situation, to *understand* what are the factors and the forces. To *look* at what your options are. To try and develop some strategy, some plan, some *awareness* of where you need to go. And, in that sense, I think that's often been lacking in riders' rights, because so much of riders' rights has been *reactive*, you know. Reactive, and dependent upon committed [individuals].

The general mood is one of considerable optimism, however, in that it is felt that

> There's all manner of positive things that we can now push along. It's a ghastly word 'proactive', but it's being able to put a positive impetus to political change, and do something about it so that bikers are getting a *better* deal, rather than joining an organisation to protect them from getting a *worse* deal.

Yet the success of the motorcycle lobby in its 'arrival' is not the whole picture. As we have noted previously, activists feel that their involvement in the lobby has given them expertise that can be carried into other areas of life, that is that motorcycle issues are just one part of riders' lives, but that their experiences there can also be fruitfully used elsewhere. The success of the motorcycle lobby, therefore lies in its rootedness within everyday life and, because of this, riders have learnt lessons they can also apply that to other areas of their lives:

> . . . let's learn the good lessons from the biking lobby, because it has *connected* a lot of people with the process, because what was proposed, they could see where it directly affected their lives, and they could join common cause with others who felt so threatened. . . . Now, if that has got them thinking about the wider political process, because bikers aren't *just* bikers, they're also citizens who live in houses, who want education, who want health provision, who want all of the other services. But their common bond is biking. And if *that alerts* them to the political process, because Martin Bangemann's stupid enough to make a stupid proposal, good. You know, let's turn that positively. . . . Find common cause and then say, 'How can we apply *those* lessons to making sure that, in future, the *positive* elements of biking are developed, in a very responsible and co-operative and joint method. And how can we apply the lessons that we've learnt from that to other aspects of our lives? And how can we *teach* that experience and lesson to other groups in society? And how can we demand that Europe becomes more responsive to lobbying, and views, and participation of all the citizens?' And it's a continuum.

Part IV
Motorcycling and its Futures

–10–

The Road Ahead

As we have seen, British riders' rights has developed within the ever-changing social and political context of British and, latterly, European conditions, and has needed to respond and grow within these moving circumstances. Yet, currently, changes within the profile of British motorcycling generally mean that the future will contain new challenges to which they must respond. In this chapter we shall examine some of these changes, and how they might affect both the motorcycling community and carry wider social, economic and political ramifications.

Unfortunately, it is not possible to reach definitive conclusions about long-term changes in the profile of the motorcycling community due to a lack of empirical data from earlier periods. As such, one can at best draw inferences as to whether the perceptions across which we have come in earlier chapters, attesting to the young and working-class nature of riders in the past, are based in actuality. However, even if differences between generations cannot be adequately ascertained, it may still be possible to gain a profile of the contemporary motorcyclist who forms the target for both legislative and lobby attentions.

The first clear factor is that, since 1995, motorcycling in Great Britain has been growing after years of decline. Overall, the motorcycle parc, that is, the number of vehicles in licensed use (including scooters and mopeds), grew from 1945 (312,844) until 1960 (1,795,000) – this latter being the highest single year for powered-two-wheeler usage. From this time there was a slight decline each year until 1972 (1,075,770) after which usage then increased slightly each year until 1981 (1,371,000). Numbers remained reasonably steady from the mid-1970s until 1987, when the numbers of motorcycles fell below one million for the first time since 1952 to 978,000, of which 712,000 were motorcycles of all capacities. The decline in use continued throughout the early 1990s to a low of 751,900 in 1994 (excluding mopeds but including scooters) before rising to 758,700 in 1995, 792,200 in 1996 and 836,100 in 1997.

Further, within this overall picture we can uncover change within patterns of motorcycle usage in that, over the last six years, whilst there has been an across-the-board increase in new motorcycle registrations by nearly 50 per cent, the biggest increases can be found in the categories of 501–700cc and over 900cc, from, respectively, 7,972 in 1993 to 28,520 in 1998 and from 6,819 in 1993 to 26,946 in

1998. This is clearly explained by the growth in super bikes sales. In 1996 supersport bikes accounted for 30 per cent of all motorcycles registrations, this rising to 33 per cent of all UK sales in 1998. This can be seen more clearly through looking at the best-selling motorcycles in 1998, which were the Honda Fireblade (3,832), the Kawasaki ZX6R G (3,558), the Honda CBR600 F (3,340) and the Yamaha R1 (3,146) (Motor Cycle Industry Association 1999).

At the other end of the scale, the picture for mopeds and vehicles under 125cc is slightly more complicated. Registrations for mopeds fell between 1989 and 1993, from 22,298 to 5,754, and held reasonably steady between 1994 and 1995, yet there was a rise in 1997, with registrations in this year reaching 12,523 and again in 1998, which saw 22,556 new registrations. The under-125cc category appears to be following this pattern of an overall decline followed by an increase since 1996 with some 17,712 in 1998 (Motor Cycle Industry Association 1995; 1998; 1999). Consequently, we can argue that the overall condition of the powered-two-wheeler market is currently very healthy and that this picture looks set to continue for '1998 saw the highest motorcycle and scooter sales for thirteen years. A total of 120,416 machines were sold, a 30% rise over the previous year' (Motor Cycle Industry Association 1999)

If we attempt to turn from the machines to look at the profile of motorcyclists themselves we uncover problems as figures for the total number, and demographic composition, of motorcyclists are not readily available. Thus, whilst a total of one million riders is generally bruited about by riders, no sources can confirm such a figure. For example, it is not possible to ascertain the total number of riders by licences as the Driver and Vehicle Licensing Agency (DVLA) keeps records of those motorcyclists who hold a motorcycle licence only, with motorcyclists who are also car drivers being subsumed within the full car-driving licence holder's category. Thus, we can say definitively that in July 1997 142,209 males and 17,145 females held motorcycle licences, including those currently facing restrictions. As a baseline, therefore, this establishes that 143,924 full licences are held in Britain. A further 354,023 provisional licences were held, 111,936 female and 242,087 males, of whom 38,999 were between the ages of thirty and fifty. Yet this tells us nothing about those riders who also hold car driver's licences. The DVLA also provide data on vehicles currently licensed. Consequently, we can argue that in December 1996 there were a total of 512,275 motorcycles licensed in Britain, excluding mopeds, of which 225,399 were over 500cc, the largest group. However, this conceals either those riders who own more than one vehicle, bikes which are being restored, customised and so on.

If we look at those passing their tests, Driving Standards Agency (DSA) statistics indicate that, perhaps contrary to popular perception, the numbers gaining a full licence have declined in recent years, picking up only in the year 1998/9. Thus, whilst in 1994/5, 54,467 men, and 5,107 women passed their motorcycle tests, a total of 84,278, (the highest number of tests passed in at least six years), by 1997/ 8 this had fallen to 28,081 men and 7,706 women, a total of 35,787, which increased in 1998/9, to 46,620 men and 9,997 women attaining their licence, a total of 56,617. As we have seen elsewhere, the most significant factor here would seem to be that the proportion for women passing their motorcycle test between 1993/4 and 1998/ 9 rose from 10.76 per cent to 17.66 per cent of all tests passed, a decrease from the previous year's figure of 21.5 per cent. Unfortunately, it is not possible to ascertain the ages of those passing tests because, according to the DSA, approximately 70 per cent of all tests were trainer booked and many of the age details were not recorded. Consequently, no adequate run of accurate statistics is available for examination.

These conclusions, therefore, do not allow us to make definitive statements about the profile of the motorcycling community. As such, we need to rely on research that is based on selective and restricted sampling, rather than figures for the entire motorcycling population. Clearly, these must be used carefully, as there may be a skew in the respondents used which may distort findings. However, they may be of help in uncovering whether, as would seem to be indicated by the profile of vehicles, we have been witnessing a change within the shape of motorcycling since the late 1980s – what Tom Waterer, the Executive Director of the Motor Cycle Industry Association (MCIA) calls the change from a 'need' to a 'desire' based market – a trend that appears to reflect a combination of factors (*Motor Cycle Dealer* July 1995).

Figure 20 The FEMA's Bob Tomlins scares the punters while Simon chats with Ruaraidh

Firstly, demographic factors have affected the profile of the motorcyclist in that the numbers of fifteen to twenty-four year-olds, the traditional core market for motorcycles, are declining in the 1990s with a resultant 500,000 lost potential riders (MINTEL Report 1993). On the other hand, however, the 'baby-boomers', those who accounted for the upturn in trends in the 1960s and 1970s, are now in the thirty to fifty-nine age range. In support of this, the report found that 78 per cent of motorcycles over 500cc are owned by people over twenty-five years old (86 per cent of whom are male). These conclusions are confirmed by the Automobile Association (AA). In their research into the profile of motorcyclists, 42 per cent had ridden for longer than ten years, with this trend being most pronounced amongst those with more powerful machines. Breaking riders into age groups, 81 per cent were over twenty-five years old, including a small, but significant, 7 per cent over the age of fifty-five.

The leisure nature of the pursuit is also supported by this research, which indicated that 51 per cent of motorcyclists also owned cars, with 21 per cent of those who did not having owned one within the last five years. The research concluded that very few motorcyclists ride from necessity, and that the pleasure element was strongest amongst more experienced motorcyclists (AA 1995). These tentative findings are supported by EMAP research which found that 80 per cent of motorcycle usage was for on-road leisure. Within the profile groups, the largest (22 per cent) was characterised as the older biker (46 per cent over forty years old) who rides tourer/sports tourers for leisure, 53 per cent of whom are AB/C1s, and the second largest group (21 per cent) who are the over thirty-year-olds, riding expensive race replicas/sports tourers as 'accessories', of whom 47 per cent are AB/C1s (13 per cent being AB) ('Bike Facts' 1995 EMAP National Publications Ltd). This is supported by the MINTEL Report which found that 40 per cent of those on bikes over 500cc fell into classes AB or C1.

Various factors would seem to support this picture. Firstly, restrictive legislation on tests and the move to car-ownership mean that motorcycling, perhaps for the first time in great Britain, is no longer a commuter necessity but a leisure pursuit. Additional factors accentuating this trend have been the great commuter distances travelled and the increase in women workers, for whom the 'dangers of motorcycling are . . . more acutely perceived' (MINTEL Report 1993). As we have already seen, women who do ride powered two-wheelers are heavily concentrated in the smaller categories. Accompanying these changes is the increasing ownership of cars, and lessening life chances, among young people:

The cost of purchase and ownership of a new motorcycle has become prohibitive for many young motorcycle owners primarily as a result of the recession and unemployment. Consequently, sales of second-hand machines are accounting for a higher proportion of sales among motorcycle owners generally but, more significantly, a greater number of young moped and motorcycle owners are opting for car ownership instead of motor-cycles. This is because of the increase of availability of reliable, low cost, used cars (MINTEL Report 1993).

Related to this, however, are both public perceptions of the dangerous nature of motorcycling, which grew in the 1970s, and the subsequent attempts of government to make the pursuit more safe. As Tom Waterer argues:

Remember the 'Think Bike' TV campaign which graphically showed a car and motorcycle colliding. Intended to raise awareness of motorcyclists among car drivers, it actually was the most negative publicity that could have been devised for motorcycling. Every mothers' son became the lad on the bike in that commercial, and so no wonder Britain's mothers put their maternal feet down and stopped their offspring from riding motorcycles. Ten years later research in schools showed that over 90% of schoolchildren were forbidden to have any form of powered two wheeler. . . . The increase in sales during the 1970s brought with it an increase in motorcycle casualties that society found unacceptable. This social concern was expressed in the media and in political pressure on MPs and the Government to 'do something about it'. That something was the 1981 Transport Act. The Act introduced the Two Part Test and the 125cc Learner bike. As a barrier to getting on a motorcycle, it proved very effective! (*Motor Cycle Dealer* July 1995).

From this we can see that the difficulties involved in starting to ride a motorcycle in the 1980s, with time limits on testing and power restrictions on small vehicles (one could no longer just buy a 250cc machine and ride it indefinitely on a provisional licence), at a time which saw the increasing availability of good second-hand cars, exacerbated the decline in motorcycling. However, as the statistics indicate, this trend is perhaps being reversed in the 1990s by the advent into motorcycling of older riders whilst young people suffer the penalties attached to riding. Put together, it would appear that motorcycling is becoming dominated by the older rider, therefore, who is the main owner of the larger, more expensive motorcycle. This appears to indicate that the polarisation of motorcycles is accompanied by a slight socio-economic trend. Big bikes have a tendency to be owned by older, higher-class males. It is these, with disposable wealth and company cars, who now constitute the major profile for motorcycling. Such conclusions are supported by motorcyclists themselves, who believe that the age structure of motorcycling has changed within recent decades. As a MAG national officer informs us:

The demographics of motorcycling has changed. There's fewer young people getting into it than there were then. Although there's an increasing number over the last few years, for instance. But if you look back to '73, then there's less young people into it.

This clearly carries consequences for the future given that young people need to have experienced motorcycling if there is to be a chance of them being 'born-again'. However, just as clearly, there is a ready understanding of the reasons that young people are no longer joining the ranks of motorcyclists, namely that changes within the testing procedure have made motorcycling a less viable option for the young, as, indeed, has the rising cost of getting a bike on the road. As the BMF's Government Relations Executive argues:

> I think it's mainly down to cost. The Transport Act 1981…. Implemented in 1982. It made access to motorcycling more difficult and, in spite of what the government said when we accused them of it, I believe, it was to make motorcycling more difficult for young people to take up.

A former editor of *Motor Cycle News* (*MCN*) explains further:

> … if you're young, whilst motorcycling is still as attractive as it always was, it's much harder to get into, like what I said earlier in terms of legislation and so on, but it's also much more expensive to get into, and the bikes you can ride are much more limited and much less exciting, and you probably can't afford to insure a big, powerful bike anyway.

Another national BMF official sums up the dilemma for young people:

> … the youngster today is faced with quite a few hurdles to get through his bike test. Compulsory basic training, in the first place. Restricted capacity limits that he's restricted to. He might *see* the Fireblades, the latest GSXRs about, but *he* can't have one of those. He's got to go through these mundane steps of run-around mopeds. I think the latest swoopy scooters, they could well bring a change about because they're very fashionable. I mean, I've looked at those and they're pretty tricked out, they are. They're very nicely styled. The Piaggios and Aprilias and whatnot. They look quite macho, don't they? They've got chunky tyres and disc brakes and upside-down forks and all the rest of it. Now, it wouldn't surprise me, you do get youngsters, in fact, I've seen one or two about, not enough to make a summer, as it were, but, as you know, in Italy, Spain and whatnot, where they've got the weather, youngsters automatically have these things. They tear around on them, popping wheelies left, right and centre. So, you might see that as being an attractive thing to do. I think ordinary, mundane utility motorbikes that the learner would have to buy otherwise, they're not very keen on. Not very good for impressing the girls and all the rest of it.

However, the cost of motorcycling has also increased due to the 'hidden' expense of prohibitively high insurance costs for younger riders. The BMF's Government

Relations Executive continues:

> The other thing is the business of insurance. I mean, some of the insurance companies seem to be quite unreasonable with their quotations. Young people get gonged something rotten. It's all bad news, and I think it's down to that. And the main problem, of course, with insurance companies is that, unlike a government, who is, in theory, answerable, insurance companies are not. You can lobby a government, but if insurance companies decide they want to jack-up premiums, then they jack them up. And if you go through someone like the British Insurance Association, then their response is, 'Well, it's not for us to tell our members what to do.'

Consequently, when adding the disadvantages together, motorcycling is being removed from the possible choices young people could make. One MAG member sums this up, whilst setting it in the context of a country where to discourage motorcycles does not make rational transportation policy:

> From those I have spoken to, it is more expensive. It's *hugely* expensive to insure a bike these days. It's a lot more expensive to take the test, and a lot more difficult to take the test. You can't just go to the local bike shop, buy a cheap bike and get on the road; which you used to be able to do virtually. That's why a lot of people took it up originally. It is no longer a cheap method of transport. It's easier to get a car and, I suppose a lot of it's a parental thing. Parents say, 'Okay. I'll buy you a car, but I'm not buying you a bike.' Though why that is I don't know, because *my* parents bought me a bike. . . . But the way things are going at the moment, where small bikes are being priced and governed to make it expensive and less interesting to start on a bike. I mean, you can buy a fairly perky car when you're seventeen and be allowed to. Whereas, at seventeen, you can buy a 125. You know. Now, if they put the same criteria to cars as they did to bikes, which would not only have the benefit of increasing the sales of small bikes, and the people who buy them, but the environmental benefits of getting some of the bloody cars off the road . . .

Yet although, by discouraging young people from taking up motorcycling, more cars may be being added to already overly congested roads, it is this same factor that lies behind the decision of other motorists to come to motorcycling. The following comments make this argument, with the last two adding additional factors, namely how road congestion is 'bad for business' but also how motor-cycling can relieve the stresses of travelling by car and allow a greater freedom of movement:

> I think, by and large, more people will go into motorcycling anyway because the roads of this country are so congested with cars. Soon, the only way you're going to move anywhere quickly will be by bike.

Mature, well-educated business men, that sit in their nice, big, expensive BMW motor cars, in their traffic jam on the M40, trying to get to work. Suddenly, 'whoom'. Motorbike goes by. And he's in work an *hour* before that business man. He's lost an hour's work, and probably a great deal of money, and he's probably thinking to himself, 'Well, if I buy myself a motorbike I, too, can go past all the business men. And I might get that deal before them. I'm not going to be held up in traffic. I'm going to get to work on time.'

In urban areas you don't get stuck in the traffic, and when you're out in the country, I remember a few years ago going to Scotland and riding along this road like a ribbon across the landscape. There were just two of us on our bikes, didn't see a car for miles. Absolutely wonderful. Yes, you get a marvellous feeling of freedom on a bike. You're sort of exposed to the elements, it's a total experience. I mean all this I'm saying is probably a cliché which everybody else says about it but, yes, that's a very positive thing about it. The freedom, both from constraints in urban areas and when you're out on the open road.

However, whilst this offers practical reasons for more people becoming motorcyclists, riders agree that the main reason for the influx of new bikers is held to be for leisure, a lure which has been exploited quite successfully by manufacturers. One rider observes, 'the manufacturers have certainly been pushing leisure quite hard, where they advertise in the Sunday supplements and that type of thing. The kind of image they're pushing is one of freedom.' What is unclear is the reasons for so doing. Another person ponders, 'I think the manufacturers, I don't know whether it's cause or effect, chicken or egg. I don't know whether they're *creating* the market or *responding* to the market.' Another rider is quite clear, that the manufacturers 'have detected that motorcycling is moving into a leisure market. "These things are smart to have."' The consequences are also seen as being quite clear, 'that with the advent of bikes like the sport bikes, the enclosed plastic things, they're more seen now as a rich man's toy, and it's a second vehicle as opposed to the only vehicle that you use.' Such views are supported by research data:

Demographic changes have changed the nature of motorcycle ownership in recent years, with a shift in emphasis in usage away from motorcycles as an economical means of utility transport to one of leisure . . . the provision of cars by companies to employees . . . has enabled a significant proportion of lapsed motorcycle owners to return to the market to own a large capacity motorcycle as a weekend leisure vehicle. Such dual ownership is particularly suited to the new father type of male consumer. The car is indispensable for family outings with babies and small children while the motorcycle lends itself to more individual enjoyment, independent of the family (MINTEL Report 1993:8).

This trend was first seen in America:

> A new creature has emerged onto the streets of New York and London. . . . Only a
> decade ago, a popular solution to the male mid-life crisis was to acquire a trophy wife.
> . . . Now, the rich man who fears fortysomething has a new, more politically correct
> alternative: the trophy bike. . . . As the limousine, car phone and bleeper become the
> degraded currency of the drug dealer and the estate agent, the new power accessory is a
> motorbike (*The Times* 20/10/93:17).

Reporting on the surging bike sales among lawyer, doctors and accountants in
America, the article reports that almost 70 per cent of Harley Davidson sales in
San Francisco and New York are to graduates, and that the average age of the
buyer is just under forty years. Anecdotal evidence comes from a 43-year-old
corporate lawyer from Manhattan:

> 'You see, while the average teenager was rebelling, we were working for straight As to
> get into Yale, and it's only now we can let it all hang out. . . . Guys my age ride in, how
> can I put it, an ironic way,' he says. 'Aside from the speed, there is no greater thrill than
> passing the waiter your helmet at a good restaurant while other people check their
> overcoats' (*The Times* 20/10/93:17).

Yet this phenomenon is not merely confined to America. Another article sums
up a British reporter's entrance into the ranks of born-again bikers, on discovering
he had ordered a Harley Davidson whilst drunk:

> I mean, look at it from my point of view: twenty years ago I'd had motorbikes because
> they were cheap, because I could build them myself from boxes of bits and because the
> Ministry of Transport could never be persuaded that I could safely drive a car. Suddenly,
> here I was with short hair, a newish Saab parked outside, a second marriage and a set of
> house deeds held by a mortgage company. You would, I promise you, have done the
> same. You and a few thousand other of the middle-class, middle-aged, middle-to-high
> income born-again bikers around Britain (*The Times* 09/07/93:WE/1).

Another attraction that is seen as bringing in new riders is the greater exposure
motorcyclists have had in recent years due to celebrities being seen on motorcycles,
which has changed perceptions of motorcycles:

> Well, it isn't a case of bikers being portrayed in the media anymore, it's a case of the
> media finds out that a *personality* has a bike, usually a Harley, and they print a picture
> of this guy, whoever it is, boxer with the silly accent, Chris Eubank, riding his Harley.
> Wearing all his horsy gear, his jodhpurs and all the other stuff that's eminently unsuitable
> for motorcycles. So they print him. They did a feature on the guy who used to be the
> Chairman at Lloyds . . . who, again, rides a Harley. They do features on Pamela Anderson
> riding a Triumph Thunderbird in whatever movie it was she made a couple of years
> ago. So all this [sort of] thing. It tends to be a case of, 'Look at all these celebs. and

look what they're doing. They're riding a bike.' So, through that, I think, people have realised that they aren't necessarily ridden by thugs. All sorts of people ride bikes.

Taken together, these comments indicate motorcycles have become fashionable consumer items. The question remains, why should this be the case? Theorists have argued that consumerism is central to developments of this nature in that, as Bauman argues:

> [it] stands for production, distribution, desiring, obtaining and using, of symbolic goods. Symbolic goods: that is very important. Consumption is not just a matter if satisfying material greed, of filling your stomach. It is a question of manipulating symbols for all sorts of purposes. On the level of the life-world, it is for the purpose of constructing identity, constructing the self, and constructing relations with others (1992:223).

In this sense, consumption is crucial to the creation, or articulation, of a sense of identity. As Baudrillard has argued, we do not buy specific things to express a pre-given sense of identity, but in order that we become that which we have bought (Bocock 1992). Individuals thus 'play the game of using things to signify who they are' (S. Hall 1989:131). Consequently, 'goods function primarily as symbols' (Lash 1990:40). To relate this to our present discussion, by their new association with high-status groups, motorcycles themselves accrue such qualities, which then transfer themselves to the rider. In so doing, the image of the motorcycle, and of the motorcyclist, may be transformed, whilst at the same time retaining a dangerous edge, to be discussed below, which merely adds to the glamour:

> Harley Davidsons became fashionable: film stars came on them. And what they started to do, the advertising people said 'Oh yeah. We'll start to use Harley Davidsons. Big, butch motorcycles' and all the rest of it. They became a fashion icon. Once that started, it started to break barriers down. And so, now, you get Triumphs latching on. You know, you wouldn't have featured a motorcycle in a film by someone like Pamela Anderson just a few years ago. It wouldn't have been a main thing of something glamorous and dynamic. The last time motorcycles were featured was in *Mad Max*, and then they were evil machines, and evil people, weren't they? So there's been this massive change.

It is because of this higher profile for motorcycles that they have now become 'trendy', they are part of being stylish in the 1990s. Thus, whilst as the following quotation indicates there are many reasons for buying a motorcycle, the style and pose of a motorcycle plays a key part, a part readily exploited in advertising:

> Yeah, it's expensive. You get some guys who are coming back, and they're buying Harleys because they want to *pose*, you get some guys who are coming back and they're buying the fastest race bikes they can get their hands on, because they were always into fast

bikes when they were bikers first-time round. You're getting other guys who're in their mid-forties that are getting old British bikes, because that's what they had first-time around. I know people like that. I know a guy who went out and bought a Royal Enfield Crusader. I know another guy who bought another small Royal Enfield simply because that were the last bike they had, when they were kids.

Further, this 'pose' is not merely about being on a motorcycle, it is about expensive machinery and accessories. The new motorcycle trend is not, therefore, for everybody, but contains strongly elitist overtones. It is the new, fashionable way of indicating financial status; a trend readily understood by manufacturing interests, as a former national official argues:

> . . . all sorts of people, who you would never even thought would get a motorcycle are getting motorcycles. . . . There is, obviously, the element of the congestion thing, a lot of people *are* turning to motorcycling because of congestion. But they ain't buying mopeds! They still want to look the business, yeah, and they're commuting on their BMs and their Harleys and their FZRs and so on. . . . I don't know what the catalyst was but there has been a change, hasn't there? You know, at one time, you went to the bike shop and there was these stereotype bikes, with a big headlamp on the front and so on, and, you know, you'd have this black leather jacket, and this black Berber jacket, and these black leggings, and these black gloves, and you look at the stuff that's available these days and there's no doubt, unfortunately, I'm a dinosaur and I still prefer the black stuff, you know, and if it ain't black it ends-up black because I bike all the year round, but, nonetheless, obviously, a lot of people want bright green leathers, and leathers that look as if someone's been sick down the back and so on. That's what people want and this is serious money, isn't it? It's a *business*. The business people are thinking, 'Actually, what do I want to sell? A £7 anorak, or a set of leathers for £500?' Difficult one this, isn't it? So serving the motorcycling community, the problem of the gear they want, has become big business. Other sorts of businesses are recognising that the people who are motorcycling have got disposable income. You cannot go out and buy those sort of leathers, and those bikes, unless you've got disposable income. You do *not* run a Genesis all the year round unless you've got disposable income. It's much easier to go and get a wreck of a car; £250, run it for a year, dump it. You know, it's silly. Businesses are recognising that and now it's okay, you know, you're a valued customer as a biker, because you've got disposable income. The whole thing's changed, and I don't know why it's changed, but it *has* changed. And it's feeding on itself. The more people who do it, if you like, supposed trendy people who do it, the more it attracts, and the more trendy it becomes. Now the bubble may burst, I'm not quite sure how. We are behind, America is two years ahead of us on this. It is a trendy thing to do.

Motorcycling is consequently becoming more socially acceptable as it becomes more fashionable in social groups with higher incomes and status. As one rider in his seventies comments, 'it's becoming more accepted. It's still got a lot of marks against it, but it *has* to become more accepted because the people who are motorcycling these days are affluent. You can't afford to spend £10,000 on a *toy* unless you've got a fairly large disposable income.' The traditional image of the scruffy, delinquent, working-class biker is thus becoming less prevalent, as it is countered by the extension of motorcycling into middle-class life. Motorcycling has grown up and become respectable. As one 'unreconstructed' biker observes:

> I think it's become more respectable. Because the average age of bikers has got older, because there's a lot of these born-again bikers, because everybody seems to know the bloke next door, or the bloke down the road, who's got a motorbike, or because they used to have one themselves, they can relate more to it.

Social exposure thus accustoms people to the new biker:

> . . . the social profile of the biker has changed. To take an extreme example, HOG members are typically middle-aged, successful business men or people in, how shall we say, aspiring forms of employment. They're not stuck in dead-end jobs as a rule. They're people who command their own destinies. You've got a lot of rock stars getting on them. You've got a lot of professional people getting on them, mostly for fun, but increasingly I see them using them to get to work, certainly in London anyway. You see more people getting off bikes and they've got suits on than ever in the past.

A further factor is that not only are contemporary riders apparently from more affluent socio-economic backgrounds, they are also, relatedly, older than the traditional market. It is, of course, important to bear in mind that this is not merely the case for new riders, but also for more experienced riders, as a 38-year-old regional official points out:

> People in the bike club have got older. I mean, there's people like me and Tod who've have been in the bike club a long time. Tod was a founder member. And when the club was started, when he became a member of the club, and later when I became a member of the club, we were both the typical age of the club – which was like twenty-something. And now we're still the typical age of the club. We've all got old.

However, it would appear to be also a factor among new bikers. A national MAG officer argues:

> There's more people getting into bikes as they're getting older. They realise they've got more disposable income, and there's a born-again biker element. So the thirties plus is the biggest growth area at the moment. I would say it's not all born-agains, and just people rediscovering it, because there's a lot of new people coming into it, realising that biking does hold something for them as well.

Thus if, as we saw earlier, younger people are discouraged from motorcycling by the expense and inconvenience of the test and the related financial costs of actually buying a vehicle, these concerns are not problematic for the older age groups. Yet whilst this indicates that there may be few objective barriers for older riders, given media attention to the issue of the returnee, or born-again, biker and of the '*nouveau*' rider, it is clearly of interest to examine some of their motivations. One factor would appear to be that motorcycles are now much more 'user friendly' than in the past. Part of this is that modern technology means that contemporary riders are less likely to carry out routine maintenance, partially because of the difficulty of working on the more complex modern machinery and also as, given greater disposable income, they do not need to. Two quotations illustrate this point:

It's obviously become more popular because the bikes are much nicer, I think, and there's not so much hard work to go into them these days, I mean, unless you want a project to rebuild, you can go into a dealer's and get something nice and the other thing, as I say, I don't know, they're becoming more user-friendly, I suppose.

There's also the cost of bikes and maintaining them, in that the manufacturers haven't really helped themselves by plugging the leisure market rather than the commuter market. Consequently, bikes have been more techno-whizz, a lot more expensive to buy, and yes, they are more difficult to maintain.

In this way, modern motorcycles are more accessible to those not mechanically minded or without the time to spend on maintenance. Into this category we could therefore place both the older rider, perhaps with a family or heavy occupational responsibilities and also women, as we saw in an earlier chapter. Thus, on a practical level, the attractions of motorcycling may be growing. One rider explains how he came across a potential *nouveau* rider:

Just a little anecdote. I was at my local Honda garage on Saturday, he's a friend of mine, just down in Hall Green, just having a little natter with him, talking about bikes in general. As I came in a very distinguished-looking chap came in and, 'Excuse me,' he said. 'Would you have a helmet bag, only I've lost mine?' To which Harvey said, 'Yep. We've got a whole range here. What sort of helmet is it?' He said 'Oh, it's not a bike helmet, it's a car-racing helmet.' He said, 'I'm not bothered about what it is as long as I can put my helmet in it,' he said. 'To stop it rolling about.' And, 'OK. Well, this one will do. It's general purpose.' 'Fine. OK. How much is that?' Bought it. And then he said, 'You've got some lovely bikes here, haven't you? What do you have to do these days to get a bike licence?' he said. 'I've been looking at these bikes and I fancy one, but I've never had one.' And this guy was nudging sixty and he had an N reg. BMW 325 coupé, but he raced a Porsche RS something or other, forget what it was. That's what he wanted a helmet bag for, his racing helmet. And there was a guy, obviously of some note. Perhaps had his own business. A lot of money. Raced a car. But he actually, for the first time, he saw these very attractive-looking bikes and he had fancied one.

For returnees, born-again bikers, motivations seem to be somewhat different. All of those interviewed mentioned family commitments and financial constraints as reasons for giving-up motorcycling in the first instance, and then a greater financial security as families grew and careers prospered. Below are a selection of such comments:

It's like a chap at training, he had a real meaty bike up until about ten years ago. He was still instructing but everyone was surprised when they had a baby and he didn't use the bike anymore. He obviously used the car, more and more and more. And he hadn't been on a bike for ages and we sort of realised what was happening when he flogged it. Got shot of the bike and we thought, 'Here we go.' Now, all of a sudden, he's decided he's going to have a bike again because the baby's older, and the wife's learnt to drive and he wants to bike again. Not to ride every day like he used to, but to bring out at weekends and have a play.

We sold off our bike to get the deposit for a mortgage and, as soon as we could, we got a bike again.

[People return] because they can afford it when you're older. I mean, *I* took a long break from biking. I took a long break because I started having children, well, my wife did actually, so, out of financial necessity, I had to get rid of the bike and have a family car, to fit them all in. However, when I got to an age, and the children got old enough, where I could afford a cheap bike again, and the kids could actually ride on the back of the bike, I got another one. And maybe it's the same with a lot of other people. There is a period in a parent's life where a lot of people can't afford both and, out of necessity, they have to have a car.

One rider explains how those years of absence felt:

[After we had an accident] my wife insisted that I sold the bike and for seven years I drooled outside motorcycle shop windows and read *MCN* and the other magazines. And decided that it wasn't enough, and I wasn't getting my fix from that and I had to get another. Initially I got a bike to build, I bought a basket case. [So I could let it in on her] gently. And with a lot of help from my friends managed to convert these half a dozen boxes into quite a smart-looking motorcycle. It took fourteen months, but we got there in the end. . . . [So] I'm one of these 'born-again' bikers, that everyone says with distaste. But, actually, a large number of people are doing it. You know, we're quite a strong band, and I don't consider myself a 'born again', I just consider myself somebody who's always loved bikes and just took a break for seven years.

Whilst returnees, like the man above, are clearly enthusiastic about their motorcycling, when discussing both the phenomenon of returnee or *nouveaux* riders or motorcycling generally, three other factors intrude, namely that of the 'different', rebellious and youthful aspects of riding – this despite, as we have seen, that motorcycling is no longer a young person's pursuit.

The first of these relates to a desire to locate a social space in which it is possible to cultivate alternative lifestyles and identities different from conventional ones (Scott 1990). As Gorz has argued, disintegration in contemporary society (for example, lack of job security, unemployment, less working hours) 'forces individuals to look outside work for sources of identity and social belonging, possibilities of achieving personal fulfilment, and activities with a purpose which enable them to acquire self-esteem and the esteem of others' (1993:352). In this sense, the 'difference' of motorcycling is no longer expressed by the social ostracism experienced by riders, particularly in the past, rather its attraction may be due to a desire to escape dull conformity of daily life wherein 'one's identity may crystallise and harden such that ennui and boredom may ensue. One is tired of ones life, of who one has become. One is trapped in a web of social roles, expectations and relations. There appears to be no exit and no possibility of change' (Kellner 1992:142–3). In this context, there is a sense in which riding a bike is associated with a denial, temporarily, of social responsibilities, for 'it is in the sphere of consumption – conspicuous leisure on the basis of adequate disposable income – that many will seek to express their sense of freedom, their personal power, their status aspirations' (Tomlinson 1990:6). To this extent, therefore, it may be argued that these new motorcyclists may be buying into the social imagery of biking and, as we saw with established bikers earlier, viewing positively the very aspects which society condemns – rebellion, irresponsibility, non-conformity and so on. The following quotations all refer both to a desire for rebelliousness and fun, either because this has been denied them in the past or because they are now mature enough to enjoy themselves, whilst also illustrating a clear link between this and a denial of age:

I think it's reliving their youth or, in many instances, living for the first time what was denied to them in their youth. Their mum and dad said, 'Oh no. You're not going out on a motorbike; horrible noise. We'll buy you a little Mini,' or whatever.

What I would say is, perhaps, but I really don't know, is that motorcycles are attractive in their appearance and, for want of a better word, they're probably 'sexy'. You know, it's something different. People *are* getting badged, I mean, the baked-bean syndrome sort of thing, you know. 'I'm in a can, I live in a house, I've got two point four children' or whatever the stats are. Perhaps people are more worldly, and thinking for themselves, and fed-up with the Thatcherite mentality of this driving yourself forward, money, money, grab, grab. Perhaps people are now standing back a little bit from it thinking, 'There's more to life than *this* . . .' I wouldn't mind thinking that they're more *relaxed* about themselves and the future. And they're thinking, 'I'm going to have some fun. The kids have grown up.' Kids are more independent these days, aren't they? Well, while they've got a job, they are. But perhaps the kids have left and they want to do something different, they had to sell the bike, or chose to sell the bike when they were setting-up home. They've now, perhaps, got some spare money and they think, 'I fancy one of these motorbike things.' Recapture their youth, perhaps.

You've got returnees, right, because, basically, biking is *enjoyable*. Now, people, when they weren't so well off gave up bikes out of necessity, they needed a family car and all the rest of it. Living standards have increased. They've got money in their pockets again. They remember they enjoyed biking. They've been through all the boredom of family life and all the rest of it, and they want a bike back to recapture a bit of the excitement and enjoyment they had when they were twenty years younger. It's as simple as that.

They see it as a way of rebelling against, perhaps, a very normal, nice family life, or escaping or whatever. . . . So they're doing this as a way to try and get some of that badness back. That anti-society thing back.

Yet what may be of interest is that not only is this a generation that is in its thirties or forties, but perhaps, more importantly, it is a *specific* generation that is of this age; a generation that was brought-up in, or in the wake of, the 'I'm going to die before I get old' hedonism of the 1960s and 1970s and after of the emergence of biking as a distinctive youth lifestyle during the new consumeristic 1950s (Bocock 1992). As Featherstone and Hepworth argue, 'the 'baby-boomer' generation which explored counter-cultural lifestyles in the 1960s are now entering what used to be called 'middle age'. As they do so they are taking with them many of the values and cultural tastes of their youth' (1991:375). Further, age-related behaviour and self-presentation are seen as in decline as 'children become more adult-like and adults more childlike' (1991:372). They argue that 'there *are* signs that, for certain sections of the population in entering *middle age* (in particular the middle classes), images and expectations are gradually beginning to change; a new language of ageing with a much greater expressive range has been gradually emerging.' Consequently, the 'public stereotype of middle age as a kind of 'mature' interlude with relatively unambiguous physical and psychological boundaries between young adulthood and declining old age has been replaced by an ideal of active, prolonged mid-life which has more in common with youth than age' (1991:383). Three quotations, two from males in their forties and the other from a female rider in her thirties, illustrate these points, whilst the latter also connects this to the resurgence of motorcycling among the thirty-plus age group. What they indicate is that part of the rebelliousness of being a rider may, to a large extent, be a rebellion against time:

> I still feel eighteen when I'm on a bike.

> An expression the station commander uses quite regularly to me at work is, 'When are you going to grow-up and get rid of that bike?' And I tell him I'm *never* going to grow up.

> You can be one of the Wild Bunch. That's why there's that resurgence in that sort of group, as a little way of stating your independence and your individuality. You're not old yet. I think that's the prime thing, you're not old. Because people these days don't get old anymore. If you were forty, forty years ago, you were old, but you're not anymore. . . . You remember people who you knew [when you were young] who were thirty-five, forty, and they were old. So, consequently, you're not old. 'I'm not old at all. I'm going to go out and blat on my motorbike . . .' we're trying to pretend that we're not this age.

As such, a denial of age, of 'not acting ones age', is perhaps explicable. This being the case, the motorcycle, with its youthful and rebellious symbolism, makes an ideal companion in this scenario for 'style is a device of conformity, or of *opposition*' (Ewen 1990:43, my italics). It still symbolises these qualities yet as, objectively, its riders are neither youthful nor rebellious, this may be seen more as a subjective attempt at wish-fulfilment. Further, motorcycling is also eminently suitable to such a task by virtue of the dress involved and the 'hidden' nature of the rider. Firstly, if, as Lurie argues, there are social beliefs concerning age-related clothing in that they 'transmit age-related messages, and when men or women do not dress to their age society may be offended' (Featherstone and Hepworth 1991:380), then motorcycling, with its uni-sex, uni-age utilitarian leathers, enables individuals to avoid such 'age-coding'. Secondly, by wearing leathers and helmet, individuals can also temporarily 'escape' their age, both to themselves and others, in that they are hidden – ageing face behind one's visor, and thickening waist within the confines of leathers. For a while, therefore, one may be a young rebel. As such, the rise of motorcycling among middle-aged, middle-class individuals may be explained by understandings of the role of consumerism in contemporary society, with it related media messages of youth and adventure, in conjunction with a specific age group with disposable income. That such people come to motorcycling may be explained by the romance and excitement of riding combined with a sense of danger not experienced in routinised daily life. What we may be witnessing, therefore, is the 'gentrification of rebellion', as older, middle-class people choose association with the imagery and lifestyle of motorcycling. It is in this sense that we can understand Tester's comment:

> Postmodernity involves acts and practices of self-definition and reflexivity. Consequently it is only possible to the extent that the resources of self-definition are already and

relatively readily available. For example, I can only choose to dress in one way as opposed to another . . . to the extent that, firstly, I possess accurate information about the symbolism and the cultural meanings of different codes of dress, secondly, I have the money or the wherewithal to be able to have access to the necessary clothes and, thirdly, that I possess the resources (which might well revolve around physical attributes as much as social and cultural ones) which will enable me to be accepted by the host community (1993:140).

On a political level, however, and irrespective of riders' wishes, the actual age of the modern rider is, indeed, of positive benefit to riders' rights in that middle-aged, middle-income riders are more likely to be listened to by politicians. As such, on one level, to have born-again and *nouveaux* riders 'in your ranks makes you stronger, it's a real asset' in that 'a lot of them hold very responsible positions, maybe in business, in commerce or whatever, and they can affect policy.' Two national officers, from MAG and the BMF respectively argue this point, the first stressing the non-aligned nature of motorcycle politics, and the second how the socio-economic profile of motorcyclists makes them a hard target for attack:

And I think that what is clear is that we don't challenge the system, we're not party-political, we're not anarchists, we will work with whatever system prevails and, because so many of our members *now*, and bikers generally, are part of the system and have prospered within it, because they're professional people and are doing okay, the possibility of nurturing and exploiting that empathy is far greater than it would have been twenty years ago.

I think it's important to recognise the *change* that has happened in motorcycling. There has been a real big change recently. And there's pointers towards telling you where that change has occurred and what has happened. In April, a 47 per cent increase in new bike sales from the previous year. Twenty-three per cent increase the previous month, in *February* for Christ's sake! We're talking Tourers, we're talking Harleys, we're talking 916s, big ones. The type of people coming to motorcycling has changed. It's because of the high insurance costs, because of the difficulties in getting licences, in so much as there is a fiscal difficulty. The age group of motorcyclists has shifted, and it's your thirties and forties, you know. The majority of bikers are in their thirties and forties now. MAG members as well! And that's a difference. So what you've got now is you haven't got a bunch of politicians passing laws against teenagers who simply want to go out and enjoy themselves. Couldn't be bothered to lobby, just want to be rebellious. The *target* is harder. [They're all tax-paying citizens], in professional jobs. It's a harder target. Motorcyclists have become, not just through the build-up in their skills in lobbying, but because of the demographic changes they've become a harder target as well. And also they've become *better*, because of that, in lobbying. [So they're harder to ignore; because of who they are, what they are and what they're capable of doing.]

The influx of these new riders into the community, in addition to bringing riders' rights into alignment with characterisations of other social movements, therefore means that the movement may be in a position to draw on their resources (educational, professional, social attributes and so on), in furthering collective goals due to their ability to associate with political elites (Melucci 1989; M.J. Smith 1995). Yet there is also considerable scepticism among riders about the new influx of bikers. Firstly, there is concern that the leisure rider will undermine motorcycle politics, in that, if motorcycling is seen merely as a hobby, political issues affecting it will not be treated seriously. One BMF national official observes:

> I mean, nowadays, one of the reasons it's slightly more acceptable, perhaps, is that people are slowly realising that a Fireblade costs a lot of money, a one-piece leather costs a lot of money, a crash helmet costs a fortune. The general public is starting to equate motorbikes with elitist leisure pursuits, and yuppies and what have you. So that's part of the reason, I believe, why we're slightly more acceptable. That's got something to do with it as well. *But,* if we carry on down that road then people are going to say, 'But motorbikes are only used for leisure so, therefore, if we're going to start banning leisure vehicles from the road, they should be the first to go, these superbikes.' So we are trying to focus people's minds on the fact, my little old 400/4 in the garage there is more important than Graham's Fireblade, because it takes me from here into work, or school or whatever *everyday*. It is an *important* form of transport to me. Without it I wouldn't have the flexibility to stay late, attend late lectures, or parties or whatever else, I'd have to worry about the appalling public transport, the possible dangers to my person and all the rest of it. So that 400/4 is a *lot* more important than Graham's Fireblade. He won't have it! But in the big scheme of keeping motorcycles on the road [it is].'

Perhaps more importantly, activists are concerned that the leisure rider is not committed to motorcycling and will therefore play no part in ongoing campaigns to protect the right to ride. Various quotations reflect this fear:

> I mean, they're generally weekend wallies. You know, 'I bought a Fireblade this week and next week I'm going to sell it and buy a jet-ski.' You know, they sell one to buy the other because it's the fashion accessory of the month.

> Clearly, if all our eggs end up in the executive basket then I think we are increasingly vulnerable. You take away his toy, or her toy, as the case may be, and what do they then do? 'Oh, I'll go and buy a yacht or learn to fly an aeroplane' or whatever the case may be, to get their thrills, their kicks. I think they're unlikely to [fight for it as much]. A lot of these executive bikers that I meet, and we've got a great deal in common, often not least of all age and some experience, I mean, they're actually relishing their new R1100, RS BMW with all its gismos, and the fact that it's got built-in leg protectors and probably next year going to have an airbag as an optional extra etc. etc. etc.. I mean, it's part of it. The throw-up display like some jet fighter pilot. I mean, it's part of it.

I mean, to a guy who goes out and spends £12,000 on a Ducati 916, or whatever they cost these days, *he*'s not going to want to get his hands greasy doing regular maintenance on it. He's going to take it into a garage. So if someone comes along and says, 'Well, we're actually bringing in a law which is going to make it impossible for you to do that, even if you *want* to,' it doesn't really matter.

Yet perhaps established bikers are being unfair here in that, after all, the new riders *have* chosen a motorbike rather than a jet-ski in the first place. Clearly, therefore, born-agains and *nouveaux* are riding because they want to. As a self-confessed rocker from the 1960s maintains:

... the bottom line is people ride motorcycles because they enjoy them. You know, they wouldn't go back on them if they didn't enjoy them in their youth and they wouldn't stay on them very long if they didn't enjoy them when they were older. ... They *know* what they want and, if they don't *get* what they want, they won't do it.

Further, riders may also be under-estimating these groups. As Bourdieu (1984) has pointed out, social groups do not necessarily unify to defend or promote their common interests without the additional influence of factors such as political mobilisation. Consequently, the extent, or not, to which new riders become part of the community may in the future reflect more on the activities of the RROs themselves: it may be up to the community to make sure that new riders feel at ease in its midst. On another note, a more pressing and practical concern is felt among riders about the consequences of high accident rates among born-again or *nouveaux* riders. There is considerable concern that the riding skills among these groups is such that motorcycling will get a bad reputation for being dangerous once more. As one Regional Rep argues:

It is changing with our leisure-pursuit motorcyclists. The rich crowd in their coloured leathers and all. Okay, they're a different breed, and they're, well, they're doing us a lot of harm, because a lot of them ride like complete twats on the road. They're doing us an awful lot of harm.

Such comments would appear to be reflected in statistical data. Britain's largest insurance intermediary estimates that whilst born-again riders represent 15.2 per cent of their clientele they constitute 27.6 per cent of fault accidents and 27.6 per cent of all thefts. Thus they are almost twice as likely to have an accident or a vehicle stolen than more experienced riders. Quite obviously, this concerns the community which feels it may face higher insurance premiums in the future. Again, notice how, in the first quotation, there is a sense of ambivalence towards the new riders, that their presence is both desirable and undesirable to the established motorcycling population:

> You've got these people . . . that are starting to ride Fireblades when they've only had a
> licence for a year or two, and they're going to have accidents, and it's going to artificially
> make the accident statistics make motorcycling appear to be more dangerous than it is,
> and that also is going to help *push* us off the road. So, unfortunately, this leisure thing,
> while it's doing us a favour on the one hand because it's getting us away from the hairy-
> arsed biker in a cut-off and loads of beer and what-have-you image, on the other hand,
> we are now being seen as not a serious form of transport, and I know there's a real fear
> that the accident statistics are going to be artificially inflated because of these [people].
> You know, it's the new hot-hatch, isn't it? And I know there were a lot of accidents
> when the youngsters started driving around in hot-hatches, so I don't see why it shouldn't
> happen now when they're riding around on their Fireblades and stuff. [So on one hand
> they're good for our image, nice middle-class people] but if they have accidents they
> could do us no good whatsoever. And also they may make motorcycling seem to be a
> trivial pursuit that, perhaps, should be one of the first things to go. You know, these
> great, big superbikes, when somebody wants to do something about pollution, 'Let's
> get rid of them.' To a certain extent, much as I don't think you shouldn't ban anything,
> how can you justify owning a superbike?

> I think one of the issues that affects ordinary people that ride bikes is the cost of things,
> and I think that's what's making biking more a middle-class, 35-year-old, professional,
> male, weekend pursuit. It's becoming like sailing or something like that. I think that's
> what is a real threat to the ordinary people who ride Guzzis, who ride old rat bikes,
> because you can't necessarily get parts, the insurance is expensive because these people
> are pushing the insurance up because they kill themselves. . . . A lot them have done a
> CBT on a course for, perhaps, a week. They've ridden a bike the bare minimum of
> times to get the licence, and they've gone out and bought themselves a status symbol,
> something they think will look a bit flash in front of their mates. And they kill themselves.

To conclude, the changing nature of the community, with the advent of the
born-again and *nouveau* rider, coupled with the decline of young riders, has skewed
the socio-economic profile of the biker in a way that presents new challenges both
to the community generally and to riders'-rights organisations. On one hand, we
have seen that these riders may be likely to add considerably to the political power
that riders'-rights organisations can bring to bear on the political process yet, on
the other hand, public perception of motorcycling may once again come to see it
as dangerous, insurance premiums may rise and there is some doubt as to whether
such riders will participate in any fight to protect motorcycling. However, should
they continue to ride, and thus become more experienced and, perhaps, come to a
greater understanding of the nature of threats posed to British motorcycling, it is
equally possible that they may come to form a crucial component in British riders'
rights in the coming years. Of one thing riders seem certain: that new riders will

have the time to achieve this integration, should they so desire:

> Despite the range of threats ahead – and over the horizon – there are also great strengths in the motorcycle community and many opportunities to make change for the good. Some people think the motorcycle is a product at the end of its 'life-cycle', but the world is not going to – overnight – run out of oil, fail to find an alternative for fossil fuels, give up its dependence on the car or lose its taste for personal mobility. The motorcycle is not an outmoded anachronism, it's a legitimate part of the jigsaw that will help us to create more sustainable transport patterns. If we didn't have them already we'd have to invent them.

Conclusion

Various themes concerning social movements were raised in the introduction which, hopefully, it is now possible to understand more clearly. Our central questions surrounded the ways in which people become involved in a community, come to identify their interests and thus become politically active. Yet there were also secondary concerns about the nature of contemporary forms of political engagement, namely whether it signifies a departure from the politics associated with the conventional political parties and the extent to which it interacts with traditional political structures.

However, our first task is to assess whether the riders'-rights movement can be seen as a valid social movement in its own right. In the introduction we looked at various factors that help establish a definition of what constitutes a social movement – such as common interests and identity, mass mobilisation potential (Scott 1990) and opponents (Tarrow 1994). In terms of goals, such movements may seek either to change society or the relative position of a group in society (Scott 1990). They are also not necessarily structured alike, but may best be viewed as forming a continuum from informal networks to formal associations. Consequently, we may additionally find that there are related pressure groups that seek to influence public policy (M.J. Smith 1995). It is believed that all of these characteristics have been discovered within the riders'-rights movement, and that it thus may be classified as a sectional social movement, acting to defend the interests of a specific social grouping both informally, at the social level, and formally, at the political level (Willetts 1982; Scott 1990). Yet our main concerns were to establish how this is experienced by the individuals who comprise the movement.

Through the testimony of individual bikers we have seen the different factors that draw people to riding and how, through their experiences as bikers, they come to perceive the threats to motorcycling. These threats were divided into two main areas. Firstly, the last forty years has seen the, now seemingly diminishing, cultural stigmatisation of biking which has exposed riders to many different types of social exclusion, albeit being barred from a pub, avoided on the street or portrayed as a mindless hooligan on television. The second type of threat is more recent and, indeed, one could argue that without prior stigmatisation this trend might not have developed as it has, that is the increasing legislative threat that is interpreted as attempts, on the part of politicians and bureaucrats, to deny bikers the rights to autonomy and self-expression. These factors provided the main reasons why our activists came to political involvement and thus lie behind the development of the riders'-rights movement.

These goals are in accord with arguments we encountered in the introduction, which proposed that, unlike the old social movements which were primarily concerned with material and political goals, the new social movements are largely concerned with the cultural expression of non-material goals (Melucci 1989; Perrryman 1994; Koopmans 1995; Plotke 1995; Routledge 1995). Clearly, in some ways we can see how the riders'-rights movement differs from traditional politics. Like many other single-issue groups, it does not have a coherent belief system, or world view, that offers explanations and solutions in all fields of life, like, for example, socialism or Marxism. Consequently, we do not hear about biker policies on third-world debt, the health service, education or whatever, except, perhaps, like anyone else, on a Friday night after a few beers. This, therefore, is a much more piecemeal philosophical position than that of the old social movements. Different bikers are free to hold differing political positions without the need to toe a party line. Yet there are some common unifying themes that form the basis for biker politics in that, as we have seen above, there is a clearly felt sense of grievance behind which lie more nebulous claims to personal freedom, justice and decent moral treatment

As such, we can see that there are strong cultural foundations underlying the riders'-rights movement. These philosophical concerns from its rootedness in the social networks and lived experience of the motorcycling community, a factor which is supported by the evidence suggesting that political involvement was greater among those riders who had a longer involvement with riding. Further, in relation to current theorisations of the politics of choice, we have repeatedly heard how important choice is for bikers, technologically, culturally and politically. As such, the political fight for the right to ride is cultural; the two are intertwined. Consequently, we might argue that the people whose stories we have heard may be activists, but they are bikers first and came to political involvement in order to defend a culture perceived as under attack, a choice which was often made at great personal costs to themselves.

This has drawn them into engagement with traditional forms of political institution, for this is where legislative and political power lie. Even here, however, the complexity of the relationship between the cultural and the political is clear for the legitimacy of the lobby politically again comes from this connectedness to the motorcycling community. We have seen that, whilst still in its infancy, the lobby is growing and becoming more sophisticated and has begun to play its part in the creation of political agenda in the EU. Whether it can continue to do this in the future will depend upon resources, in terms of money and personnel, yet this itself will depend upon whether the lobby can maintain the support of bikers themselves. In this equation the actions of the new generation of riders will be critical; whether they will view motorcycling merely as a weekend pastime or whether they will be prepared to defend their rights to ride if necessary.

The possibilities for this occurring depend upon the one question that it has not fallen within the remit of this work to answer, for, whilst we can see the dialectical relationship between the culture and politics of motorcycling through our examination of those who have made the transition from merely 'being a biker' to 'being a biker politically', we have not been able to answer what, perhaps, may become the more salient question in the future: why do not all bikers make this quantum leap? Thus, our final question mirrors our first: for if we can now see why some people come to act on behalf of all then why, like a car driver when confronted by the bright headlights and insistent growl of an oncoming motorcycle, do other people seem to be able to see nothing at all?

Useful Addresses

The British Motorcyclists' Federation
Jack Wiley House
129 Seaforth Avenue
New Malden
KT3 6JU
Tel: 020 8942 7914
Fax: 020 8949 6215
E-mail: bmf@compuserve.com

Federation of European Motorcyclists' Association
Rue des Champs 62
1040 Brussels
Belgium
Tel: 00 32 2 736 9047
Fax: 00 32 2 736 9401
E-mail: fema_ridersrights@compuserve.com
Web site: http://www.fema.ridersrights.org

Motorcycle Action Group
MAG Central
P O Box 750
Rugby
CV21 3ZR
Tel: 0870 444 8448
Fax: 0870 444 8449
E-mail: maghq@mag1.demon.co.uk

Bibliography

Adams, J. (1995), *Risk*, London: UCL Press.

Aronowitz, S. (1992), *The Politics of Identity: Class, Culture, Social Movements*, London: Routledge.

Automobile Association, unpublished report, compiled in 1995.

Barrington Moore, Jr. (1978), *Injustice: The Social Bases of Obedience and Revolt*, Basingstoke: Macmillan.

Bauman, Z. (1989), *Modernity and the Holocaust*, Cambridge; Oxford: Polity; Blackwell.

Bauman, Z. (1991), *Modernity and Ambivalence*, Cambridge; Oxford: Polity; Blackwell.

Bauman, Z. (1992), *Intimations of Postmodernity*, London: Routledge.

Becker, H. (1963), *Outsiders*, New York: Free Press.

Blasius, M. (1994), *Gay and Lesbian Politics: Sexuality and the Emergence of a New Ethic*, Philadelphia: Temple University Press.

Bocock, R. (1992), 'Consumption and Lifestyles', in R. Bocock and K. Thompson (eds.), *Social and Cultural Forms of Modernity*, Cambridge; Oxford: Polity; Blackwell.

Bourdieu, P. (1984), *Distinction: A Social Critique of the Judgement of Taste*, London: Routledge.

Bradley, H. (1996), *Fractured Identities: Changing Patterns of Inequality*, Cambridge: Polity.

Brunt, R. (1990), 'The Politics of Identity', in S. Hall and M. Jacques (eds.), *New Times: The Changing Face of Politics in the 1990s*, London: Lawrence & Wishart.

Cohen, A.P. (1985), *The Symbolic Construction of Community*, Chichester; London: Ellis Horwood; Tavistock.

Cohen, S. (1980 edn), *Folk Devils and Moral Panics: The Creation of the Mods and Rockers*, Oxford: Martin Robertson.

Collyer, D. (1973), *Double Zero: Five Years with Rockers and Hell's Angels in an English City*, London: Fontana.

della Porta, D. (1992), 'Life Histories in the Analysis of Social Movement Activists', in M. Diani and R. Eyerman (eds.), *Studying Collective Action*, London: Sage.

Downes, D. and P. Rock (1982), *Understanding Deviance: A Guide to the Sociology of Crime and Rule Breaking*, Oxford: Clarendon Press.

Eder, K. (1993), *The New Politics of Class: Social Movements and Cultural Dynamics in Advanced Societies*, London: Sage.

EMAP National Publications Ltd, 'Bike Facts', research presentation, compiled in 1995.

Ewen, S. (1990), 'Marketing Dreams: The Political Elements of Style', in A. Tomlinson (ed.), *Consumption, Identity and Style: Marketing, Meanings and the Packaging of Pleasure*, London: Routledge.

Featherstone, M. and M. Hepworth (1991), 'The Mask of Ageing and the Postmodern Life Course', in M. Featherstone, M. Hepworth and B.S. Turner (eds.), *The Body: Social Process and Cultural Theory*, London: Sage.

Friedman, J. (1992), 'Narcissism, Roots and Postmodernity: The Constitution of Selfhood in the Global Crisis', in S. Lash and J. Friedman (eds.), *Modernity and Identity*, Oxford: Blackwell.

Gallie, D. (1983), *Social Inequality and Class Radicalism in France and Britain*, Cambridge: Cambridge University Press.

Garner, R. (1996), *Contemporary Movements and Ideologies*, New York: McGraw-Hill.

Giddens, A. (1979), *Central Problems in Social Theory*, Basingstoke: Macmillan.

Giddens, A. (1990), *The Consequences of Modernity*, Cambridge; Oxford: Polity; Blackwell.

Goffman, E. (1963), *Stigma: Notes on the Management of Spoiled Identity*, Harmondsworth: Penguin.

Gorz, A. (1993), 'The Condition of Post-Marxist Man', in T. Docherty (ed.), *Postmodernism: A Reader*, London: Harvester Wheatsheaf.

Hall, M.F. (1995), *Poor People's Social Movement Organizations: The Goal is to Win*, Westport: Praeger.

Hall, S. (1989), 'The Meaning of New Times', in S. Hall and M. Jacques (eds.), *New Times: The Changing Face of Politics in the 1990s*, London: Lawrence & Wishart.

Hall, S. and D. Held (1990), 'Citizens and Citizenship', in S. Hall and M. Jacques (eds.), *New Times: The Changing Face of Politics in the 1990s*, London: Lawrence & Wishart.

Hall S., D. Held and T. McGrew (eds), (1992), *Modernity and Its Futures*, Cambridge; Oxford: Polity; Blackwell; Open University Press.

Harris, I.R. (1986), 'Myth and Reality in the Motorcycle Subculture', University of Warwick, (Unpublished PhD).

Hebdige, D. (1990), 'After the Masses', in S. Hall and M. Jacques (eds.), *New Times: The Changing Face of Politics in the 1990s*, London: Lawrence & Wishart.

Hogg, M.A. and D. Abrams (1988), *Social Identifications: A Social Psychology of Intergroup Relations and Group Processes*, London: Routledge.

Inglehart, R. (1977), *The Silent Revolution: Changing Values and Political Styles among Western Publics*, Princeton: Princeton University Press.

Kellner, D. (1992), 'Popular Culture and the Construction of Postmodern Identities', in S. Lash and J. Friedman (eds.), *Modernity and Identity*, Oxford: Blackwell.

Klandermans, B. (1997), *The Social Psychology of Protest*, Oxford: Blackwell.

Koopmans, R. (1995), *Democracy from Below: New Social Movements and the Political System in West Germany*, Oxford: Westview Press.

Lash, S. (1990), *Sociology of Postmodernism*, London: Routledge.

Mayer, M. (1995), 'Social Movement Research in the United States: A European Perspective', in S.M. Lyman (ed.), *Social Movements: Critiques, Concepts, Case Studies*, Basingstoke: Macmillan.

Mazey, S.P. and J.J. Richardson (1993a), 'Interest Groups in the European Community', in J.J. Richardson (ed.), *Pressure Groups*, Oxford: Oxford University Press.

Mazey, S.P. and J.J. Richardson (eds), (1993b), *Lobbying in the European Community*, Oxford: Oxford University Press.

Melucci, A. (1989), *Nomads of the Present: Social Movements and Individual Needs in Contemporary Society*, London: Hutchinson Radius.

MINTEL, 'Motorcycles in the UK', unpublished report, compiled in 1993.

Mulgan, G. (1994), *Politics in an Anti-political Age*, Cambridge: Polity.

Pakulski, J. (1995), 'The Decline of the Marxist Paradigm', in L. Maheu (ed.), *Social Movements and Social Classes*, London: Sage.

Parkin, F. (1971), *Class Inequality and Political Order: Social Stratification in Capitalist and Communist Societies*, London: MacGibbon & Kee.

Perryman, M. (ed.), (1994), *Altered States: Postmodernism, Politics, Culture*, London: Lawrence & Wishart.

Plotke, D. (1995), 'What's so New about New Social Movements?', in S.M. Lyman (ed.), *Social Movements: Critiques, Concepts, Case Studies*, Basingstoke: Macmillan.

Routledge, P. (1995), 'Resisting and Reshaping the Modern: Social Movements in the Development Process', in R.J. Johnston, P.J. Taylor and M.J. Watts (eds.), *Geographies of Global Change: Remapping the World in the Late Twentieth Century*, Oxford: Blackwell.

Rush, M. (1992), *Politics and Society: An Introduction to Political Sociology*, Hemel Hempstead: Harvester Wheatsheaf.

Rutherford, J. (1990), 'A Place Called. Home: Identity and the Cultural Politics of Difference', in J. Rutherford (ed.), *Identity: Community, Culture, Difference*, London: Lawrence & Wishart.

Scott, A. (1990), *Ideology and the New Social Movements*, London: Unwin Hyman.

Seidman, S. (1992), 'Postmodern Social Theory as Narrative with Moral Intent', in S. Seidman and D.G. Wagner (eds.), *Postmodernism and Social Theory*,

Oxford: Blackwell.

Smith, M.J. (1995), *Pressure Politics*, Manchester: Baseline Book Co.

Smith, S.L. (1998), 'Athletes, Runners, and Joggers: Participant-group Dynamics in a Sport of "Individuals"', *Sociology of Sport Journal*, Vol. 15, no. 2, 174@93.

Tarrow, S. (1994), *Power in Movement: Social Movements, Collective Action and Politics*, Cambridge: Cambridge University Press.

Tester, K. (1993), *The Life and Times of Postmodernity*, London: Routledge.

Thompson, H.S. (1966), *Hell's Angels*, Harmondsworth: Penguin.

Thompson, K. (1992), 'Social Pluralism and Post-modernity', in S. Hall, D. Held and T. McGrew (eds.), *Modernity and Its Futures*, Cambridge; Oxford: Polity; Blackwell; Open University Press.

Tomlinson, A. (1990), 'Consumer Culture and the Aura of the Commodity', in A. Tomlinson (ed.), *Consumption, Identity and Style: Marketing, Meanings and the Packaging of Pleasure*, London: Routledge.

Touraine, A. (1992), 'Beyond Social Movements?', in M. Featherstone (ed.), *Cultural Theory and Social Change*, London: Sage.

Ware, A. (1986), 'Political Parties', in D. Held and C. Pollitt (eds.), *New Forms of Democracy*, London: Sage.

Willetts, P. (1982), 'The Impact of Promotional Pressure Groups on Global Politics', in P. Willetts (ed.), *Pressure Groups in the Global System*, London: Pinter.

Willis, P.E. (1978), *Profane Culture*, London: Routledge & Kegan Paul.

Yearley, S. (1991), *The Green Case: A Sociology of Environmental Issues, Arguments and Politics*, London: HarperCollins Academic.

Index

Index